How the Beatles Rocked The World

Other books by Stephen F. Kelly

The Korean War: Memories of Forgotten British Heroes
Recollections of the 1950s: Home, Family and New Horizons
Bill Shankly: The Biography
Forty Years of Coronation Street
Idle Hands, Clenched Fists
The Victorian Lakeland Photographers
A Game of Two Halves
The Bootroom Boys
Dalglish
Souness: A Soccer Revolutionary
Fergie, The Biography of Alex Ferguson
Red Voices
Backpage Football
You'll Never Walk Alone

Novels
Mr Shankly's Photograph
A Very Secret Life

How the Beatles Rocked The World

Stephen F. Kelly

WHITE OWL
AN IMPRINT OF PEN & SWORD BOOKS LTD.
YORKSHIRE - PHILADELPHIA

First published in Great Britain in 2024 by
White Owl
An imprint of Pen & Sword Books Limited
Yorkshire – Philadelphia

Copyright © Stephen F. Kelly 2024

ISBN 978 1 39903 606 1

The right of Stephen F. Kelly to be identified as
Author of this Work has been asserted by him in accordance
with the Copyright, Designs and Patents Act 1988.

A CIP catalogue record for this book is
available from the British Library

All rights reserved. No part of this book may be reproduced or
transmitted in any form or by any means, electronic or mechanical
including photocopying, recording or by any information storage and
retrieval system, without permission from the Publisher in writing.

Typeset by Mac Style
Printed in the UK by CPI Group (UK) Ltd, Croydon, CR0 4YY.

Pen & Sword Books Limited incorporates the imprints of After
the Battle, Atlas, Archaeology, Aviation, Discovery, Family History,
Fiction, History, Maritime, Military, Military Classics, Politics,
Select, Transport, True Crime, Air World, Frontline Publishing, Leo
Cooper, Remember When, Seaforth Publishing, The Praetorian Press,
Wharncliffe Local History, Wharncliffe Transport, Wharncliffe True
Crime and White Owl.

For a complete list of Pen & Sword titles please contact

PEN & SWORD BOOKS LIMITED
47 Church Street, Barnsley, South Yorkshire, S70 2AS, England
E-mail: enquiries@pen-and-sword.co.uk
Website: www.pen-and-sword.co.uk
or
PEN AND SWORD BOOKS
1950 Lawrence Rd, Havertown, PA 19083, USA
E-mail: uspen-and-sword@casematepublishers.com
Website: www.penandswordbooks.com

Contents

Acknowledgements   vii

Chapter 1   Where The Sixties Began   1

Chapter 2   A New Decade, A New Era   8

Chapter 3   The Mersey Sound   16

Chapter 4   A Cultural Revolution   33

Chapter 5   'What the hell is going on in this country?'   50

Chapter 6   Jobs for All   62

Chapter 7   We Gotta Get Out Of This Place   72

Chapter 8   Top of the Form   79

Chapter 9   Youth On The March   91

Chapter 10   'I Get High With A Little Help From My Friends.'   108

Chapter 11   'Ho, Ho, Ho Chi Minh!'   115

Chapter 12   With God on Our Side   127

Chapter 13   Social Changes   135

Chapter 14   The Ticking Time Bomb   144

Chapter 15   Beatniks and Biba   169

Chapter 16   A Shared Culture   186

Chapter 17	'We played it because we loved it'	203
Chapter 18	The Fifth Beatle	209
Chapter 19	The Beatles are Coming!	220
Chapter 20	Conclusion	230
Bibliography		235
Index		237

Acknowledgements

I began writing this book in 2019, before the pandemic struck and changed the lives of so many of us. During Covid, however, I seemed to lose the motivation to write, preferring instead to sit in the garden and read during that long spell of sunshine of the first lockdown. Such was the effect Covid had on so many of us. Although largely written by then, the book lay dormant on my computer and I did not finally pick it up again until 2022, thanks primarily to my wife and publishers Pen & Sword. So I would like to thank them for their belief in this book and for setting me a deadline (always a good thing for any journalist). In particular, their Commissioning Editor, Jonathan Wright, has encouraged and overseen progress, while Charlotte Mitchell, Junior Commissioning Editor and Production Assistant, has had to put up with many largely irrelevant phone calls, requests and emails from me. Thank you especially to my copy-editor, Tony Walton, whose thoroughness regarding detail and helpful comments will surely have added to this book. His work is much appreciated.

During the course of writing this book, I have spoken to and interviewed numerous people about their memories of The Beatles and their importance to a youth revolution that swept the world. But in particular I would like to thank the following for their support and contribution to this book.

Barbara Weber and Manfred Weber, for their memories of student days in Germany; Clare Jenkins, for her recollections of Birmingham and life as a young woman in the Sixties; television producer Johnnie Hamp, for his inspiring Little Richard and Jerry Lee Lewis programmes at Granada TV and for being the first producer to invite The Beatles into a television studio; Mike Prior, for his CND and student day memories; Christine Parkinson, for her recollections of her teenage years in Newcastle; Annie O'Malley, for memories of Manchester, fashion and occasional illegal substances; Thelma McGough (nee Pickles), for her interview about her life in Liverpool during the 1950s and 60s and tales of her first boyfriend, John Lennon, and her Cavern days; Jean Birkett, for memories of her student days; Veronica Palmer, for recollections of tough times at convent school; Bob Jones (not his real name), with thanks for his memories of Birkenhead; Cliff Butler, for his reminiscences of travelling abroad to watch Manchester United; Janice Finch, for her memories of seeing The Beatles at Granada Television; Chris Prior, for his dread of National Service; Leslie Woodhead, for his memories of making the only film ever showing The Beatles at The Cavern, as well as his researches on the Soviet bloc and permission to quote from his book; Roger McGough, for his memories of Liverpool; Melanie Tebbutt, for her thoughts about the 1960s and permission to quote from her book; and Brian Trueman, for his memories of both The Beatles and The Rolling Stones at Granada TV. Other thanks go to John and Gillian Jones for their kind hospitality and memories of Liverpool.

I have also consulted a number of Facebook sites, especially that of Bill Harry, the founder and editor of *Mersey Beat*, who still maintains links with the surviving Beatles and other Liverpool groups of the era. His knowledge of The Beatles and that period is second-to-none. And inevitably, I have consulted far too many internet sites to mention individually, though an especial mention should go to the Granadaland website. My thanks to all those who maintain and update these sites.

Thanks also to Jon Savage, Jane Brown, Gavin Hodge, Joe Moran, Michael Grade, Dominic Sandbrook, David Remnick, James Rosen, Candy Leonard, Artemy Troistsky and James McGrath.

Thanks also to my two children, Nicholas and Emma, for their technical support as well as their encouragement and good humour; and to their partners Tsugumi Nakasako and Lily Huggins. And finally, but never least, to my wife and best friend, Judith Jones, who encouraged me to revisit the book and to help find a new publisher. Without Judith's help, this book would never have come to fruition.

April 2024

Chapter 1

Where The Sixties Began

Mathew Street, Liverpool; home of the Cavern. This is where it all began. The Sixties, that is, and the revolution that would sweep through Britain, Europe, America, the Eastern Bloc and much of the rest of the world. Of course, it's not really true that this was precisely where it all started, but I like to think so, and it's as good a starting point as any for re-examining the Sixties.

I am walking up Mathew Street, as I have so many times in the past. I am showing around some German friends who are visiting Liverpool for the first time. Overhead there is a seamless sky of grey cloud and the cawing of seagulls; both awaiting the tide and an inevitable change of weather. As we stroll up Mathew Street with other camera-popping tourists, I point out the Grapes pub where The Beatles and other well-know Liverpool bands and personalities would drink. I also point to the original entrance to the Cavern, some 20 metres or so down from the new entrance. It's just an old iron door now; tourists are mingling up and down the street, cameras at the ready. They are taking photos of each other alongside the John Lennon statue and outside the new Cavern entrance. Most are unaware of the former entrance lower down the street.

I queued in this street so many times to get into the Cavern that I feel as if I've leaned against every stone. Friday lunch hour, but especially every Sunday night, I would be here as a young teenager, waiting to watch The Beatles, along with The Searchers, maybe The Big Three, The Merseybeats or some other band – though we called them groups in those days. Indeed, the last time I ever went inside the Cavern was on Bonfire Night in 1963 to hear The Rolling Stones, a new band from London who, the newspapers told us, were even scruffier than The Beatles but had a very authentic blues sound to their music. Well, maybe they were a little shabby, but they created a terrific sound. They, too, were destined for fame.

By then, the Beatles had smartened up. Brian Epstein had fitted them out in Fancy Dan matching suits without lapels. They looked silly: John Lennon hated them, as many of us Liverpudlians did, and in a famous *Rolling Stone* magazine interview years later claimed that this was the start of their decline. 'We were the best rock and roll band in the world,' he said, 'doing two-hour sessions and then Brian put us in suits and we were doing 20-minute sessions.' There were a few expletives in there as well. Maybe he was right. They did go a bit soft under Epstein, although at the time it didn't feel soft.

But back to The Rolling Stones. Bill Wyman seemed to enjoy it enough. 'While some people were building a wall, metaphorically, dividing the north from the south in pop music,' he wrote in his autobiography, 'we found no barriers whatsoever from Merseyside fans. Walking around the city we were stopped and chatted to by friendly Liverpudlians. In the evening our show at the Cavern was fantastic, with a marvellous crowd.'

Mick Jagger revelled in it as well. 'Man was it hot!' he later wrote. 'We almost sweated away. They've had so many big groups at the Cavern that you've got to prove yourself. They asked us back so they must like us.' We did, but they never came back.

As we approach the new entrance of the Cavern, you can see that it is open and people are pouring out up the stairs. We can hear music, so I encourage my visitors to come with me down the winding stone staircase. Once inside, I am swept back fifty years or more to around 1962, when I was a 16-year-old who had been caught up in the music and the atmosphere. It's not the real Cavern, but it's not that much different. A low-ceilinged brick wall structure (I'm told the same bricks from the original Cavern) with mind-blowing acoustics. There is a band on stage, playing some typical R'n'B track from the Sixties.

The original Cavern was much more cramped and I don't remember a bar, just a minute cloakroom, said to have been manned by a young girl called Priscilla White, who later changed her name to Cilla Black. I often wonder if she picked the name from the fact that we were all dressed in black back then; Chelsea boots, tight corduroy trousers, polo-neck top, duffle coat and scarf. Why a scarf? I don't know. And for that matter, why a duffle coat? No wonder we were hot! The moisture dripped incessantly down the whitewashed walls and there was a constant smell of rotting fish; when you walked outside, your clothes stuck to your body. I assume, though I cannot really remember, that we all puffed on our cigarettes down there. If we did, the air must have been thick with smoke.

Suddenly, all these memories are sweeping back. I remember standing by the small stage, mesmerized by John Lennon, who was always my favourite, and being taken with the bass playing of Johnny Gustafasson, the legendary saxophonist Howie Casey and the Dominoes' guitarist, Kingsize Taylor. There were others such as Billy J. Kramer, Lee Curtiss and Beryl Marsden, rated by many as the best female singer to ever come out of Merseyside. Dancing in the narrow confines of the cellar, we even had our own dance, commonly known as the Cavern Stomp, that did not require too much space as we tried to chat up girls over the deafening sound of the various bands on stage. A wave of nostalgia sweeps over me. It is as if I am a teenager again, rebelling against the old order, desperate to escape suburbia and my dreary job in a shipyard and make something of my life. I was a typical child of the time, not unlike Arthur Seaton in Alan Sillitoe's *Saturday Night, Sunday Morning*, a teenager and a bit younger than Seaton, but not giving a damn, just wanting to change the world.

And that world was indeed ready for change.

The twentieth century had thus far not been kind to young people. Almost an entire generation had been wiped out in the First World War, and those who did survive returned to a nation supposedly 'fit for heroes' but which actually was far from it. Many suffered from the traumas of the trenches, and those who didn't struggled to find work. Education was poor, with all but a few leaving school at 14. Then came the Depression and the 1930s. Money was desperately short, dole queues were long, families were means tested and there was barely anything to feel optimistic about. It was little wonder that many young people turned to extreme varieties of politics. Some, including young Liverpool docker Jack Jones, opted to go to Spain to fight fascism, whilst others took up the cause of fascism, which at the time seemed so seductive. Young people were trapped in a cocoon of poverty and zero opportunities. And then, just as the economy began to pick up, there came the Second World War. If poverty had not subjected you to dejection and hopelessness, Hitler's guns and bombs soon would. Once again, a young generation was expected to fight for King and country. For six years, Britain's youth was engaged on battlefields across Europe, the Middle East and the Far East. There was no time to think of fun or the future.

In 1945, Britain emerged victorious from a war that had seen homes destroyed and lives torn apart. At least between 1914 and 1918, cities and towns had suffered few consequences. There had been little or no bombing, apart from the Zeppelins dropping the occasional bomb over London, and hardly any civilian fatalities. But the Second World War had been six long years when everyone's life had been severely disrupted one way or another. Young men, expecting to start work, had instead been thrown into the forces and gone off to battle. And young women, perhaps anticipating married life and some degree of happiness and tranquillity, found themselves forced to work long hours in factories to help the war effort. Those who were married had waved goodbye to their husbands, many not seeing them again for years, sometimes forced to put family plans aside. Instead, they were left to fend for themselves, often with young children, little money, and death staring them in the face. They also had to cope with the hardships of war, such as rationing, incessant bombing, scurrying to air raid shelters and the constant worry of where their loved ones might be. Homes had been destroyed, city centres left in ruins, people maimed and killed. Around Liverpool, the scars left by German bombs were evident everywhere.

Many children, particularly those living in the major industrial cities, were evacuated to the quieter countryside, leaving memories and pain that would last a lifetime. In most instances they were away from their homes for months, in some cases even years. They lived with new families, went to new schools and had to make new friends. For many it was a traumatic period, being taken from the city and planted in the countryside, away from their family. Education was severely disrupted, and for teenage boys there was the daunting prospect of having to go into the army, navy or air force when you had finished your education.

The late 1940s and 1950s offered some respite from the challenges of war, but life was still hard going. Money was short, rationing was still enforced and educational opportunities remained few and far between. There wasn't much to make you laugh, apart from Arthur Askey on the radio or an evening at the cinema watching George Formby. Young people were still trapped in a straitjacket of conformity and obedience. The Catholic Church dictated a set of stringent rules for its followers, whilst the Church of England remained supreme for most others. If you got into trouble with the police, you could expect the worst. And of course there was National Service too. It was a world longing to break out of itself.

The music and youth revolution had, in truth, begun in the 1950s, principally with the release of Bill Haley's smash hit record 'Rock Around the Clock'. The Decca label recording shot to the top of the charts in both the United States and Britain and caused a sensation. Rock and roll had arrived. The film *Blackboard Jungle*, featuring Bill Haley and the Comets, was released a year later and caused a furore in Britain. Initially it was banned, but once it was released it led to Teddy Boys dancing in the aisles and ripping up seats. The newspapers were full of it. Grandparents were shocked, vicars horrified, and politicians talked of the need to ban such films. It seemed as if rock and roll had released some kind of post-war anger and energy. And then came Elvis Presley, whose 'Heartbreak Hotel' shot to number one in the charts in 1956. With his swinging hips, dark clothes, sulky looks and sexually provocative style, Presley looked and played the rebel. He was just what young people in post-war Britain and America were searching for. Presley, even more so than Bill Haley, was the teenage heartthrob. Haley – with his round, chubby face, kiss curl and dickie bow tie – was hardly rebel material. But Presley was different. Like James Dean, he spoke for a generation. But it was still a voiceless generation.

Prior to the 1960s, young people had little or no say in society. The authoritarian nature of the state – with its discipline, belief in the political system, the police and other forms of Establishment control – regarded young people as irrelevant. Few had been educated beyond the age of 15. Their role in society was limited. You were caned in school, respectful of your parents, fearful of the police and beholden to the Church. Nobody wanted to know what young people thought. You didn't have the vote until you were 21, so politicians had no reason to be interested in you. The chief, and only, recognized role of young people was as army fodder, and during the First World War, hundreds of thousands of young men had been sent to their deaths on the orders of their military commanders. The 1930s similarly gave little voice or opportunity to the young. They were jobless, disenfranchised and of little economic or cultural importance.

It was no different for young women; indeed, it was worse. Their role was to be a wife and mother. If they had jobs, it was usually prior to marriage or pregnancy, and in Northern Britain generally in a cotton or woollen mill or in service to some rich family. And if they didn't marry, then they lived at home, looking after their parents. Sex was frowned upon, not to be enjoyed but for procreation. Women especially, if they did indulge, were likely to be left with the consequences.

Most revolutions are started by young people demanding more than their elders have been able to offer. They are largely about aspiration. The elderly always have much more to preserve. They have jobs, families, status; the young have nothing but their dreams and ideals. What was set to happen in the Sixties would reshape society, even if it did not turn out quite as anticipated.

Journalist Andrew Marr summed up the Sixties perfectly:

'If you weren't listening in the Cavern Club in the early days or at the Isle of Wight when Dylan went electric, if you never dodged the police horses at Grosvenor Square. Or heard Adrian Mitchell and Allen Ginsberg in the Albert Hall, or sashayed out of Bazaar with a bright bag of swirly-patterned clothes ... then sorry Babe, you missed it. And you missed it forever. Most of us did miss it – too young, too old, too living in the wrong place. But then most people missed the Wild West and the French Revolution, and the rest of the events that come with capital letters.'

But for those who did witness it, the Sixties would never be forgotten.

'The Beatles changed our society,' says my German friend Manfred Weber. 'After the war we were so repressed. There were things we didn't mention, questions we daren't ask. But the Beatles released us from that straitjacket and young people began to talk about these things. It was so liberating.' His wife, Barbara Weber, a student at Bonn University in the 1960s, agrees: 'There were student demonstrations and other political activity. We needed to confront our past.'

Lower down in Mathew Street, I point out to my guests a bust of Swiss psychoanalyst Carl Gustav Jung. It seems a strange place for him to be remembered, especially as he had never visited the city of Liverpool. The clue is in his 1962 book *Memories, Dreams, Reflections*, in which he described a dream he had:

> 'I found myself in a dark, sooty city. I was in Liverpool ... I walked through the dark streets. The various quarters of the city were arranged radially around the square. In the centre was a round pool, and in the middle of it, a small island. While everything around was obscured by rain, fog, smoke and dimly lit darkness, the little island blazed with sunlight. On it stood a single tree, a magnolia, in a sea of reddish blossoms. It was as though the tree stood in the sunlight and was, at the same time, the source of light.
>
> 'My companions commented on the abominable weather, and obviously did not see the tree. They spoke of another Swiss who was living in Liverpool, and expressed surprise that he should have settled here. I was carried away by the beauty of the tree and the sunlit island, and thought, "I know very well why he has settled here." Then I awoke.
>
> 'This dream represented my situation at the time. I can still see the greyish-yellow raincoats, glistening with the wetness of the rain. Everything was extremely unpleasant, black and opaque – just as I felt then. But I had had a vision of unearthly beauty, and that was why I was able to live at all. Liverpool is the "pool of life".'

It may have been a dream, but they would be prophetic words. Liverpool would indeed turn out to be the pool of life, and through The Beatles the world was about to be changed.

Chapter 2

A New Decade, A New Era

As young people woke up to a new decade in January 1960, they would have found a Britain not much changed since the post-war years. Britain was still a nation dominated by class and obedience, seeped in its traditions and royalty. Prime Minister Harold Macmillan (Eton and Oxford) relaxed by going grouse shooting and worrying about his wife's affair with one of his ministers, Robert Boothby (also Eton and Oxford). Macmillan had succeeded Sir Anthony Eden (Eton and Oxford), and in turn Macmillan would be succeeded by cricket lover Sir Alec Douglas-Home (also Eton and Oxford). The composition of the governing Conservative Party was dominated by men educated at public schools who had trodden the same paths from Eton to Oxford or Cambridge. The judiciary was similar, as were the highest offices of the military and the civil service. Britain was ruled by a tight-knit Establishment, much as it had always been. And as 1960 began, it seemed there was little chance of that ever changing. There were few women Members of Parliament, even fewer in government posts and hardly any in the senior ranks of the civil service, the Church, the police or the judiciary.

Britain was an obedient and subservient society. The Church of England and the Catholic Church were powerful institutions whose messages were of obedience and acquiescence. Churchgoing was at a peak. Crime was low, confined generally to petty thefts, burglary and the occasional street fight. There were few cars on the road, so car and driving crime was still in its infancy and would not rise for some years until vehicle ownership became more widespread. Of course, that had its benefits; you could play in the streets without fear of being knocked down and drive safely on major roads without the need of eyes in the back of your head! And when necessary, the courts doled out severe punishments.

Schoolchildren were kept on a tight rein, with schools serving up a diet of corporal punishment in order to maintain strict discipline. The slipper, the cane and expulsions were common, few boys escaping their education years without ever having at least suffered the pain of a good thrashing from some sadistic teacher. A grammar school selection system in education meant that two-thirds of students were promptly assigned a poorer education and the prospect of a non-skilled occupation.

The pubs closed at 10.30 pm and nobody under the age of 18 was even allowed inside a public house. Walk past any pub at the time and you would see young kids outside waiting for their parents. For young people, recreation was limited to television, the cinema, youth clubs, the local YMCA and a few music venues. For older people, the pub was often the centre of their lives.

At the Cavern Club in Liverpool, an all-night session on New Year's Eve had featured a line-up that included the Micky Ashman Jazz Band, The Swinging Blue Jeans, the Dallas Jazz Band and the Yorkshire Jazz Band. The Cavern was very much a jazz haunt at that time. The following night, the Swinging Blue Jeans, then a folksy jazz group, were back alongside the Cy Laurie Jazz Band.

The Cavern at the dawn of the Sixties was just not for young teenagers. Thelma McGough (nee Pickles), later to become girlfriend of both John Lennon and Paul McCartney, recalls going to the Cavern when she was at art college:

> 'But it wasn't the Cavern it later became. It was a jazz club then. Acker Bilk and George Melly played and I disliked jazz, I thought it was awful. There were Chianti bottles in raffia on the tables holding candles. Men in jackets smoking pipes. Lord, to me it was boring. That's what the Cavern was like then.'

In a way, it neatly summed up Britain, while Thelma's attitude to it all equally summed up the frustrations of a new teenage generation, ready to explode.

Meanwhile, elsewhere in Liverpool, a gang of young lads who during the previous year had formed a band and called themselves The Quarrymen, and had made their first appearance at the Cavern, were at home celebrating with their parents or relations, no doubt downing a beer or two before stepping outside with a bucket of coal to herald in the New Year and listen to the fog horns of all those ships in the River Mersey celebrating the incoming year.

For The Beatles, 1960 was to be a formative year. Another young art school student, Stuart Sutcliffe, was about to join them. When he did, he suggested they change the name of the group from The Quarrymen to The Beatles. They would soon become The Silver Beetles and later that year just The Beatles. They were also booked to follow a number of other Liverpool groups who were playing in clubs and bierkellers in Hamburg's red light district. Time spent there would hone their abilities as musicians.

Bill Haley and Elvis had come and gone. Haley had visited Britain once, in 1957, but Elvis had never visited, and was now in the US Army stationed in Germany; hair shorn, and making few recordings. He was now very much the typical soldier. Britain had spawned its own rock and rollers, but they too were clean-cut and hardly a threat to society. Tommy Steele was chirpy, while Cliff Richard was a mum's favourite.

The music at the time was generally tame; jazz was popular, as were ballad singers and pianists like Russ Conway and Winifred Atwell. Skiffle was also popular, with Lonnie Donegan regularly featuring on television and being a big influence on Paul McCartney. Emile Ford and the Checkmates topped the hit parade with 'What Do You Want To Make Those Eyes At Me For?', with Adam Faith, Cliff Richard, Frankie Laine, Neil Sedaka and Max Bygraves not far behind. American music remained popular – Connie Francis, The Everly Brothers, Eddie Cochran, Duane Eddy, Guy Mitchell and Ricky Nelson.

In January 1960, Prime Minister Harold Macmillan was about to start a six-week, 20,000-mile tour of British colonies in Africa, including Ghana, Nigeria, Rhodesia and South Africa, where the demands for independence were reaching new heights. Increasing calls for nationalism, coupled with serious disturbances elsewhere across the African continent, brought into question British rule. During his trip, Macmillan, addressing a meeting in South Africa, talked of the 'winds of change' sweeping through the British Empire. The legacy of the Empire was causing major issues back in London too, and Macmillan had concluded that it was no longer viable in its current form. With African nationalism on the rise, the issue needed to be addressed. Countries needed to be given their independence, though many in Macmillan's own Conservative government strongly disagreed. It was to be a turning point in British history, one that would reverberate through British politics and society for the next fifty years.

D.H. Lawrence's novel *Lady Chatterley's Lover* remained banned, regarded as obscene, but plans were quietly underway at the Penguin publishing house to publish the novel later that year. They knew that the novel might be illegal, but were prepared to challenge any actions taken against it. Little did they know that it would lead to a sensational court case that would have the nation aghast. It would redefine obscenity and have a bearing on all future publications. Although written thirty years earlier, the novel in many ways still astutely reflected the same social class divisions in British society.

Britain was very much a rigid, authoritarian society, full of traditional values and refusing to change or even budge a few inches. It was a nation in need of a good shakeup.

Thelma McGough remembered:

'I don't know if it was only in my house but we weren't allowed to do anything. I think that's why John [Lennon] and I got on so well. You weren't allowed to wear makeup. You weren't allowed to wear drainies [drainpipe trousers], it was in that crossover period between that generation who got the key of the door at 21 and became instant adults and were allowed to do everything grown-ups did. But before that you weren't allowed to do anything. Not in the class system that we were brought up in anyway.'

What was different was that there were now 5 million teenagers living in Britain. It was the highest number of that age group ever in British history, caused by bulge years of births immediately after the Second World War in 1946 and 1947. Once this generation had left school and started work, they had money in their pockets. It sowed the roots of a social revolution.

Britain's towns and cities were full of terraced houses in back-to-back streets, usually with no gardens or inside toilets, and mostly built between 1860 and 1920. It hadn't changed much since the First World War. The big cities had at least begun some modernization, but it was only limited. Bomb sites and derelict land shaped the landscape, a hangover from the destruction of the Second World War.

Britain was a class-ridden society. On one side was a small, elite, aristocratic upper class, with all the privileges that accompanied the label. They mostly owned the nation's businesses and land, and enjoyed good housing, cars and a wealth of consumer goods, as well as the best of education, usually private.

In contrast was a working class, living mainly in the North, centred in the big, dark, industrial cities or large manufacturing towns, where housing was poor, wages low and deaths premature. In between was a middle class, aspirational and beginning to enjoy the proceeds of a university education or professional job, but still at this insignificant stage. It was little wonder that politics was dominated by two ideological parties. 'The real England is not the England of the guidebook,' wrote George Orwell. 'Blackpool is more typical than Ascot.'

The often nightly bombing raids of the Second World War had brought about considerable destruction for the cities of London, Liverpool, Manchester, Glasgow and Sheffield. The post-war years were a time of austerity, and although the 1945–51 Labour government had made a considerable commitment to rebuilding, it was a slow and expensive business, with the Conservative Party also struggling with the issue.

It was much the same across Europe. It may have been fifteen years since the end of the Second World War, but its legacy still blighted much of the continent. A humiliated Germany was beginning its slow climb back to economic sustainability, thanks in main to the Marshall Plan. The war had left a terrible scar, not just on the landscape but also on the German people. In their homes and workplaces, nobody talked of the war, such was the shame. But what Germany lacked in confidence it made up for with its economic endeavours, quickly growing an economy that would thrive throughout the Sixties and Seventies.

In Spain, fascist dictator General Franco continued to rule. Seizing power following the Spanish Civil War, he governed over a terrified population. Spain's economy remained agrarian and backwards. It was a country of weeping Madonnas, witchcraft and authoritarian Catholicism. The writer Jimmy Burns noted:

'Far from magnanimous in his hour of victory, Franco emerged in 1939, at the end of the Spanish Civil War, determined to rule his country with an iron fist. Spaniards were divided between those who continued to support him and the military rebels and those who had fought against him on the side of the democratically elected Republican government. The former were rewarded with jobs, social security benefits and new houses. The latter faced imprisonment, execution and social exclusion, including exile.'

There were few political rights, no free elections, and prisons were crammed with left-wing political agitators. The legacy of its own terrible internal conflict would leave the country divided and isolated until Franco's death in 1975.

It was much the same in Portugal, where another fascist president ruled over a nation even more in need of social and economic reform than its Iberian neighbour. Portugal was a nation of impoverished agricultural workers and rural villages. It was isolationist, known for little other than its most famous export, port. President António de Oliveira Salazar had been installed as President since the early 1930s and would continue his reign of brutal totalitarianism until his death in 1970. It would not be until four years later, in 1974, that Portugal finally threw off the noose of fascism.

In Greece, a civil war following the Second World War left the country divided. Although some social progress was made in the 1950s, a military junta led by the Colonels seized power in 1967 and imposed yet another fascist regime in Europe. It too would remain in power until 1974.

In the Soviet Union, a communist system had ruled since the 1917 revolution, but following its military gains during the Second World War, Moscow extended its influence across much of Eastern Europe. Poland, Yugoslavia, Albania, Bulgaria, Romania, Czechoslovakia and others all fell under the influence and control of Moscow. Even Germany itself was divided between East and West, with the former capital, Berlin, split between two sectors and only limited freedom of movement between East Berlin and West Berlin. Much of that came to an end in 1961 when a wall was thrown up overnight by the Soviets, dividing families and businesses for the next twenty-eight years.

It was ironic that despite the Allies having fought the Second World War to protect liberal democracy from German fascism, much of Europe in 1960 was under the yoke of totalitarian regimes of one kind or another. And if right- or left-wing dictatorships did not rule, then the Catholic Church generally did. Ireland stood in fear of God, its population slavishly adhering to the dictates of the Church. In France, too, the Church was a major power. General De Gaulle may have favoured secular Republicanism, but his vision of France was deeply infused with the country's Catholic heritage and his own Catholic devotion. In Italy, meanwhile, it was impossible to escape the influence of the Vatican, much as it had been throughout the country's history.

In all these regimes there was only limited political and social freedom. Voting rights, abortion, divorce, women's rights, contraception; all barely existed. Freedom of the press was limited, popular music was banned, films were censored and young people didn't have the vote. It was a bleak picture of the state and Church controlling all aspects of life. Few dared to challenge the *status quo*.

As 1960 dawned, a handsome, young, well-connected Democrat senator from Massachusetts was beginning his campaign to become the next president of the United States. Nobody gave him much chance, but in the elections that took place in November 1960, John F. Kennedy defeated his Republican rival, Richard M. Nixon, by the narrowest of margins. It seemed that the youthful Kennedy had ushered in a new liberal dawn. Yet three years later, troubled by a growing war in Vietnam but having evaded a potential nuclear holocaust over the siting of Soviet missiles in Cuba, he would be gunned down on the streets of Dallas. Kennedy seemed to offer some hope of a youthful, energetic future. His assassination temporarily dampened that enthusiasm, setting America on course for greater involvement in Vietnam and yet more civil rights disturbances. But the arrival of The Beatles was to push American youth in a new direction in their search for answers.

Chapter 3

The Mersey Sound

Where to begin? Well, let's stick with music. Let us go back to where we started, to Liverpool.

The year is 1960. Liverpool is still recovering from the war. There are bombed-out buildings and derelict bombsites peppered across the city centre's elegant streets. It's a grey city still full of smoke and smog, with a damp mist that regularly rolls in from the Mersey with every incoming tide. The docks are pre-eminent, the lifeblood of the city, employing thousands of men who each day jump aboard the overhead railway to make their way to whatever dock has a newly arrived ship. But it's casual labour. You turn up and you get called for a job. It's well known that certain docks and gang leaders choose their favourites. In some places, if you're a Catholic you haven't got a chance of being chosen. And of course black people do not work on the docks. The work is not regular, being dependent on the tide, the availability of berths and the arrival of ships in the Mersey Bar. Ships did not run to an exact timetable. Bad weather, the tide and mechanical problems meant any ship could easily be a day or more late. You might turn up for work one morning and there would be nothing; another day, there would be a dozen ships docking. Nevertheless, the docks and ships are what Liverpool is about. Over the water from the imposing Pier Head lay Birkenhead, with its sprawl of docks, as well as Cammell Laird, shipbuilders, at the time one of the most eminent shipbuilding companies in Britain, with a worldwide reputation for building the finest ships. It had just launched its latest and what would turn out to be its last-ever liner, the *Windsor Castle*. But it was about to secure a contract to build two nuclear-powered Polaris submarines for the Royal Navy, which promised to keep the shipyard busy for a good few years. Liverpool is a port, a city dominated by the sea; always has been and always will be.

It was from these ships that young Liverpool lads would disembark, clutching a suitcase full of records. Going to sea as a marine engineer or apprentice of some sort was a well-known job opportunity for Liverpool school-leavers. Some joined the cargo fleets of Elder Dempster, Holt, Harrison's, Blue Funnel and the Bibby Line. Others preferred the liners of Cunard, P & O, White Star or Canadian Pacific. Many of these ships plied their trade with the east coast of the United States and Canada, visiting New Orleans, Philadelphia, the Gulf of Mexico, New York, Boston and Montreal. It was in these east-coast city ports that the young sailors, visiting bars and record shops, happened upon the latest music. They would purchase recordings by many lesser-known performers such as Bo Diddley, The Coasters, Chuck Berry, The Isley Brothers, Barrett Strong, Carl Perkins, Howlin' Wolf, Muddy Waters and Larry Williams. They would also purchase records, not available in the UK, by artistes who had enjoyed some minor successes in Britain such as Little Richard, Jerry Lee Lewis and Frankie Lymon.

It's important to understand that in the early 1960s, American music was not readily available in British record shops. Some top artistes like Elvis Presley, Perry Como and Buddy Holly had international recording contracts and did sell their records in the UK, but unless you had a contract with one of the major international recording companies, such as RCA or Capitol, there was little chance that any of your music would be heard outside of your own locality. As a result, many American artistes were recording and selling their records on a local basis. Sun Records, for instance, was based in Memphis, Tennessee, with many of its performers coming from the region itself, while the Blues label Chess Records was based in Chicago.

And so the Liverpool-based sailors disembarked from their ships and brought their records home, introducing them to family and friends, playing them on their new portable record-players. The few record shops that there were in the city centre might try to order some of these records, but generally they had little success.

There had always been a thriving music scene in Liverpool, whether it was in the pubs or local clubs. Folk music, often associated with seafarers, had long been popular, while groups such as the Spinners, formed in the late 1950s, made a good living from their recordings and appearances. In the 1950s, skiffle had also been a popular music genre in Liverpool, encouraged by the recordings which many sailors brought back to the city from places like New Orleans. Indeed, both The Spinners and The Beatles themselves had begun life as skiffle groups. Skiffle legend Lonnie Donegan, a major star of the late 1950s, was to be an acknowledged inspiration for most of the bands that would emerge out of Liverpool, but in particular was a major influence on Paul McCartney and The Beatles.

Those sailors doing the transatlantic run to New York initially tended to bring jazz records back, following visits to the wealth of jazz clubs on 52nd Street as well as in and around Harlem. Clubs such as the Royal Roost, Five Spot, Birdland and the Half Note. It was said that almost any night you could walk up and down 52nd Street and hear the likes of Duke Ellington, Charlie Parker, Thelonious Monk and Miles Davis. But by the late 1950s and early 1960s, the sailors' tastes had shifted to rhythm and blues recordings.

The Cavern Club in Liverpool's Mathew Street had been set up in 1957 by Alan Sytner specifically as a jazz club. Jazz fanatic Sytner, who already ran a couple of jazz clubs in the city, had visited Paris and been taken to Le Caveau Francais and other Parisian jazz clubs housed in cellars. He loved their authenticity and wanted to recreate the same in Liverpool. The Cavern was perfect for him. Housed in the cellar of an old warehouse in the centre of the city, you descended a narrow passageway of stone steps and found yourself in a cavernous space. The Cavern opened its doors in January 1957. One of the regular bands was The Merseysippi Jazz Band, which had been going since 1949, and The Coney Island Skiffle Group. The Cavern continued to exist as a jazz venue until 1959, when Sytner, faced with some hefty repair bills, decided to sell up and move to London. During its time, the club had featured some of the jazz greats, including Americans Sister Rosetta Tharpe, Earl Hines, Zoot Sims and Jack Dupree, as well as major British jazz bands such as those of Humphrey Lyttleton, Johnny Dankworth, Ken Colyer and Ronnie Scott.

The venue was then taken over by Ray McFall, a young accountant who had been working at the club as a cashier a couple of nights a week. McFall kept the club going in much the same vein, playing jazz music, but by 1960 some of the jazz bands were beginning to expand their repertoire and experiment with rock music. Rory Storm and the Hurricanes, then a jazz band, for instance, decided to test the water one night at the Cavern by singing the Jerry Lee Lewis favourite 'Whole Lot of Shakin', but the jazz fraternity didn't like it and hurled old copper coins in their direction. McFall didn't like it either, but faced with increasing financial difficulties he decided to give rock 'n' roll (or beat music) another try by introducing it for just a couple of nights a week. The first official beat night was held on 25 May 1960, with Rory Storm and the Hurricanes and Cass and the Casanovas. Although the jazz fanatics stayed away, the gig attracted hundreds of other young people. McFall was soon convinced that there was a market here that could potentially solve his continuing financial difficulties, so one evening of rock 'n' roll a week soon became two, then three, four and five evenings, with jazz eventually becoming just an occasional event.

Nor was the Cavern the only music venue in Liverpool. Other clubs such as the Blue Angel, the Jacaranda, the Locarno and the Iron Door were all getting in on the act of featuring rock 'n' roll bands. Across the water in New Brighton, the Tower Ballroom offered a larger venue and later featured gigs with the Beatles and Little Richard. And in Birkenhead there was the rather glitzy Majestic. Before long, there would be well over twenty music venues peppered around Liverpool and Merseyside. Liverpool was on the verge of a music revolution that would take the world by storm. It needed just one more ingredient.

Liverpool had never been short of its own pop stars. Frankie Vaughan had been performing and recording since the early 1950s and had his first hit, 'Green Door', in 1956. Billy Fury from the Dingle was another Liverpool lad who had shot to fame as a recording artiste with 'Halfway to Paradise', which became a smash hit in 1961.

But now Liverpool was about to unearth a pop group that would not only change music, but would create such an unrest among young people that it would generate a revolution which would sweep the world.

The story of the rise of The Beatles has been well told. They had begun life as a skiffle group calling themselves The Quarrymen, playing Lonnie Donegan numbers and simple Buddy Holly songs. Initially, there were five of them – John Lennon, Paul McCartney, George Harrison, Pete Best and Stuart Sutcliffe. Lennon and Sutcliffe were students at the Liverpool College of Art, while Paul McCartney attended the Liverpool Institute. McCartney had passed his eleven-plus exam, but, typically for the time, was only one of three from his school year to pass. George Harrison also attended the Liverpool Institute, like McCartney being another rarity as a working-class boy who had passed the examination. Drummer Pete Best was another grammar school boy attending Liverpool Collegiate College, proving a useful member of the band given that his mother owned and ran the Casbah Club in Liverpool, which would be a perfect venue for the band to practice.

The Beatles played around various music venues, including the Casbah, before securing a booking at the Cavern in February 1961. By then, they were beginning to generate a following in Liverpool, which by mid-1963 had turned into mass adulation across the country.

As the local music scene began to escalate, a fortnightly newspaper, *Mersey Beat*, appeared on the newsstands. It was edited by Bill Harry, an art college friend of John Lennon and Paul McCartney. Bill Harry had met Stuart Sutcliffe and John Lennon when they were students at the Liverpool College of Art, and they had all become friends. Also in their 'gang' was Thelma McGough. Bill Harry was a huge fan of the Beatles, and as their popularity – and that generally of the Liverpool music scene – began to increase, he decided to produce a paper to list the growing number of gigs in the Liverpool and wider Merseyside area.

The first issue of *Mersey Beat* appeared on 6 July 1961, with a photograph of Gene Vincent on the front page. The American rock star, who had just appeared at Liverpool's Rialto Ballroom, was shown, cigarette in hand, signing autographs for a couple of young admirers. There was also a story about a young girl called Cilla Black who was beginning to sing at various venues, including the Cavern. Also on the front page was an article by a certain John Lennon, headlined 'Being a Short Diversion on the Dubious origins of the Beatles'. The article went on: 'Many people ask, what are Beatles? Why Beatles? Ugh, Beatles, how did the name arrive? So, we will tell you. It came in a vision – a man appeared on a flaming pie and said unto them "From this day on you are the Beatles with an 'A'."Thank you Mr Man, they said, thanking him.' It was typical John Lennon humour.

There were also features about the various groups and many photographs, along with all the latest news. Although its importance has never been properly recognized, *Mersey Beat*'s role in publicizing the growing Liverpool music scene was crucial. In its second issue, dated 20 July 1961 a front-page headline reported that The Beatles had secured a contract with the German recording company Polydor to make four records per year.

The very first issue of *Mersey Beat* was also important because Bill Harry visited the NEMS (North End Music Stores) record shop on Whitechapel, in the city centre and just down the road from the Cavern, and asked to see the manager, a Mr Brian Epstein, to see if he would sell copies of the paper in the shop. NEMS was the major record shop in the city, with teenagers packed in there listening in the booths to whatever they fancied, before usually leaving without buying anything! Epstein reluctantly agreed to Bill Harry's request and took a dozen copies. They sold out within minutes of going on display, so Epstein ordered 100 more and asked Harry to drop around for a meeting. Epstein may not have been much older than Harry, but he was a million miles apart when it came to background and taste. Epstein's father owned the NEMS business and the family, who were Jewish, lived in a large house in the leafy suburbs. Brian was more likely to be found at the Philharmonic Hall listening to a classical music concert rather than down some city centre dive. Epstein was also gay, which was a closed world in those days. But Brian was intrigued by the interest in the local pop scene and wanted to know more. It was the beginning of something that was to change music and society forever. And principal to this would be The Beatles.

The popularity of The Beatles and the availability of venues prompted a surge in the number of groups in the Liverpool area. Over the next few years, many would go on to fame and fortune. They included Gerry and the Pacemakers, Billy J. Kramer, Cilla Black, The Fourmost, The Big

Three, The Searchers, The Undertakers and many more. All the group members were young, working-class lads from around the suburbs of Liverpool. They had picked up guitars, amplifiers and drums cheaply or on the 'never-never' from the music store Hessys, across the road from NEMS in the city centre. They had formed their own bands, rehearsed in garages or front rooms and found themselves bookings at youth clubs, church halls or more professional venues such as ballrooms or places like the Iron Door and the Cavern. The music wasn't difficult; a good beat on the drums, a few chords and someone singing, and you were away. The guitar was as easy an instrument to play as any. Buddy Holly had got away with playing only three chords. You didn't even have to be able to read music. You could sit on the bed and strum away, carry it around easily, knock out a few chords with your mates and have a sing-a-long. The guitar was a highly sociable instrument. It wasn't like a piano, which was expensive to buy and difficult to play, or even the saxophone, which was also expensive. You could be taught a decent tune on the guitar in a single evening. Neither did you need a professional teacher. Your mates could easily teach you. All you had to do was to learn a handful of chords from the cheap 'teach yourself guitar' books. It was just a matter of practicing. Within a few years, there were hundreds of bands on Merseyside, all playing the same numbers, mostly R 'n' B or rock 'n' roll, by the likes of Chuck Berry, The Coasters, Little Richard, Jerry Lee Lewis, Carl Perkins and Bo Diddley.

Forming a band became an escape route from the drudgery of school life, the office or the factory floor. It was exciting, and there was always a chance that you might just make it. Whereas boxing had once been the gateway to escaping the poverty of the big cities like Liverpool, it was now music. Initially, of course, they did it for fun and the local adulation that went with it. But once the Beatles and others had topped the charts, it seemed fame and possible fortune were beckoning for almost anyone who had the ability to learn half-a-dozen guitar chords.

The Cavern was certainly not the biggest of music venues, but the atmosphere and acoustics were infinitely better than anywhere else, either in Liverpool or possibly the UK for that matter. It had been an old warehouse and really did look like a cavern. It was long, thin and had a ceiling no more than 12 feet high. In order to enter, you went down a flight of narrow steps and then paid on the door. If ever there was a fire risk, this was it, but in the 1960s nobody cared much about such things. Life itself was a risk.

Inside was hardly pleasant; condensation dripped down the walls and there was always a distinctive smell. Most people wore the same style of clothes; the men wore skinny black corduroy trousers, Chelsea boots, black polo-necked sweaters and quite often duffle coats. It was commonly called the beatnik style and was one The Beatles had adopted, although they were soon able to afford black leather coats. The girls wore dresses, with their hair in a bun, and often danced barefooted. But what made the Cavern so special was the sound it generated. The noise resonated around the walls: it was loud, clear, exciting.

Over the next few years, all the leading Merseyside groups would play the Cavern, as well as bands from around the country and the USA who would go on to top the charts. They included The Rolling Stones, The Hollies, Manfred Mann, Gene Vincent, The Who, The Kinks, John Lee Hooker, Howlin' Wolf, The Yardbirds and so on.

The Beatles had spent time abroad in Hamburg, playing nightly in various bierkellers, such as the Indra, alongside other Merseybeat groups. Many of the sessions they played went long into the night. Thelma McGough saw a distinct change in them after their German trips:

'Privately John and the others might have had aspirations but there was no indication that they were going to be that big. I think Hamburg changed that. If you think of Tiger Woods or Andre Agassi with their family and fathers training them day after day, that's the equivalent of what The Beatles underwent in Germany. Practice, practice for hours on end, every day. It was that practice that made them better.'

Others also saw a change in them. They had gone to Germany as boys but came back as men, hardened by the experience.

In January 1962, Brian Epstein secured a major recording contract with Parlophone for The Beatles. Their first release, 'Love Me Do', became a number one hit on the *Mersey Beat* chart, but fared less well on the national charts. And then in March 1963 came 'Please, Please Me'. That soon became a national number one. Neither music, nor society, would ever be the same again. A revolution was about to begin.

What was revolutionary in terms of music was that four lads – sometimes five, and in the case of the Big Three, just three – were not only singing together in harmony, but playing instruments. With most groups it was now more than one person singing, with no individual playing the starring role. Prior to The Beatles, it had tended to be an individual backed by instrumentalists, like Bill Haley *and* the Comets, Buddy Holly *and* the Crickets or in the case of Britain, Cliff Richard *and* the Shadows. But with the new genre, it was everyone singing and playing.

While a music revolution was going on in Liverpool, it was being copied around the country as the Sixties progressed. In nearby Manchester, a plethora of clubs opened up on the back of the Beatles' success. They included the Twisted Wheel, Oasis, the Ritz, Time and Place, all featuring local bands such as The Hollies, Wayne Fontana and the Mindbenders, The Dakotas, John Mayall and Freddie and the Dreamers.

Clubs were springing up everywhere, many of them featuring local bands as the music craze spread among young people. It was a quick way to make some money, and who knows, perhaps one day a recording contract and fame.

With their jobs and new-found disposable income, teenagers could afford to buy records and go to the clubs and coffee bars that were springing up to meet the demand. If you lived in a small town or rural community, many churches were seizing the initiative and running dance nights.

Teenager Christine Parkinson remembered:

'When I was in my late teens we used to go to a club in Newcastle called La Dolce Vita and that felt really grown up. We used to dance round our handbags us girls and used to eye up any boys loitering around the edges. The Animals I liked because they were a homegrown group from Newcastle and we felt a bit of ownership. They were our lads.'

In Middlesbrough, the Outlook Club even hosted a gig which it called 'North v South', with The Hollies representing the North and The Rolling Stones representing the South. It's not known who won or how the winner was to be chosen. Admission price for members was 7s 6 pence, and 10 shillings for guests.

Clare Jenkins recalled:

'There were two clubs in Birmingham called Mothers and The Factory, which is where some people I knew went to listen to that kind of music and hippy bands like Quintessence, who I saw in concert. But I never went there. I was more middle of the road, going to the Top Rank dance club and when I was a young teenager the Catholic youth club, where we'd listen to nice pop music.'

In London, the Marquee Club had opened in Oxford Street in 1958, hosting a range of jazz, blues and skiffle groups, such as Johnny Dankworth, Chris Barber, Muddy Waters, Sonny Boy Williamson, Alexis Korner and later, of course, The Rolling Stones. The Stones had made their debut at the Marquee in January 1963, supporting harmonica player Cyril Davies, and would go on to play a number of gigs at the venue. In 1964, the Marquee relocated around the corner to Wardour Street in Soho, and like the Cavern in Liverpool began to shift away from jazz to reflect the current musical trends. Manfred Mann, The Yardbirds, The Who, David Bowie and Eric Clapton would all become regular performers before the decade was out.

Publicity manager Greg Tesser remembered the Marquee from its halcyon days in the 1960s:

'In London terms, it was the centre of all that was innovative in rock and R and B. Just down the road, of course, was The Flamingo, which had all-night sessions featuring Georgie Fame and Zoot Money, but their fan-base was completely different to the Marquee, which was in a big way sowing the seeds that led *Time* Magazine in 1966 to tell the world that London was the hip capital of the world. Within the feature, the writer coined the phrase "Swinging London".'

Music fan Tony Edwards remembered:

'[During 1965 I] became a regular at the club, attending at least 3 nights a week, with groups such as Long John Baldry (various incarnations), Gary Farr and the T-Bones, Spencer Davis Group, Alex Harvey Soul Band, The Moody Blues, Jimmy James and the Vagabonds, Graham Bond Organisation, and of course Manfred Mann, The Yardbirds and The Who. Every so often there would be a visit by someone special, such as Buddy Guy, T-Bone Walker, Memphis Slim, and I do remember a great showman Soloman Burke doing the James Brown entrance and exit with crown on head. An absolutely brilliant show, which was made even better, by having Jimmy James and the Vagabonds as support group.'

Because the Marquee was situated in Soho, it encouraged the development of Carnaby Street. Teenagers would flock to the street during the day, buying their clothes, and in the evening would parade their new outfits at the Marquee. The Rolling Stones had actually begun their career at the Crawdaddy club in Richmond in February 1963, although some members of the group had played the Marquee the previous summer. They also played at the Ealing Club, the Red Lion in Sutton and the Manor House pub in north London. Young people couldn't get enough of live music in small venues with their intimate atmosphere.

In his autobiography, Stones guitarist Keith Richards remembered the impact of the new music on young people, particularly girls: 'It was like somebody had pulled a plug somewhere. The 50s chicks being brought up all very jolly hockey sticks, and then somewhere there seemed to be a moment when they just decided to let themselves go.'

But not everyone was quite as taken with the Stones as they were with The Beatles. Clare Jenkins recounted:

'[I] always watched Top of the Pops. My parents were very patient; they'd even sometimes watch it with us – though we didn't always agree about the singers or groups we were watching. They thought The Rolling Stones were an extremely bad influence, for instance – but we weren't into them, so it didn't matter. We weren't that kind of rebellious though my brother did go to the 1970 Isle of Wight Festival, with Hendrix, The Doors, etc., and has very vivid memories of that.'

Christine Parkinson also had reservations about them:

'I found The Rolling Stones a bit dangerous, they had that feel about them and they looked so different to me. Mick Jagger and the way he moved, a bit dangerous. Being a convent schoolgirl, it made me feel a bit uncomfortable. There were a few girls who were into the Stones but they were a little bit too edgy and uncomfortable for me. I was a good girl. I wanted the reasonably clean-cut Beatles.'

The Beatles' music may have been revolutionary, but their politics were hardly radical and rarely vocalized until much later into the Sixties. John Lennon was the only stand-out political one among them. They may have joked with Harold Wilson on TV or at functions from time to time, but there were no signs that they were in any way Labour supporters. They probably always voted Labour simply because that was what their parents or family back in Liverpool would do. Only John ever said much that was radical or appeared to have any political commitment about him. He was the one who always looked the most moody – he had attitude coming out of his ears.

When Thelma McGough first met John Lennon, she was taken with that attitude. It was her first day at Art College in Liverpool. She was standing in the queue waiting to enrol when she was introduced to him:

'Another girl I was at school with came in and she said to John: "I believe your mother's dead." And he didn't bat an eyelid. Honestly his mouth didn't twitch, his eyes didn't move, he was sitting on a trestle table and he just carried on swinging his legs. She wouldn't let it go, and said "It was a policeman who knocked her down, that's right isn't it?" And he said "yeh." But there was not one iota of discernible emotion that something major had happened in his life. And she continued, "When was it?" and he said "July." She just kept going on and he was impervious. I was mesmerized by what I believed was bravery, his ability to not be marred or injured by such a traumatic event. He showed no visible reaction to any of it even though she kept going on and on and on. I was gobsmacked. I thought "my God, this guy's unique." I started going out with him the week after that.'

It was unusual that given their working-class Liverpool background, The Beatles were neither much interested in politics or football. But although they may not have shown much interest in football (which was strange, because at the time both the city's clubs, Liverpool and Everton, were riding high), the fans of Liverpool Football Club demonstrated their love of The Beatles by singing their songs on the Kop at their ground. In 1964, in an iconic edition of BBC's *Panorama* programme, a reporter is seen in front of the Kop immediately prior to kick-off with 27,000 Beatle-haired fans behind him rhythmically swaying and singing 'She Loves You', followed by 'Anyone Who Had A Heart', a recent smash hit for Cilla Black.

But what was truly important about The Beatles was that they were not afraid to voice their opinions. They certainly had plenty of them, even if they were not political. In doing so, they gave a voice to a new generation of young people who hitherto had been neither heard nor listened to.

What's more, the Beatles had long hair; far longer than the norm. That long hair left them open to criticism from parents, elders, teachers and employers. Onstage they might have looked reasonably smart in their measured suits, but offstage they were likely to wear black – a sure sign of evil – as well as leather coats and boots. And there was usually a cigarette hanging from their lips. Britain's youth soon began to copy the image.

British bands may not have been overtly political, but in America there were signs of singers becoming more aware of politics. Leading the charge was Bob Dylan, a young folk singer from Duluth in Minnesota. Bill Haley, Elvis Presley and Jerry Lee Lewis may have headlined the invasion of rock 'n' roll, but none were in any way radical. Dylan was a different matter. The American singer began his recording career in 1962 with his self-titled debut album. The cover showed a young, moody-looking Dylan sporting a black sailor's cap, clutching his acoustic guitar. He had a 'couldn't care less what you think' attitude, an image that seemed to resonate with young people. The record was not an immediate hit, but over time it sold in huge numbers. Dylan toured the UK in December 1962, staying a couple of months until January 1963. He mainly played small folk clubs around the London area, but his music did not go down that well with the traditionalists, who were more into sea shanties and tales of crofters than the moody grunting of an American teenager. But if his first visit was hardly successful, his return two years later was very different. By then he was a major star and his songs were resonating with young people. Dylan had begun writing his major hit, 'The Times They Are a Changin', in 1963. He said at the time that he wrote the song 'as a deliberate attempt to create an anthem of change for the moment'. Many years later, he claimed that it 'was definitely a song with a purpose ... the civil rights movement and the folk movement were pretty close for a while and allied together at that time.'

Dylan, however, later denied that the lyrics were as overtly political as many assumed. He had already created a stir with his 'Blowin in the Wind' album, released in 1962, with the title song regarded as something of a statement urging change. But whatever Dylan may have argued about not being political, young people had a very different view and clearly regarded his lyrics as meaningful. Indeed, they soon became an anthem for a disaffected young generation, hell bent on change. Other American singers also began to emerge; some, like Joan Baez, with politics firmly written across their foreheads. Baez, at one point a girlfriend of Dylan, became involved in the American Civil Rights Movement, recorded

'We Shall Overcome' and 'Joe Hill', and joined the Freedom March on Washington as well as many anti-Vietnam War demonstrations.

Back in Britain, although groups like The Beatles, the Stones, The Who and others might not have been overtly political, their dress code and attitude suggested otherwise. They were definitely anti-Establishment.

The tabloid press demonized the likes of Jagger and John Lennon, making them out to be a threat to society. By doing so, however, they simply made them into even greater anti-heroes.

In July 1965, The Animals released the single 'We Gotta Get Out of This Place'. Its lyrics, possibly more than any other at that time, spelled out their anxieties and fears:

> 'Watch my daddy in bed a-dyin'
> Watched his hair been turnin' grey
> He's been workin' and slavin' his life away.'

It was a cry for change, and the chorus line suggested a solution:

> 'We gotta get out of this place
> If it's the last thing we ever do
> We gotta get out of this place
> 'Cause girl, there's a better life for me and you.'

It was to be another anthem for Britain's youth, trying to escape the drudgery of provincial working-class life.

By late 1963, The Beatles had become the biggest thing British music had ever witnessed. Their second single, 'Please, Please Me', had topped the hit parade, and an album under the same name quickly became the biggest-selling album ever released in the UK. Their rise to fame was meteoric as one hit followed another.

Suddenly, everyone was talking about them, as Beatles fan Christine Parkinson recounted:

'I was so aware of The Beatles. My favourite was George Harrison. We were very excited about The Beatles; we each had our favourites. We knew all the songs. I wanted the reasonably clean-cut Beatles. I only had a mum, my dad died when I was about four and a half. She was an older mum and didn't care much about music. I had two older sisters and a brother, so I didn't have too much disapproval. My sisters were into the same kind of thing.'

Every Beatles fan had a favourite Beatle, and that was what was unique about them. It's hard to think of any other pop group of four distinctly identifiable members who all seemed just as popular as each other. There was George, who was cool; Ringo, with his humour and sense of mischief; Paul, with his good looks; and John, who was the tough guy. There was no leader, just four guys who got on well and seemed to enjoy each other's company. What's more, this appeal was shared by both men and women. The girls all fancied one or other member of the group, whereas the boys simply wanted to be a Beatle, with the fame – and the girls – that accompanied it. Sex was a vital ingredient to their act. They became international sex symbols.

Beatlemania had been born. Girls screamed so loud at their concerts that you couldn't hear the music. They were a sensation. Wherever they appeared they were mobbed by huge numbers of girls, pushing and swaying in vast crowds that the police tried to control. Girls fainted on the roadside or had to be carried out of theatres, such was the excitement. Every day, one newspaper or another had a Beatles story or photograph. Later that year they toured Sweden, returning to a phenomenal reception at Heathrow airport. It soon became the norm for thousands to meet or wave goodbye to them at some airport or other.

Their rise to fame in the United States, however, was slower as contractual problems delayed the release of recordings. It eventually took a few well-known DJs to acquire bought-in copies of their records from the UK and to have them copied and passed on to other radio stations. Once the various issues had been resolved, their records were released in the United States and swept to the top of their charts. In February

1964, The Beatles flew to America for the first time, waved farewell by 4,000 screaming teenage girls at Heathrow airport, only to be greeted at JFK airport in New York by just as many fans. The youth revolution was spreading. Needless to say, however, they weren't popular with everyone in America. Baptist preachers denounced them from the pulpit, newspapers called them debauched and even TV show hosts commented about their long hair. Society was split: the elderly were appalled, but the young identified with them and loved them.

Chapter 4
A Cultural Revolution

In those heady days of the early 1960s, I spent many an evening not only at the Cavern, but the Everyman Theatre as well. One of the attractions was the weekly poetry evening at the Everyman, where poets like Roger McGough, Brian Patten, Adrian Henri and others would read their latest poems in the Bohemian atmosphere of the downstairs bar. It would be filled with smoke, pints of beer and beatnik-dressed young people sitting on the floor or on the few available chairs. In many ways it was the same audience as frequented the Cavern or many of the other clubs in the city centre. But what made the evening so rewarding for me was that everyone was invited to read their own poems. When the readings ended, everyone would roundly applaud. The poetry was not that of Shelley or Keats, but rather poetry that resonated with ordinary young people. Roger McGough wrote of the first plastic daffodils of the year on the supermarket shelves, while Adrian Henri wrote of love being like 'fish and chips on winter nights'. Others, meanwhile, wrote of schooldays or unrequited love. But whatever it was, it always seemed to be meaningful, funny and part of their lives.

Roger McGough was the driving force behind the Liverpool poets. In a *Guardian* article years later, he remembered those Sixties evenings:

'I was living in the centre of town and we started going down there. Brian Patten, Adrian Henri and I had started doing poetry readings in various venues around the city. We'd take over folk clubs on a quiet Monday night. We started doing events – or "happenings" as they were known in America. This being Liverpool, there was always a lot of humour. In the bar downstairs there'd often be a band on – and a dance. We generally put on readings and sketches downstairs.'

McGough also distinctly remembered that 'Paul McCartney and George Harrison would come to the readings and hang around'. It was all part of the Liverpool scene that encompassed not only music but writing, theatre and art. And at the centre of this thriving arts scene was the Cavern and the Everyman Theatre.

The poets were so popular that in 1967, Penguin published a collection of their poems called *The Mersey Sound*. It was of course derided by the poetry Establishment, but it went on to become a bestseller, with McGough becoming recognized as a serious poet and commentator. McGough also later joined forces with John Gorman and Paul McCartney's brother, Mike McGear, to form the Scaffold and went on to record a number of hit records, including 'Lily the Pink'.

Paul McCartney and John Lennon had been composing their own songs almost from the moment they met and started strumming their guitars. They were mostly simple, unsophisticated tunes, which they never played at any of their sessions at the Cavern or elsewhere. Indeed, it wasn't until 'Love Me Do', their first British recording, that anyone realized that they composed their own songs. The lyrics and music were shared, depending on who came up with something first.

John, in particular, was always scribbling things down. Long before The Beatles had become nationally known, he was writing snippets of poetry and other witty, often satirical, pieces for the *Mersey Beat* newspaper. In 1964, a collection of his writings, *In His Own Write*, was published, followed two years later by *A Spaniard In The Works*. Lennon was also drawing on a regular basis, usually humorous sketches of people he knew or incidents he remembered. He would continue to sketch throughout his life, often claiming that he loved art more than music.

Further uptown from the Cavern in Liverpool, the Everyman in Hope Street nestled between the imposing Anglican Cathedral and the awesomely striking Catholic Cathedral. In 1960 it was called Hope Hall, having gone through a variety of lives. It had originally been built as a dissenters' chapel, then became a church, followed by a concert hall and in 1912 a cinema, which is how it continued until it closed in 1963. It was to reopen a year later as a theatre, the inspiration of Peter James, Martin Jenkins and Terry Hands. Roger McGough recalled:

'Before the Everyman opened up in the mid-60s there was the Playhouse, which had an older audience. It was regarded as elitist – the actors came up from London, did the shows and then went back on the next train. The Everyman was different. The actors came and stayed in Liverpool. They put on proletarian, socially conscious stuff.'

The aim of the new theatre was to be different, by presenting new plays or fresh interpretations of old plays and to employ young actors, many of them recent graduates. There were to be no stars and everyone was to be paid the same: £5 a week during rehearsals and £8 during the actual production. The theatre itself was rather drab and rundown, totally unlike your usual venue, but that in itself was an attraction. Young people felt far more at home in its shabbiness than sitting in the front stalls or gods of some ornate Edwardian edifice.

In its first season in 1964, the Everyman opened somewhat traditionally with Shakespeare's *Henry IV Part One*, but then presented Ibsen's *An Enemy of the People*, followed by Pinter's *The Caretaker* and a little later T.S. Eliot's *Murder in the Cathedral*, *Waiting for Godot* (Samuel Beckett) and *Look Back in Anger* (John Osborne). The Everyman was indeed very different, and was soon attracting audiences of young people as well as comments in the national press. Even the traditional Playhouse audience began to switch allegiance.

There were other art-associated venues in town, such as the Kardomah cafe in Bold Street, where you might spot one of the Beatles or a poet, and where young people simply 'hung out'. There were also pubs, like the Philharmonic in Hope Street and Ye Cracke just around the corner from the College of Art, where John, Paul and Stuart would drink at lunchtime. In addition there was the Grapes in Mathew Street and the White Star lower down, where the Beatles drank following their sessions at the Cavern.

It was without a doubt The Beatles who created and inspired this art scene. They were at the core of it, especially John, Paul and George, with their own brand of humour and irreverence helping to drag the arts into the late twentieth century and away from the elitism that had so often stifled any development.

Typical of this was the banning of D.H. Lawrence's novel *Lady Chatterley's Lover* and the sensational trial which followed in 1960. Lawrence's novel concerned a love affair between the aristocratic Lady Chatterley, whose husband had been paralyzed from the waist down during the First World War, and the estate's gamekeeper, Mellors. The book described their illicit relationship with explicit sexual language. A private edition had been printed in Italy in 1928 shortly after it had been written, but due to its sexual content, a British edition had never been openly published. Other editions had been published in Britain, but were highly censored, with many of the explicit passages omitted. No uncensored version had ever been openly available in Britain. In 1960, however, Penguin Books decided to publish an unexpurgated edition of the novel. When it appeared, it was promptly banned under the Obscene Publications Act 1959 and its publishers, Penguin, were charged under the Act.

The trial at the Old Bailey began on 20 October 1960 before twelve jurors and lasted for two weeks. During that time, a series of well-known artists and writers testified before the court in its favour, including E.M. Forster, Cecil Day-Lewis, Rebecca West, Richard Hoggart and Raymond Williams. What was at stake was whether the book had any literary merit. If it did, then under the terms of the new Act, it could be freely published. On the one side were the literary intelligentsia arguing for its publication, whilst on the other side was the Establishment, the traditional conservative forces of old Britain, who at times seemed more shocked by the fact that an aristocratic woman could possibly consider a sexual relationship with someone who was basically a servant than by any language used in the book. The trial began with the prosecuting counsel's first request that a clerk in the Director of Public Prosecution's office should carefully count the number of obscene four-letter words in the book. In his opening speech to the jury, the prosecuting counsel then played them as if they were trump cards: 'The word "fuck" or "fucking" appears no less than

30 times ... "Cunt" 14 times; "balls" 13 times; "shit" and "arse" six times apiece; "cock" four times; "piss" three times, and so on.'

The Chief Prosecutor, Mervyn Griffith-Jones, who had been a war hero and awarded the Military Cross after his service in North Africa and Italy, was totally out of his depth. It was almost in desperation that, in high-Victorian style, he asked the jury: 'Would you approve of your young sons, young daughters – because girls can read as well as boys – reading this book? Is it a book that you would have lying around in your own house? Is it a book that you would even wish your wife or your servants to read?' To much amusement, he then begged the jury to 'think of the factory girls, reading the book in their lunch-hour'. Once these words were out of his mouth, the case was lost.

It was clear from the prosecution that its case was hardly in keeping with the changing times. There was a clear division in the court. The jury had no Establishment connections, being twelve ordinary citizens. They deliberated for just three hours before making up their minds and returning to deliver a unanimous verdict of 'not guilty'.

The trial had been a sensation, hitting the headlines throughout its duration. When the book was rushed out for publication following the verdict, it became an instant bestseller, selling over three million copies in three months, although most people were still inclined to hide it beneath a brown paper cover. On the first day of publication, it sold its entire print run of 200,000 copies.

'The Innocence of Lady Chatterley,' ran the headline in London's *Evening Standard*. 'Jury reach historic decision after three hours,' it reported, adding that applause broke out in court after the verdict was revealed.

Most ordinary people in 1960, however, remained deeply conservative, and the Home Office was flooded with letters of protest. In Edinburgh, copies were burned on the streets; in South Wales, female librarians asked permission not to handle it; from Surrey, one anguished woman wrote to the Home Secretary, explaining that her teenage daughter was at boarding school and she was terrified that 'day girls there may introduce this filthy book'.

What the publication of *Lady Chatterley's Lover* did was to breach a barrier. After the trial, there was a reluctance to venture down that banning route again, and the Obscene Publications Act became discredited and only rarely used. 'No other jury verdict in British history has had such a deep social impact,' wrote the respected lawyer Geoffrey Robinson in the *Guardian* some years later. It set a trend for Britain in the 1960s and a society that would be more liberal, free-thinking and less judgmental.

Such was the trial's significance that the poet Philip Larkin later wrote:

> Sexual intercourse began
> In nineteen sixty-three
> (which was rather late for me) –
> Between the end of the 'Chatterley' ban
> And The Beatles' first LP.

The seeds of the 1960s cultural revolution had been firmly sown in the mid to late 1950s. John Osborne's play *Look Back in Anger* had opened at London's Royal Court Theatre in May 1956, albeit to mixed reviews. Kenneth Tynan described it as 'a minor miracle' and Harold Hobson as 'a landmark', but they were among the few who immediately recognized its importance. The BBC's Ivor Brown and the *Daily Mail* took a very different, more conservative view. Perhaps of even more importance than *Look Back in Anger* was Shelagh Delaney's *A Taste of Honey*, which opened at the Theatre Royal in Stratford East in 1958. Salford-born Delaney had begun writing her play in a school exercise book at the age of 16 after a visit to the Opera House in Manchester to see a Terrence Rattigan play. Unimpressed by Rattigan's take on the world, she returned home convinced that she could write something better, more relevant, and set about doing so. She was just 18 when her play premiered in London. It featured racism, homosexuality, sex, abortion and working-class life in the North, subjects largely shunned in British theatres up to that time. The *Daily Mail* hated it. Their reviewer, Edward Goring, wrote: 'Once, authors wrote good plays, set in Drawing rooms. Now, under the Welfare State, they write bad plays set in garrets.' He added that it 'tastes of exercise books and marmalade', concluding that 'if there's anything worse than an angry young man, it's an angry young woman'. It was typical of the kind of London elitism that pervaded the British theatre at that time.

Joan Littlewood's Theatre Workshop was also significant, featuring plays by the former IRA activist and prisoner Brendan Behan. Meanwhile, Arnold Wesker, whose *Chicken Soup With Barley* and *Roots* added a political dimension to theatre, later founded the Roundhouse Theatre at Chalk Farm in an old railways turntable shed outside Euston station that had lain derelict for a few years. In 1960, Wesker persuaded the Trades Union Congress to back a resolution (Resolution 42) calling for an inquiry into the arts. Wesker saw the building as perfect for the staging of plays and other events. Above all, Wesker wanted to shift the arts away from its elitism and into the community. The venture became known as Centre 42.

The TUC also backed the project by injecting cash. Joan Littlewood had been a member of the Communist Party, and as such was quietly shunned by the BBC. Both she and Wesker took a radical approach in terms of content and production.

In 1963, Littlewood adapted a radio play by Charles Chilton called *The Long, Long Trail*, which had been broadcast two years earlier. Littlewood's adaptation became known as *Oh, What A Lovely War!* and was an immediate hit. Perhaps more importantly, the play rewrote the history of the First World War. It was the story of the war from the soldiers' standpoint, rather than that of the generals, and gave a fresh interpretation of events. It was about writing history from the bottom upwards and helped set a style that would change how we interpreted history.

But if Littlewood and other radical playwrights had caused a minor sensation in the early 1960s, it was a musical, *Hair*, later that decade that really hit the headlines. Conceived by two American actors, James Rado and Gerome Ragni, *Hair* opened in New York's East Village in 1967. The musical was about hippie counterculture and the sexual revolution. The following year, it transferred to Broadway and was the theatrical sensation of the year. What caused the uproar was the show's content of nudity, explicit language, sex, drugs, anti-Americanism and race. Actors – male and female – cavorted naked on stage, indulging in a narrative of free love, threesomes, homosexuality, sodomy, desecrating the American flag and drug-taking. It was enough to make Middle America and the Home Counties of England shocked to the core. But for young people, *Hair* was a breath of fresh air, a vivid depiction of what their generation was up to. And the music was straight out of the charts.

In September 1968, the production opened in London's West End just one day after the abolition of theatre censorship. Prior to that, it would almost certainly have been banned. Generally, the reviews were less hostile than might have been expected. Irving Wardle in *The Times* said: 'Its honesty and passion give it the quality of a true theatrical celebration – the joyous sound of a group of people telling the world exactly what they feel.' In *The Guardian*, Phillip Hope-Wallace wrote: 'It is funny, and even charming at times. Much play is made with dashing about the auditorium, with wandering flower people hobnobbing with those in aisle seats. It is all a good deal less awful than it sounds.' In *The Financial Times*, B.A. Young agreed that *Hair* was 'not only a wildly enjoyable evening, but a thoroughly moral one'. However, the 78-year-old W.A. Darlington of the *Daily Telegraph* found it 'a complete bore – noisy, ugly and quite desperately funny'.

Whatever the critics may have thought, the public certainly loved it. Young people flocked to see the show, with it running to almost 2,000 performances. Its songs climbed the charts and the album sold in its millions. The psychedelic poster for the show became a huge seller as well, adorning student bedrooms around the world.

Hair had pushed the boundaries, and a short time later Kenneth Tynan's *Oh! Calcutta!* pushed them even further. Staged in 1969, initially off Broadway, the musical transferred to London in 1970. What shocked was extended scenes of nudity, language and references to masturbation. The show ran for over 3,000 performances in London and remains one of the longest-running shows ever on Broadway.

The cinema also had strict controls on what could or could not be seen by the public. All films were rated by the British Board of Film Censors: an 'X' film could only be seen by adults (those over 18 years of age); an 'A' film could be seen by a younger person, but only if accompanied by an adult; and a 'U' film could be seen by anyone. The Board of Film Censors also had the powers to ban any film which it believed to be obscene. This usually meant that there were explicit sex scenes, violence or offensive language. In addition, local authorities had the powers to ban films from being shown in their areas. In such instances, the local Fire Brigades Committee or some form of Watch Committee would have the powers to view and ban a film. These committees would be constituted by representatives of the fire brigade, local councillors and, more often than not, a policeman or two. The release in 1967 of *Ulysses*, the film loosely based on the James Joyce novel, caused considerable controversy. It may have been given an 'X' certificate by the Board of Film Censors after a number of changes had been enforced, but it was nonetheless proscribed by many local authorities. In Birkenhead, the film was banned by the local Fire Brigades Committee, causing one reader of the *Birkenhead News* to write to the paper in protest.

In literature, Colin Wilson with *The Outsider* in 1956 and John Braine with his novel *Room At The Top* a year later set a new trend by writing about working-class life, as observed by those who were themselves working class. Wilson was from Leicester, the son of a factory worker, while Braine, from Bingley in Yorkshire, had begun life as a shopworker and was subsequently a librarian. Others soon followed in their path. Many had little more than a formal education and only a few had been to university. They included Nottingham's Alan Sillitoe, who penned *Saturday Night, Sunday Morning* and *The Loneliness of the Long Distance Runner*. These authors became known as 'The Angry Young Men' for their approach to literature. It was an approach that had taken the theatre out of the drawing rooms of Belgravia and onto the streets of Salford, Manchester and Yorkshire for their storylines. With it, new audiences were attracted. It was the same with novels. The comic novels of Kingsley Amis – *Lucky Jim* (1954) – and Keith Waterhouse, with *Billy Liar* (1959), also attracted a new class of reader.

The trend had been established, and during the 1960s others added to the genre, such as David Storey (*This Sporting Life*), Nell Dunn (*Up the Junction*), Muriel Spark (*The Prime of Miss Jean Brodie*) and Anthony

Burgess (*A Clockwork Orange*). *This Sporting Life* featured the northern game of rugby league, with its hard drinking, sleazy club chairman and sycophantic local sports journalist, while *Up The Junction*, based in the slums of Battersea, gave readers, and later viewers, a stark portrayal of backstreet abortions.

Irish writer Edna O'Brien gave voice to the emotions and feelings of women, particularly in *The Country Girls* and *August Is A Wicked Month*. Although O'Brien found fame in Britain, many of her writings were banned in her native country due to their sexual content. If Britain was set to become more liberal-minded in the 1960s, Ireland would lag a couple of decades behind.

Clare Jenkins, a young schoolgirl at the time, remembers reading 'daring' books:

> 'I read a lot of Edna O'Brien – I remember being shocked by certain aspects of her books, like when her heroine goes to the toilet at a party and doesn't flush the toilet afterwards because the hosts of the party haven't been nice to her. That seemed outrageous.
>
> 'I remember also reading a lot of D.H. Lawrence and my French pen-pal's father – they were devout Catholics who lived in a farmhouse in northern France, where I stayed for a month – being shocked to see I was reading *The Virgin and the Gypsy*, and telling me so in no uncertain terms. I didn't tell him I'd also read *Women in Love*. Mind you, I had to hide books like that from my mother as well, who was terrified we'd be corrupted by many things in the sixties – as were the mothers of most of my schoolfriends, many of whom were Irish Catholics. I remember a friend being given the book of *Bonnie and Clyde* for her birthday and passing it round to all of us because there were some sexy scenes in it. Trouble is, when it got to me, Mum found it, stuffed behind a cushion, and it immediately fell open at a much-thumbed page. She threatened to burn it, and I had to plead with her to give it back to me so I could return it to my friend.

'I would also have read those classic books like *Saturday Night & Sunday Morning, A Kind of Loving,* because we were always at the library, borrowing books – and I was desperate for knowledge, and those wider horizons. I used to discuss them with my school friends – we were all curious about the world. Some girls were more outspoken, more daring, than my gang of five were, but we heard them talking about books and records and TV, in the classrooms, so we'd sometimes then look into what they'd been talking about.'

Many of these novels were turned into highly successful films, again reaching out to a new and wider audience of young cinemagoers. They were also directed by a wave of young film directors such as Tony Richardson, Ken Loach and Ken Russell, whose innovative approaches were more direct and realistic.

Annie O'Malley remembers going to see many of these films as a teenager and how she could relate to them because they were about the kind of life she led; working class, northern and 'about the issues faced by many young people. They weren't Hollywood, they were Salford, Nottingham, Leicester, places I knew.' Many of them featured young actors with northern working-class roots, including Albert Finney, Tom Courtney, Glenda Jackson and of course Welshman Richard Burton.

The Beatles, of course, were also getting in on the act. In 1964, they starred in the movie *A Hard Days Night,* directed by Richard Lester with the screenplay by fellow Liverpudlian Alun Owen. It was a film about thirty-six hours in the life of The Beatles and centred around Paul's trouble-making grandfather, played by Wilfrid Bramble. It predictably featured a host of new Beatles songs, which were simultaneously released on an album that also became an instant best-seller. The film was a huge success, grossing more than £10 million worldwide, and was also critically acclaimed and nominated for two Academy Awards. The film is credited as being one of the most influential musicals ever, inspiring The Monkees' television show as well as a whole genre of pop music videos. In 1999, the British Film Institute ranked it the eighty-eighth greatest British film of the twentieth century. The Beatles, it seemed, could do no wrong. The following year,

A Hard Days Night was followed up by *Help!*, again directed by Richard Lester along, with another new album from the soundtrack. More films followed, including *Magical Mystery Tour*, and then John Lennon starred without his fellow Beatles in *How I Won The War*. The latter, described as a black comedy, was directed and produced by Richard Lester, based on the 1963 novel of the same name by Patrick Ryan. The film, however, was not highly rated by the critics.

Television also began to feature hard-hitting, well-written dramas that portrayed working-class life. BBC's *Z Cars*, written by Elwyn Jones, was based in the fictional Newtown, somewhere in the North of England, and recounted the daily activities of the police, with the focus around their patrol car. It was a far different approach to the traditional image of the police which had been portrayed in earlier programmes such as *Dixon of Dock Green*. Nell Dunn's TV play *Up The Junction* highlighted appalling backstreet abortions, while *Cathy Come Home* depicted the dire housing problems of 1960s Britain.

And of course there was *Coronation Street*. It may have been what was to become known as 'soap opera', but nobody could ever deny its importance. The Street began in December 1960, produced at the studios of Granada Television in Manchester. It was the creation of Tony Warren, who initially conceived it as a sixteen-part series to be called *Florizel Street*. Within Granada itself there was opposition to the programme, with fears that it was too dreary and not what people would want to watch. In the end, Granada's then head of programmes, Dennis Foreman, managed to persuade his colleagues to give it the go-ahead. The one compromise was that they needed to find a better title. They considered the name 'Jubilee Street', but in the end opted for 'Coronation Street'. Cecil Bernstein, part of Granada's controlling family, remained sceptical and told the press department not to give it too much pre-publicity to save any embarrassment should it flop. The programme was to be transmitted twice a week, with the first show to be broadcast live. Because it was 'live', Granada scoured the repertory theatres of the north-west in search of talented actors who could perform under pressure and cope with any kind of mishaps. And mishaps did occur; ornaments fell off walls and occasionally actors forgot their lines and had to ad lib. Granada, which had won the franchise to operate in the North in 1955, deliberately wanted authenticity and a soap opera that would appeal to its viewers, something they could identify with.

It was set in a row of terraced houses in a cramped little street, supposedly somewhere in Salford but never really identified as such, with a corner shop, a pub and a church hall. Because its precise location was never acknowledged, anyone, anywhere, could identify with it. It opened with Elsie Tanner haranguing her neighbours. All the characters were sharply defined and rang true. Every street had a woman of 'questionable morals' like Elsie Tanner; a harridan like Ena Sharples; an irascible old codger like Albert Tatlock; and upright pub landlords like Jack and Annie Walker. Elsie Tanner also had a teenage son, Dennis, who, like so many of his age, was kicking against the system and his family.

The show very much mirrored life in Northern working-class Britain, and although many no longer lived in the terrace streets, they could still identify with them. They may have moved on to the suburbs and their three-bedroom semi-detached houses, but most had been born in places like Coronation Street and could readily remember and identify with the characters and the issues that preoccupied them. The Street was cast in the mould of a kitchen-sink drama of angry young men and tough northern women, and as such very much caught the mood of the times.

Ken Farrington, who played landlord's son Billy Walker, called it a 'documentary drama', while the poet Sir John Betjeman likened it to Dickens' *The Pickwick Papers*.

But not everybody was impressed. Ken Irwin in the *Daily Mirror* wrote that 'there is little reality in his [Tony Warren's] new serial which, apparently, we will have to suffer twice a week. The programme is doomed from the outset – with its dreary signature tune and grim scene of a row of terraced houses and smoking chimneys.'

But if the *Daily Mirror* and other newspaper critics didn't like it, The Beatles certainly did; they were known to be avid viewers. At one point it was mooted that they might even feature in the show. Bill Harry, editor of *Mersey Beat* and friend of The Beatles, remembered:

'Corrie was planning on introducing a character called Walter Potts who wore a Beatle jacket and aspired to be a pop star ... Harry Kershaw, the programme's original script editor, remembers that they received a message that the Beatles wouldn't be averse to appearing on the show ... The Beatles would be travelling to a concert in Manchester by car, which would break down near the back door of the vestry where Ena Sharples worked. Crowds would begin to gather, which unsettles the police and they knock on Ena's door asking whether she can give the four lads sanctuary. She agrees and John, Paul, George and Ringo file past her into the vestry.

'In the next episode, Ena would charm them into agreeing to give a concert that evening for the local Over-Sixties club. But when a 14-year-old girl hears about it, she tells all her friends and the Under-Sixteens join the Over-Sixties in a concert at which The Beatles perform. When it's over, the police arrive and the group sets off, rather late, for their other concert ... Reluctantly, because it was felt that more rehearsal time was essential as The Beatles weren't actors, the plans were dropped.'

Stuart Sutcliffe will always be remembered as the fifth Beatle. Born in Edinburgh, his family moved to Liverpool when he was very young. Sutcliffe subsequently attended the Liverpool College of Art, where he soon befriended John Lennon. In May 1960, he was recruited to join John, Paul, George and Pete Best in the group, even travelling to Germany with them. Shortly after they had returned from their stint in Hamburg, Sutcliffe decided to quit the band. It was generally acknowledged that he was a somewhat mediocre guitar player. Anyhow, Sutcliffe's great love was art. In 1961, he had entered for the John Moores Painting Prize, an event held every two years at the Walker Art Gallery in Liverpool, coming runner-up in the junior section to Peter Blake. The John Moores Painting Prize for new artists was one of the most prestigious in Europe, and was largely for abstract painting. The winner in 1959 had been Patrick Heron, while David Hockney's career was greatly enhanced when he won in 1967. Sutcliffe's prize was £60, a not inconsiderable amount in those days, which went on purchasing new equipment for the band. John Lennon even visited the exhibition to see his friend's painting. John Moores, owner of the Littlewoods Pools company and sponsor of the prize, purchased one of Sutcliffe's paintings as a gift for his son. The Walker Art Gallery itself also bought one. Sutcliffe subsequently enrolled in the Hamburg College of Art, but died tragically young of a brain haemorrhage in April 1962, aged just 21.

Sutcliffe's girlfriend, Astrid Kirchherr, also earned her place in Beatles history. It was Kirchherr who took many of the early photographs of The Beatles, often depicting them in urban scenes with stark backgrounds, wearing their leather gear, with cigarettes and guitars casually strewn around. It was a radical approach to pop group photo-shoots that helped move them away from soft, colour studio portraits to harsh, exterior black and white pictures.

The 1960s saw a revolution in British art, certainly helped by the John Moores Painting Prize, with the emergence of a number of important young artists. Francis Bacon's reputation was already growing. His 'Three Studies for Figures at the Base of the Crucifixion' had been painted towards the end of the Second World War and had firmly established him as a leading artist, while his paintings of the screaming pope during the 1950s had proven him as a major international name. Bacon enhanced his reputation throughout the 1960s with a variety of portraits. Indeed, his 'Three Studies of Lucian Freud', painted in 1969, would become the most expensive painting ever auctioned at that time when in November 2013 it fetched $142.4 million.

In America, a young artist named Andy Warhol shot to fame in the 1960s with his advertisement paintings. The simplicity, style and subject matter of many of Warhol's works appealed to young people. Portraits of Marilyn Monroe, Mao Tse Tung, Elvis Presley and other iconic figures of the era soon found their way onto mass-produced posters and onto the bedroom walls of the young. Warhol was himself still young, political and a pioneer of style and subject matter. He even ventured into film, directing a number of movies that explored sexuality in an open and controversial way.

Although Bacon was well established before the 1960s, he would be joined in that era by a number of prominent artists in Britain. Others such as Lucien Freud, Frank Auerbach and Ronald Kitaj were also beginning to establish themselves and became major recognized artists during the 1960s, being joined by a number of other young artists, including David Hockney and Peter Blake. Had Sutcliffe lived, he might well have joined this distinguished group.

Bradford-born Hockney had studied at the Royal College of Art in London in the early 1960s, alongside Peter Blake, but moved to Los Angeles in 1964 before returning to Britain four years later. Hockney took the art world by storm, producing a number of highly regarded works whilst he was in America, which began to attract great interest and high prices. Hockney, like Bacon, was also gay at a time when homosexuality was still an offence. It would not be legalized until 1967. Neither Hockney nor Bacon made any attempt to hide their sexuality and were brave enough to confront any prejudices that might have impinged on their reputations.

This group of artists became known as the School of London. Prominent among them was Peter Blake, a 'pop artist' whose work mixed pop culture with fine art, including advertisements, collages and record covers. It was Blake who had pipped Stuart Sutcliffe to the John Moores Prize, later generously arguing that Sutcliffe really should have won it. Blake retained an interest in The Beatles and Liverpool, and later teamed up with them to design the famous cover of the 'Sgt Pepper's Lonely Hearts Club Band' album. Released in 1967, the cover featured a wide range of celebrities and other iconic images, one of whom was Stuart Sutcliffe himself.

The pop art movement stretched into other areas, producing posters, psychedelic art, comics, adverts and a whole range of designs. It was about young people and fresh approaches, particularly in areas that hitherto had not been influenced in any way by art.

Also worthy of mention was *Private Eye*, the satirical magazine first published in 1961, with Christopher Booker as editor. It was initially a vehicle for juvenile jokes: an extension of the original school magazine, full of cartoons, a modern version of *Punch* magazine. Under the later ownership of Peter Cook, and with Richard Ingrams as editor, it shifted direction in 1962 and began to lampoon the Establishment by exposing the hypocrisy of politicians, the press, the law and other aspects of previously untouchable echelons of British society. *Private Eye* was not only at the forefront of trying to knock down authoritarianism and the Establishment, but was catching the mood of young people. More than half a century later, it remains as strong as ever, with a fortnightly circulation of almost 250,000.

In less than a single decade, culture had shifted from its previous elitism to a vibrant, new influence, led largely by young people. There was a morphing in many areas of the arts between music, drama, art, poetry and film. Traditional boundaries were crossed, with pop art and television leading the way in making art more accessible to the ordinary person.

Chapter 5
'What the hell is going on in this country?'

'I was forced to spend a great deal of time today over a silly scrape (women this time, thank God, not boys) into which one of the ministers has got himself.'
When Prime Minister Harold Macmillan wrote the above entry in his diary on the evening of 15 March 1963, he was either being totally naïve or simply denying the truth. The 'silly scrape', as he called it, would some months later lead to his downfall, the resignation of his Defence Secretary, John Profumo, allegations of spying, a scurrilous court case, call girls, a murder, a suicide, a public inquiry, acres of headlines in the papers and a general election that would sweep the Tories out of office. It was a 'silly scrape' that even fifty years later continues to intrigue and titillate the nation. It had everything. But it would also underline and expose a rottenness that pervaded aristocratic England and British politics. The old order was about to be exposed and ousted, and the new order of youth was ready to take over.

Revelations of the 'Profumo affair', as it became known, began with a question in the House of Commons from George Wigg, the backbench Labour Member of Parliament. Wigg was close to the British security services and was known around Parliament for his gossip. He had clearly got wind of an affair in the highest Tory circles, and although the Labour Party was reluctant to pursue the issue, Wigg himself had no such reservations. A massive scandal was about to break.

Harold Macmillan's Secretary of State for Defence, John Profumo, first met Christine Keeler at Spring Cottage, a small lodge on Lord Astor's Cliveden estate in Berkshire which was temporarily leased by the London osteopath Dr Stephen Ward, who had been treating the estate's owner. It was said that Stephen Ward and John Profumo met when the latter was a guest of the Astors at Cliveden. Lord Astor and Profumo had wandered from their dinner party down to the Lodge, where Ward was entertaining his friends. Profumo had apparently watched in admiration as a young Christine Keeler swam naked in the Spring Cottage swimming pool. It was known that parties regularly took place at Ward's cottage involving notable members of the aristocracy and attractive young girls. Keeler was a dancer who mixed in the highest circles. Profumo was so taken by Keeler that he later asked Ward how he could get in touch with her. Thus began an affair that was to have devastating consequence for all concerned, leading to just about everybody's downfall. What made the story so sensational was that Keeler was also having an affair with a high-ranking Soviet official known as Captain Yevgeny Ivanov, who also happened to be the naval attaché at the Soviet Union's embassy in London. Clearly there was a security risk involved, and Ivanov, who was also known to British security services as an intelligence officer with the Soviet GRU, was now a man under heavy surveillance.

Keeler had been a dancer at Murray's Cabaret Club in Soho for some years, where she met society osteopath Stephen Ward and fellow dancer Mandy Rice-Davies, who would also be caught up in the web of intrigue that later broke. Murray's was frequented by the most glittering of people in London, including royalty in the shape of a young Princess Margaret, financiers, industrialists, show business stars and politicians. At Murray's you could drink legally until 2.30 am, at a time when pubs had to close at 10.30 pm. You could also dance with the half-naked hostesses and mingle with the best in society. In its heyday, Murray's Cabaret Club was one of the most discreetly risqué establishments in London, a place where society could rub shoulders and drink vintage champagne with scantily clad showgirls and hostesses. There was said to be a pervasive atmosphere of sex, with one customer describing it as a 'visual brothel'.

It was here that Keeler befriended Ward and later went on to share a flat with him, although she always insisted that they never shared a bed. Keeler also joined Ward for weekends at his cottage on the Cliveden estate. Other girls from Murray's would be invited along too, including Mandy Rice-Davies.

Profumo's affair with Keeler did not last long, but what made it complicated was that Ivanov, knowing that she was also seeing Profumo, asked Keeler to ask the Cabinet minister about defence secrets concerning the British nuclear capability. This was at a time when the Cold War was at a new height following the Cuban Missile Crisis. At this point, MI5 became aware of Profumo's affair with Keeler and may well have warned him off. Rumours about Profumo's affair and the link with the Soviet naval attaché circulated around Westminster and in newsrooms for some weeks, but with little evidence to support the tittle-tattle, nothing could be published.

The story eventually broke when George Wigg, under Parliamentary privilege, began to ask questions in the House of Commons. In a statement to the House, Profumo denied everything, but his words only added to the intrigue as Fleet Street knew better. Eventually, the story began to unfurl in the public domain and Profumo was forced to return to the House of Commons, admit the truth and make a full apology for his lies. He immediately resigned his post as Secretary of State for Defence.

The newspapers were now full of the story, leading to a huge scandal and acres of newsprint. Like all the other newspapers, the Labour Party-supporting *Daily Mirror* carried the story of Profumo's resignation on its front page. 'Profumo Quits, He lied to MPs over Christine to save his family,' ran their headline. The *Mirror* was not impressed, and in a comment column also on the front page it wrote: 'There can be nothing but pity for a suave but tarnished politician who had to admit – in a letter to the Prime Minister – that he is guilty of lying, of misleading, of deception, and of a grave misdemeanor.' It then asked the question that just about summed up the 1960s: 'What the hell is going on in this country?'

The older generation was shocked at such goings-on. Newspapers, particularly the sensationalist Sundays, were hidden from inquisitive children, while teenagers giggled, barely imagining that such things were happening in the families of their elders and supposed betters. 'Well, if they can do that, why can't we?' they wondered. Another seed had been sown.

The scandal would lead to the trial of Ward for pimping, with the doctor reckoned by many to be the scapegoat of the Establishment. At his trial, which was a further sensation, Ward was found guilty but then, before he could be sentenced, committed suicide in his prison cell. Ivanov, the Russian spy, was recalled to Moscow by Soviet officials and disappeared overnight, while Keeler and Rice-Davies both faced court appearances and imprisonment.

There were further accusations that MI5, the police and civil servants had played a less-than-honest role in proceedings, at times trying to either cover up events and individuals or lay blame where it was not deserved. It was an immensely complicated tale that, over the years, has continued to intrigue, with more than a few questions still unanswered. Even an inquiry under Lord Denning never fully revealed all. It was, without doubt, one of the most sensational stories the British press had ever encountered, with the public intrigued by the daily outpourings and revelations.

The commentator and journalist Malcolm Muggeridge in the *Sunday Mirror* called it 'the slow, sure start of the death of the upper classes'. It certainly was. Harold Macmillan, who initially had called it all 'nonsense', may have not been too fussed about Profumo's affair, but he was clearly worn down by the media's constant and insatiable interest. Following a brief illness, which was nowhere near as serious as he believed, Macmillan decided that it was time to stand down, and in October 1963 he resigned as Prime Minister. Although he was briefly replaced by the aristocratic and fellow Etonian Sir Alec Douglas-Home, it was clear that the old order was crumbling.

Within a year, the scandal and its repercussions would lead to Harold Wilson's Labour Party being elected to government, with the Tories shunted into the wilderness for the next six years. When they did return to office in 1970, it would be under the leadership of a working-class grammar school boy. The scandal had exposed the old aristocratic order and its hypocritical attitudes. It had become a laughing stock, satirized each Saturday evening in the BBC Television show *That Was The Week That Was* (popularly known as 'TW3') and ridiculed in most of the newspapers. Whereas the aristocracy had previously managed to carry on its misdemeanours behind closed doors, it was now fully exposed. Upstairs downstairs had been blown wide open.

In November 1960, John F. Kennedy had been elected President of the United States. At just 43 years of age, he was the youngest ever president of America, succeeding Eisenhower, who at 63 was the oldest ever president up to that time. Kennedy was seen as the dashing young prince; handsome, rich, Harvard-educated, from one of the most powerful families in America and surrounded by admiring courtiers. And of course he had an adoring, beautiful, well-connected and equally wealthy wife. For America, he heralded the beginning of a new era, with even the elderly looking on in admiration. He was what every young man aspired to and the template of what every young woman desired.

The presidential election had been a tight contest, with Kennedy winning by the narrowest of margins, though there is much evidence to suggest that his father, Joe Kennedy – the former US Ambassador to Britain – had 'bought' votes for him in Chicago's crucial Cook County through his friend, Mayor Richard Daley. Nonetheless, JFK's election heralded a new era of youth in politics.

However, the assassination of President Kennedy in Dallas in November 1963, just three years into his term of office, seemed to destroy that dream of youth succeeding and temporarily sent America into a spin of self-doubt and recrimination. There was a view that the old forces still held power. When youth had surfaced, it had been shot down.

In Britain, the assassination of Kennedy was equally disturbing. It may be a cliché, but everyone really did remember precisely where they were and what they were doing when they heard of his death. Bob Jones from Birkenhead, who was 17 years old at the time, recounted:

> 'I was on a bus coming back from technical college. When I got home there was somber music being played on the television. I was going away that evening on a YMCA trip. When I got to the YMCA an hour or so later there were some who had not heard. We were all devastated. He was young and we all identified with him.'

But it was not long before the British public also opted for a younger man. The election of Harold Wilson in 1964 at a mere 48 years of age was a breath of fresh air in British politics. He was not only the youngest British Prime Minister since Lord Liverpool in 1812, but was a northern working-class lad, even though he had been educated at Oxford. He was likened in some newspapers to John F. Kennedy, though in truth, apart from their youthfulness at the time of office, they had little else in common. Nevertheless, Wilson was undoubtedly an integral part of the trend towards youth in British life.

He had been born in Huddersfield in West Yorkshire, the son of an industrial chemist. He passed his eleven-plus examination attending Royds Hall Grammar School, but at the age of 16 the family moved to the Wirral as his father went in search of work and Harold Wilson continued his education at the Wirral Grammar School. From there he progressed to Jesus College, Oxford, where he read Politics, Philosophy and Economics. He attained a brilliant first and quickly became one of the youngest dons in the university's history.

When Wilson had been elected leader of the Labour Party in 1963 following the death of Hugh Gaitskell, the *Observer* saw him as an appropriate choice in a changing social climate, while the *Daily Telegraph* claimed that he had a 'youthful, bubbly quality'. Even the Trotskyist newspaper *International Socialism* was impressed, commenting in 1963 that Wilson was a far different breed from his predecessor Hugh Gaitskell, noting that 'in the portly lineaments and plummy accents of the late Gaitskell, the world could detect more than a mite of the amateur gentlemanly, public school tradition'. Wilson, however, looked and sounded quite different.

For the satirists and cartoonists, lampooning the elderly and aristocratic Eden, Macmillan and Alec Douglas-Home had been easy, but Wilson was not such a soft target. Not only did he have a sharp intellect, but he had worked his way up from the bottom. Wilson certainly played on his working-class background and his Yorkshire accent. He was also a football fan, at a time when the game was very much a frowned-upon working-class activity, and a keen supporter of his home team, Huddersfield Town. His party campaigned for the poor and for major reforms in society, and had picked up on many of the issues that dominated at the time and which television programmes like *That Was The Week That Was*, *Poor Cow* and *Cathy Come Home* had highlighted as iniquitous in Britain. Apart from his propensity to smoke a pipe (not unusual at the time), his Labrador dog Paddy and his slightly whining Yorkshire accent (still a problem in many walks of life), there was little else with which to ridicule him. 'TW3 and Harold Wilson had much in common: both were cheeky, chirpy upstarts,' wrote Ben Pimlott in his biography of Wilson, even going on to compare Wilson to the show's host, David Frost.

Wilson was scathing of the Tories and the Establishment. In his book *The North*, Paul Morley quotes Wilson in the 1964 general election campaign as saying: 'We are living in the jet age but are governed by an Edwardian establishment ... they cling to privilege and power for the few, shutting the gates on the many. Tory society is a closed society, in which birth and wealth have priority ... their approach and methods are fifty years out of date.' It was a view that found accord with many.

Wilson won the election by the narrowest of margins, ending thirteen years of Tory rule, or as he called it, 'Tory misrule'. Two years later, having acquitted himself with some style, he was re-elected with a more workable majority. Labour and Wilson would remain in office until June 1970, making the Sixties the years of Labour.

With Liverpool and The Beatles so much in the limelight, Wilson, not unnaturally, played on his strong Liverpool connections. He had spent much of his youth on Merseyside and was the Member of Parliament for Huyton, a suburb of Liverpool. He had his photograph taken with The Beatles whenever he could, made frequent references to them, and in 1965 lobbied the Queen to recognize their contribution by awarding them MBEs. Most of the country shared Wilson's delight, but there were others who saw it as demeaning the honours system. Colonel Frederick Wagg even sent back the twelve medals he had earned fighting in two world wars, while others wrote bitterly to the newspapers. And after the Cavern had briefly closed in 1966 due to financial difficulties, it was reopened a few months later by Harold Wilson, flanked by his wife Mary and rising Liverpudlian comic Ken Dodd.

The Labour MP Eric Heffer, who was elected to Parliament in 1964 for the Liverpool constituency of Walton, was certain that young people and the Liverpool music scene had played an important role in Labour's election, writing many years later in his autobiography:

> 'There is no doubt in my mind that the astounding Merseybeat boom had a big effect on the outcome of the general election. The groups were young, vibrant and new. They were in tune with the desires of the people. They asserted working class values, they looked to the future. I believe The Beatles made a powerful contribution to Labour's victory.'

In his biography of Wilson, Ben Pimlott details how society was fundamentally changing and how Wilson cleverly used this to enhance his prospects of attaining office: 'The fashion was progressive in the sense of being questioning and irreverent, and against the authority of Church, school, social hierarchy and government. It affected attitudes, not just to sex, censorship and popular music, but also to privilege, social class and opportunity." He adds that Wilson 'sensed … that the tide could be harnessed to his advantage'.

Once in office, Wilson surrounded himself with a team of young people. Richard Crossman, Roy Jenkins, Jim Callaghan, Tony Benn, Dennis Healey and Barbara Castle all became Cabinet members. It was a far cry from the Establishment figures who had huddled around the Cabinet table in the days of Macmillan and Alec Douglas-Home. Politics was now a young person's game. Even the Downing Street civil servants remarked on the change and how much more relaxed and informal things were.

Had The Beatles voted in the 1964 general election, it hardly takes a great leap of the imagination to assume that they would have voted Labour. Given their Liverpool roots, it's hard to envisage that they would ever have considered voting Conservative, and there is no evidence of them having ever met Alec Douglas-Home or having their photograph taken with him, as they had with Wilson. If they did have any love affair with Wilson, however, it was to be short-lived. By 1966, they were scathingly recording 'Taxman' for the 'Revolver' album, complaining of the high rates of tax they were paying.

Yet for many teenagers, the 1964 and 1966 general elections simply passed them by. Had they been able to vote, then it seems a fair assumption that Wilson would have achieved a more workable majority. But in 1964, teenagers were not allowed the vote; it was not until the 1970 election that the voting age was lowered from 21 to 18. Ironically, those young people then failed to support the very Prime Minister who had given them the vote and seemed to be on their side. By 1970, however, they had concluded that Wilson was most definitely not on their side and had been something of a disappointment.

For many young people, the Labour Party in Britain towards the end of the Sixties did not fully represent their views. The Establishment political parties were never really trusted by young people. They never had the vote, so it was hardly worth joining them and becoming active. 'What was the point of knocking on doors asking people to vote for Labour or whatever when you couldn't even vote yourself?' remembered one young person at the time. It was thus hardly surprising that young people opted for something radically different when it came to politics. The obvious left-wing alternative was the Communist Party, but they had lost much support after backing the Soviet invasion of Hungary following the uprising in 1956 and then repeating its stance regarding the takeover of Czechoslovakia in 1968.

For young people, politics had instead taken new directions, with a plethora of left-wing organizations springing up. They included Trotskyist groups such as the Workers Revolutionary Party, the International Socialists, the International Marxist Group and other Leftist parties like the Revolutionary Communist Group, the Communist Party of Great Britain (Marxist Leninist), the Socialist Workers Party, the Socialist Party of Great Britain and so on. Although they attracted plenty of young people to their ranks, they did not attract much in the way of parliamentary votes. Mostly, they had been fuelled by protests surrounding Vietnam, anti-apartheid and Northern Ireland, and looked to be doing something while Labour stood on the sidelines.

In Northern Ireland, the 'troubles' again came to the fore, with young people prominent in the campaign for civil rights. Bernadette Devlin, a young student at Queen's University in Belfast, had become active in the newly formed student-led civil rights organization People's Democracy as well as the Northern Ireland Civil Rights Association, which had been formed in1967. Devlin was subsequently excluded from the university, but it did not stop her campaigning for greater rights for Northern Ireland's Catholic community. There were marches and ugly outbreaks of violence, with campaigners shot, buildings burned down and a confrontation between the Protestant community and the Ulster Constabulary, as well as the British Army. It was a disturbing time, but it demonstrated that young Catholic people in Ulster had had enough of deprived housing, poor education, limited job opportunities and being categorized as second-class citizens. Devlin was an outstanding orator, full of energy and passion, and in 1969 she successfully stood for Parliament and was elected at the age of 21, making her the youngest female MP in history. Her maiden speech broke with all the traditions of impartiality, being described by Labour's Michael Foot as the finest speech he had ever heard in the House of Commons.

With the voting age having been lowered, one might have expected a flurry of young voters to support Wilson and Labour at the 1970 general election, but instead a Conservative government, under Edward Heath, was elected with a healthy majority. Heath had links with Liverpool, having served in the city during the Second World War with an anti-aircraft battery as a 2nd lieutenant in the Royal Artillery. It may well have been that many young people did vote for Wilson, but by then the nation had – temporarily – grown weary of his brand of politics and duplicity. Labour's promises had never fully materialized. Instead, Wilson had supported nuclear weapons, an anathema to those young people who marched with CND, and had looked to introduce legislation to regulate trade union activities. On the other crucial issue of the day, Labour had supported America's involvement in Vietnam, although, much to his credit, Wilson had forcefully rejected any involvement by British troops in Vietnam, despite much American pressure. It is a fact that has never been fully appreciated.

While the Labour Party may have elected some youthful leadership in the Sixties, the same could not be said of the trade unions. The old barons still remained in place, wielding considerable power and influence. The unions were strong in their industrial bases, yet there was a reluctance to support youth, and in particular the unions showed little interest in equality issues.

In 1968, however, there was a major step forward when women machinists at Ford's Dagenham plant went on strike, demanding equal pay. The women who made car seat covers had discovered that men carrying out the same work were paid more, so in June 1968 they went on strike. Such was the impact of the strike that car production was eventually brought to a halt when they ran out of material. The strike ended when the Secretary of State for Employment, Barbara Castle, intervened to negotiate a settlement, although she faced fierce opposition from within her own government. The strike was to have an enduring legacy. Spurred on by the Dagenham women's example, other female trades unionists, rather than rely on the unions, founded the National Joint Action Campaign Committee for Women's Equal Rights, which held an equal pay demonstration attended by 1,000 people in Trafalgar Square in May 1969. It was to be a wake-up call to the unions.

The ultimate result was the passing of the Equal Pay Act 1970, which came into force in 1975. In the second reading of the bill, the Ford machinists were cited by Labour MP Shirley Summerskill as playing a 'very significant part in the history of the struggle for equal pay'.

Nevertheless, for much of the Sixties equal pay and women's rights remained low down the agenda, with trade unions boasting few women members and barely interested in recruiting more. It was little wonder that women chose an alternative route in their fight for recognition.

The main push behind the demand for female equality was the growth in young women graduates. For the first time, women were emerging from the universities with good degrees and were not looking to go into traditional areas of female employment such as teaching, nursing and secretarial work. Instead, they wanted to go into business, finance and the public sector. They wanted equal pay, equal opportunities and maternity rights. They wouldn't get any of it in the 1960s, and would have to wait until the 1970s for a start to be made.

The decade of youth rebelliousness seemed to draw to a close in the late Sixties, at least in some respects. In America, the Republican Richard Nixon was elected to the presidency, while in Britain, Edward Heath's Conservatives had come to power. Wilson and his Labour government had run out of steam and the electorate seemed unsure of what it wanted. British politics remained rooted in tradition, with Labour representing the working classes while the Tories represented those with power and money. The Liberals sat somewhere in-between, not really sure of their position and without a great deal of support, while the radical parties of the Sixties slowly lost popularity. The 1970s would continue as years of turmoil, involving strikes, economic uncertainties and demonstrations that would culminate in 1979 with the election of Margaret Thatcher and a radical change of direction.

Chapter 6

Jobs for All

In July 1957, Conservative Prime Minister Harold Macmillan told a packed Conservative Party meeting in Bedford that in Britain 'you will see a state of prosperity such as we have never seen in our lifetime – nor indeed in the history of this country'. Ever the showman, Macmillan paused and then added: 'Indeed let us be frank about it – most of our people have never had it so good.' Macmillan was to be forever associated with the phrase 'never had it so good'. And he was right. After the Second World War and years of austerity, rationing and rebuilding, the British economy was at last booming – and it was to continue into the Sixties and beyond.

Jobs were aplenty, and for any young person leaving school at 16 (as indeed most did) there was always a wide choice of jobs available. Stephen Platt remembers leaving school in the early Sixties: 'I had a choice of jobs – one in Liverpool and another as an apprentice draughtsman in the local shipyard. I chose the latter. I never heard of anyone being on the dole.'

It was the same for girls. In Manchester, Annie O'Malley also left school when she was 16: 'There were lots and lots of jobs. My sister worked in a bank. I thought that sounded cool so I got a job in a bank. I got the job in the bank without even having Maths or English "O" level!'

This also meant that teenagers, for the first time in history, suddenly had disposable income. They could go out and buy records or clothes and pay to go to clubs like the Cavern. As a consequence, record shops sprang up on high streets. Peep inside and there would be teenagers in the sound booths listening to the latest hit music. Coffee bars also became haunts on the high street, where teenage boys and girls would congregate and mix, making their cappuccino last half the night.

Between 1955 and 1966, unemployment was at the lowest ever experienced in the UK, before or since. Unemployment among young people was virtually non-existent. Throughout the Sixties, unemployment never exceeded more than 2.7 per cent of the workforce. During the early years of the period, it stood at 2 per cent, before declining between 1964 and 1966 to around just 1.3 per cent. It then began to rise steadily, with small peaks and troughs, until it stood at 2.7 per cent in 1970. Most of this could be attributed to people in the process of leaving one job for another and being recorded as unemployed for just a short period of time. Long-term unemployment was similarly at an all-time low.

You only had to read the newspapers to see how many job vacancies there were. The *Daily Telegraph* was crammed with adverts most days, and all the local papers would have at least half-a-dozen pages of job ads. You could take your pick, and there was certainly no need to accept just any job. Britain had a booming economy, with lots of jobs, high exports, decent wages and plenty of overtime. Britain had become a consumer society like never before.

The massive growth in consumerism focused primarily around the so called 'white goods' which had first started to appear on the market in the late Fifties and could now be found on sale in every high street. Vacuum cleaners, steam irons, fridges, radios and so forth were being snapped up by every household, eager to be the envy of their next-door neighbour.

The introduction of the transistor radio also helped the boom in music. The radios were small and cheap, running off batteries. With most teenagers in employment, it meant that they were easily affordable. Teenagers could carry them around and listen to music in their own bedrooms. Listening to records also changed. Out went the fragile old 10-inch 78rpm records and in came the smaller plastic 7-inch 45rpm singles, as well as the long-playing 12-inch vinyl, all of which were within the price range of young people. As a consequence, the antique wind-up gramophone player was superseded by an electric, lightweight record player.

There was also an explosion in the acquisition of television sets, with almost every household boasting one by the end of the decade. But more importantly, it was cars which were leading the economic boom, with ownership beginning to penetrate all strands of society. In particular, the working classes were digging deep into their pockets or more likely taking out hire purchase loans – more commonly known as the 'never-never' – and acquiring cars. In the 1930s, it had been a stain on families to be buying anything on credit, that is if you could even get it, but in the 1960s it became far more acceptable. Indeed, paying out a substantial sum for the likes of a car through hire purchase was the norm. To have a car sitting outside your house was proof of both affluence and aspiration. The 1960s was the decade of the car. The manufacturing and purchasing of cars was a development which was to have far-reaching social consequences.

The car was the road to freedom. Suddenly, you could easily escape suburbia, even if it was only for an afternoon in the countryside. It may not have been cheap to buy a car in the first place, but once it had been purchased, taxed and insured, it offered affordable travel to wherever you wanted. Even petrol was cheap. If you were sharing it with others, it meant an easy and inexpensive escape from the grime of the cities, with its connotations of work and drudgery.

Plus, of course, you could go on holiday in the car. It was cheaper and gave you so much more mobility. Families piled into their cars and drove south to the resorts of Devon and Cornwall. Previously, people had crammed into trains or onto buses and made for their nearest coastal resorts, where they would remain fixed until the end of their holiday. With the car, you could move around; a day or two here and a few more days somewhere else, or maybe using your hotel or B&B as a base and then venturing further afield each day to a different spot.

A few were even more adventurous and drove acrossing the Channel on the continent. 'We had a car early on,' remembered Judith Jones, 'and we would go on holidays in Britain, usually to Cornwall but then after a few years of bad weather we started venturing further afield, to France in particular. Driving abroad however was unusual in those days.'

More importantly, the car could lead to better jobs and social mobility. Suddenly, people could commute and were often prepared to consider jobs miles away from where they lived. Whereas a 10-mile journey to work may once have been expensive and taken too long on public transport, in the car it was often cheaper and certainly a good deal quicker than travelling by bus or train. Aspirations could be realized. No longer were you confined to a narrow geographical area with its limited employment opportunities.

The car also took on a new role in leisure activities. Football fans, for instance, abandoned the regular British Rail football specials and instead travelled by car, cramming it full with friends and following their teams to visit away grounds at half the cost. It would eventually lead to social problems in the form of hooliganism, but in the 1960s it was still generally quiet on the terraces.

Football wasn't the only leisure activity to thrive with the car. Film and theatre-going also became more accessible. Instead of waiting for public transport or racing for the last bus home, young people were able to journey to places they would normally not have been able to go.

'I remember my 21st birthday party in 1967,' recalled Bob Jones. 'After the party, at about midnight, we all piled into cars and went off to New Brighton to go ten-pin bowling. And then came back home at about 2.30 am. Now that's something you could never have done on public transport.'

To help the surge in motoring, a programme of motorway construction had begun. The Preston bypass had been opened in December 1958, with the first full-length section of the M1 motorway, between Rugby and Watford, following in November 1959. Later in the Sixties, the M1 would be extended to Leeds. Other motorways, including the M6, would also open during the decade, making travel that much easier. Instead of taking the train from Manchester or Leeds to places such as London, it was now just as easy – and certainly cheaper – to go by car.

If any single car was to symbolize the 1960s, it was the Mini-Minor. Designed by Alec Issigonis, it was produced by the British Motor Corporation at their Cowley plant in Oxford and the Longbridge plant in Birmingham. It first rolled off the production lines in 1959 and was as radical a design as any car that had been produced in the decades before. Above all it was small. It wasn't an old person's car at all, but instead a young person's vehicle. Indeed, older people struggled to get in and out of it. It was also cheap, attractive and generally reliable, making it an even more obvious attraction to young people. The arrival of the Mini encouraged freedom-seeking teenagers to discover a new world. Brian Epstein was so taken by the car that in 1965 he bought one for each of The Beatles. It was all part of branding The Beatles and was wonderful publicity for the manufacturer. The Beatles were soon photographed peering through the wound-down windows of their new cars. There were also plenty of photographs or mini-skirted young women sprawled across their bonnets. Little wonder young people flocked to buy the new car.

In 1960, the car sold for around £500, and although it was not easy for young people to afford that amount of money, with a hire purchase agreement in place it became considerably more manageable. There was also a Mini Cooper version, more expensive, which was much coveted by aspiring young people, more likely at the time to be men than women. But the cost of a Mini, as well as other cars, was certainly within the reach of many young people, particularly those who had been working since the age of 16. It was to be a liberating force. If teenagers had not been able to escape the suburbs in the 1950s, they certainly could in the Sixties.

The British economy was booming. As the demand for new cars rocketed, car manufacturers opened new plants, creating new employment possibilities in some of the traditionally deprived areas. At Halewood on Merseyside, Ford opened a plant in October 1963 to produce the new Ford Anglia, while over the River Mersey on the Wirral, Vauxhall opened a factory at Ellesmere Port.

If unemployment was at an all-time low, the same could not be said of prices, which rose steadily throughout the Sixties, peaking at around 3 per cent in 1970. Much of this rise was due to the demand for white consumer goods and the increase in disposable income. Wages had increased to keep pace with rising prices, leading the Wilson government to introduce a prices and incomes policy in the hope of maintaining some control. The policy had only moderate success. Nonetheless, Britain boasted one of the fastest-growing economies in the world, although France and West Germany were beginning to catch up by the end of the decade.

But for all the growth and boom, Britain was still primarily a heavy industry economy. The traditional 'dirty' industries of coalmining, shipbuilding, rail and steel – which had been the mainstay activities of the economy since the turn of the century – continued to be the major employers, although they had been added to during the late Fifties and Sixties with car manufacturing. Aerospace was also becoming important, along with the computer industry, although this was still very much in its infancy. The financial and service sectors, however, remained small.

Many of the country's major industries were under national ownership, having been taken into public control by the 1945–51 Labour government. Most prominent were coalmining and the railways. In 1968, some 450,000 were employed in coalmining and quarrying, with almost 2 million in transport. Yorkshire, South Wales and Scotland were still the largest areas supporting coalmining, under the direction of the National Coal Board. British Railways remained one of the largest single employers in the country. In engineering alone, there were over 1.5 million employed in dark and dirty workshops up and down the country. The steel industry employed 250,000, with its steel mills centred primarily in the Sheffield and South Wales localities. Even shipbuilding, then beginning to go into decline, could boast 130,000 workers, while the cotton and textile industries still had over 100,000 employees, even though they had been in sharp decline for a number of years.

The TUC annual report for its 1969 conference reported trade union membership of 8.8 million. Most of those members belonged to unions in the major industrial sectors. There were over 370,000 members in the mining industry alone, 1.4 million in engineering, 1.5 million in transport and 300,000 in the railways. British trade unions were as strong and powerful as ever, although they would become even more powerful over the next ten years. The unions reflected their memberships – male-dominated and working class. Few unions were interested in equal pay for women, maternity leave or any other women's issues. Trade union leaders were powerful barons, with the likes of Lord Cooper, Lord Delacourt Smith, Lord Ted Hill and Sir Tom O'Brien already ennobled. Others would soon been become ennobled or knighted.

The picture of the economy in the Sixties was thus generally a male-dominated one of heavy industries and manual labour, with much of it in the North, Midlands, Scotland and South Wales. The public sector was beginning to grow, and would develop through the late 1960s and Seventies at an impressive rate, with more and more women coming into the employment market. Work was still labour-intensive, with major factories employing thousands of workers, although new practices and equipment were beginning to be introduced that would, in time, reduce the workforce. When the shipyard gates opened at 5.00 pm or the car factory day came to an end, thousands of workers would pour out onto the streets, either on their bikes or racing across the road to join the bus queues.

By the end of the decade, computers were also slowly being introduced, but they were enormous in size, taking up vast amounts of space, and usually had to be stored in clean areas. Freda Gill remembered a computer being installed in the office where she worked:

> 'It had on it all the members' names and addresses. It was revolutionary. It took up an enormous space – about two or three of the old offices and it had to be vacuum sealed. Out went all the old filing cards and here was this new piece of equipment that could store them all and be updated very easily. It saved so much time and effort. Before that we had had to fill in all the data on a card which was a boring and tedious task. Strange to think that today you could get all this into a small laptop.'

There was also considerable concern that the introduction of computers would take away jobs. Indeed, many workers and trade unionists fiercely opposed the introduction of computers, not just on the factory floor but also among professional workers. There were concerns that computer-mechanized machinery would one day lead to a virtually automated production line. Mike Cooley, President of the draughtsman's union, DATA, was warning in the newspapers about computer-aided design and how it would lead to the disappearance of draughtsmen. Many of the warnings would eventually ring true, but new jobs, many ironically in the computer business itself, would eventually replace those jobs.

Most shop floor workers were paid weekly and in cash. Paid overtime was common and in abundance. Clocking-on was also an everyday occurrence on the shop floor, workers being provided with a card each week so that they could formally register on a clock the time they arrived at work and the time that they left. Apprentice Bob Jones at the Cammell Laird shipbuilders in Birkenhead recalls that he had to sign in on a clock:

'Sometimes we would sign someone else's name in if we knew they were going to be late. If you were more than about ten minutes late, they would dock your pay by an hour. Of course, when it came to signing out there would be a long queue at the clock and it could take you ten minutes but they didn't give you an extra hour's pay for that!'

The factory floor was not the healthiest or easiest of places to work. Health and safety was poor, with accidents galore, particularly in the construction industry. The Trades Union Congress of 1968 debated the issue and was told that there had been 304,000 industrial accidents in the preceding year, compared to 296,000 in 1966. The figures for fatal accidents made for grim reading too. In 1963, 610 people had died, and in 1966, a total of 701 had been killed in the workplace, although the figure for 1967 showed a decline, dropping to 564. The fall was due in main to a sharp decrease in the construction industry, where fatal accidents declined from 288 in 1966 to 197 the following year. Shocked by these figures, the Labour government had been persuaded to introduce new and tougher legislation to replace the existing Factories Act.

On top of these fatalities were industrial diseases such as pneumoconiosis, which affected at least one in every two coalminers, while in the steel industry workers suffered a variety of deadly lung diseases. Watch any film of a steel factory at the time and you will see giant ingots and steel bars being dragged out of bright orange furnaces by men in overalls, with white sparks flying in all directions. Today it seems inconceivable. Asbestosis was another killer disease, although imports of asbestos were falling dramatically by the end of the decade as industrialists realized its danger. Dockers in Liverpool went on strike, refusing to unload a containment of asbestos, and were heavily criticized by employers and the media. But for most of the Sixties, asbestos was used frequently in the construction of schools, offices, ships and so forth. There were other toxic and chemical diseases, particularly in the dyeing industry. It was little wonder that young people wanted to shun the shop floor when working in an office offered far better conditions.

If cars were widening people's horizons, so too was the airplane. As the Sixties began, international travel was split evenly between sea and sky. Only a handful of ordinary people would have flown anywhere as the decade began, but by the end of the Sixties, flying was becoming a possibility for most people. 'I didn't go on a plane until 1967 when I was 20 when I flew to the Costa Brava for a holiday,' remembers Jean Birkett. 'I can't think of many of my friends at the time who had ever flown. But within a couple of years, I had flown to Canada and many other places.'

Suddenly, the European holiday market was opening up. Between 1961 and 1971, the number of people holidaying abroad leapt from just under 4 million to almost 8 million. There were flights to Spain, Greece and Italy as British holidaymakers took advantage of venturing abroad, where sunshine and sandy beaches could be guaranteed. They were lured by sun-drenched posters of blue seas, soft sand and bikini-clad girls. Most of the trips were all-inclusive package holidays, making travel a lot easier. They were also cheap, with a week in Spain costing as little as £20. A coach met you at the airport, with an English-speaking courier to take you to your hotel and look after your every need, including three meals a day. In most of these countries, alcohol and cigarettes were considerably cheaper than back home. And, of course, there was all that sunshine.

Most people loved it and went again the following year. But there were those who found foreign countries rather too different. 'I had an uncle who went on a coach tour to Austria,' recalled Bob Jones. 'When they got there, he got the next coach home leaving his sisters to holiday by themselves. He came back complaining that the beer just wasn't the same!'

Interestingly, it was football that introduced many to their first air travel as they followed their teams around Europe in various competitions. Manchester United fan Cliff Butler remembers going to see his team in Madrid: 'It was my first ever trip abroad to see United. In fact, it was my first ever trip out of the country. I had never been on a plane. It was a real adventure. I think it cost about £20 which was a lot of money in those days ... it was really an amazing experience.'

What The Beatles did was to give hope to a generation. If they, four working-class lads from the North, could make it, then almost anyone could, no matter what school you had been to. But it wasn't quite as simple as that. For a start, you had to have a talent, plus a considerable amount of luck. In the music industry, dozens, if not hundreds, of young local musicians were 'making it' and becoming stars overnight. The number of successful bands soared. From Liverpool there was Gerry and the Pacemakers, The Big Three, Billy J. Kramer, Cilla Black and The Searchers, while elsewhere there was The Rolling Stones, The Who, Herman's Hermits and The Animals. While boxing had been the one escape route from the slums during the 1930s, in the 1960s it was music.

Apart from the car and holidays abroad, the only other way that people could boast their status was in their homes. Britain's housing at the beginning of the 1960s was still largely Victorian, cramped and decrepit, not helped, of course, by the German Luftwaffe, which had wrought large-scale destruction on most of Britain's large cities, especially Liverpool. Over 4 million homes had been destroyed. That might have been twenty years earlier, but Britain had still not built or replaced many of the ruins. Bombed sites and wrecked buildings still scarred the landscape of our cities and towns. With a booming population following the end of the war, who were getting married in the Sixties and looking to buy their first homes, there was a general outcry for more new housing.

Chapter 7

We Gotta Get Out Of This Place

The Beatles had come mainly from ordinary homes. Only John Lennon could boast anything that might be called middle class, living in a semi-detached house on Menlove Avenue in the leafy suburb of Woolton. The house which was owned by the family even boasted a porch and stained glass windows. His girlfriend at the time, Thelma McGough, describes it as 'quite posh". It was typical suburbia. Paul McCartney, meanwhile, lived with his brother, Mike, and parents in a rented semi-detached house in Allerton, also in south Liverpool, which had been built in 1949. 'Whilst we weren't a poor family,' remembered Paul later in life, 'we weren't rich by any means, so we never had a car, or a television till the coronation in 1953. I was the first one in the family to buy a car with my Beatle earnings. My mum, as a nurse, rode a bike.'

George Harrison lived his early years in a small rented terrace house in Woolton with only an outside toilet, again not so far away from John and Paul. When George was aged 4, the Harrisons had moved to a slightly larger council house in Speke, which at the time was considered semi-rural. Ringo (born Richard Starkey, his stage name being adopted in the late 1950s), on the other hand, had lived in a two-up, two-down rented terraced house in the Dingle, close to the docks. All their homes had been built during the inter-war years, apart from Ringo's, which had been built much earlier.

As befitting his family status, Brian Epstein lived in a large, expensive detached house on Queen's Drive in Childwall, close to their local synagogue. Epstein also had a small flat of his own in the centre of the city, where he could discreetly live a private life.

All the boys' parents were hard-working, though not particularly well paid, with Ringo, George and Paul all growing up in rented homes. Both John and Paul had lost their mothers when they were teenagers, and in the case of John his father had also left home when he was young. Ringo had spent much of his childhood ill and in hospital, missing out on his education. They had few consumer goods, no cars, no telephones, and television came late to their homes. It may have been better than their parents had experienced when they were young, but somehow it was stifling. The general attitude of parents was 'do your homework, pass your exams, get a decent job, get married, settle down'. And that was your lot. It was typical for so many kids up and down the country.

There was little that demonstrated the poverty and iniquity that existed in Britain better than the state of the nation's housing.

At the dawn of the Sixties, more than one-third of Britain's population were unable to either afford to buy a home of their own or find private rental accommodation. House ownership was still a dream of the future, although that dream would begin to be realized by more and more families as the decade rolled on. There was also, of course, a private rented sector, where some landlords charged extortionate rents and there were few rights for tenants. In 1967, around 25 per cent of all homes in the UK lacked a bath or shower, an indoor WC, a hand washbasin or hot and cold water (by 1991, that figure was only 1 per cent). Again in 1967, only half of homes were owner occupied.

After the war, the Labour government had begun a massive house-building programme that promised a new home for everyone who needed one, and whilst this policy was highly successful, with a massive increase in the number of houses built, it had begun to tail off in the 1960s. Britain still needed housing, and quickly. This led to two initiatives. The first was the development of housing estates on the outskirts of towns, and the other was high-rise blocks of flats that could house hundreds of occupants.

High-rise flats (defined as blocks of six storeys and more) seemed the obvious answer. Construction methods had revolutionized building techniques, making the construction of tower blocks not only considerably easier but also cheaper. High-rise blocks would also help maintain a working population in the town and city centres, whereas the out-of-town estates shunted the population into green belt areas and were not favoured by everyone. In 1953, just 3 per cent of new council housing approved had been high-rise flats. By 1966, however, high-rise housing accounted for 26 per cent of all council home starts. It was a massive change in the housing market. In 1960, high-rise became the vogue word in urban architecture. New blocks, some twenty storeys or more high, were flung up in cities across the country, including Liverpool, Newcastle, Manchester, Southampton and Edinburgh.

Teresa Flynn in Liverpool was quite taken by them and summed up their appeal neatly. 'I am the mother of seven children and I need fresh accommodation,' she told the *Liverpool Echo*. 'I like the flats and I would go anywhere if I could find accommodation for my family.' Indeed, everyone the *Echo* spoke to seemed extremely pleased at the prospect of moving. Who could blame them? The city-centre slums were well past their time, with rotting window frames, damp walls and ceilings, no inside toilets, damaged roofs, rat infestations and small backyards. True, there were dynamic communities in many of them, but there was also a multitude of problems.

One of the most notorious among the new high-rise projects was the Park Hill flats in Sheffield. Perched high on the rise overlooking Sheffield railway station, the Park Hill flats were officially opened by Labour leader Hugh Gaitskell in 1961. It was the largest housing development of its kind anywhere in Britain, and the first residents had already moved in as the Opposition leader unveiled a plaque to commemorate the occasion.

Park Hill flats began, as so often these things do, with genuine optimism and good intentions, though Gaitskell sounded a note of caution: 'I agree there are dangers in multi-storey developments. Sometimes I must admit blocks built up high remind me of nothing but barracks. Those no doubt are better than nothing but not especially pleasant to live in or look at. But may I say how well you in Sheffield have avoided these dangers.' He added that the people of Sheffield should be proud of the new development. Largely, they were.

In December 1940, two nights of German bombing had wrought ruin and destruction on Sheffield, destroying many of the Victorian terraced streets of the city centre. The Park Hill flats were to be a new beginning. They were based on the concept of French architect Le Corbusier, whose 'streets in the sky' were the current trend in France. The idea was to replace the slums with ultra-modern flats and facilities, creating the same communities that flourished in the back-to-back houses of the pre-war city centre.

Park Hill consisted of two-, three- and four-bedroom flats and maisonettes that would house almost 3,000 people. It was to be a town within a town, with shops, a doctor's surgery, dentist, clinic, nursery, school, pubs and police station. Instead of the traditional 4-foot-wide decks, the access area outside the flats would be 10 feet wide, providing a communal area where children could play and families socialize.

The *Sheffield Telegraph* described them as the 'super flats of the future'. There was barely a word of criticism from anyone. The *Sheffield Star* went further, calling it 'a breath-taking dream'. Residents talked about the magnificent view over the city and the Pennines, where on a clear day 'you could see as far as Derbyshire'. Meanwhile, awards were being foisted on the designers.

For ten years or more, the Park Hill flats were deemed a huge success, until a combination of an infestation of cockroaches, vandalism and crime led to growing unpopularity. Once the decline had begun, it accelerated at a rapid pace. By the mid to late 1970s, nobody wanted to live in Park Hill. Nonetheless, in the 1960s, Park Hill was a brief answer to the city's housing problems.

All over Britain, local councils followed the example of Sheffield with blocks of flats that could rehouse thousands from the city centre slums. In some cities, people were rehoused in 'prefabs', quickly constructed temporary bungalows which were seen as a short-term solution though many of them lasted into the 1960s. Liverpool's Belle Vale, one of the largest prefab estates, proved surprisingly popular with their small gardens away from the city centre slums.

The other initiative by urban local councils was to construct large-scale housing estates on the outskirts of towns. One such scheme was in Birkenhead, where, after the war, the council began constructing the massive Woodchurch estate that would house most of its council tenants. It was a glowing success to begin with, but as time marched on, social problems began to emerge. In Liverpool, estates were built at Netherley, Kirlby, Speke and Belle Vale.

During the 1950s and 1960s, a series of new towns were also constructed. These included Skelmersdale, which was designed to house an overspill population from the north Liverpool conurbation. Elsewhere in the country, Washington, Runcorn and Peterlee were among many others.

As Britain entered the Sixties, housing was still a national disgrace. A report in 1966 claimed that more than a quarter of houses in Liverpool had no hot water. Two per cent didn't even have a toilet to call their own, and one-in-ten households were living in overcrowded conditions. The report stated: 'A couple with their 5 children are all living in one room ... They all sleep in one big bed behind a partition, making a room 4 foot wide. Seven people sleeping in one bed in a room 4 foot wide.' It was a long way from what John, Paul and George had ever experienced.

Although many families had been rehoused in the new suburb estates or the city centre high-rise blocks, there were still massive problems. Not enough homes were being built to accommodate the burgeoning population, and many families were still housed in decrepit, Victorian, town centre terraced streets. Granada TV's Coronation Street was typical of its kind.

Such was the crisis in Britain's housing that it prompted a young author, Jeremy Sandford, to get together with film director Ken Loach and producer Tony Garnett to write a play for the BBC. Although Sandford came from a wealthy background, he had deliberately gone to live in Battersea in order to experience the social deprivation and was shocked by what he witnessed, particularly when it came to housing. What Sandford wrote was so realistic that at times it was hard to tell what was real and what was fictional. It was called *Cathy Come Home* and told the tale of a couple and their three children who, through no fault of their own, were forced out of their home and into slum lodgings, then a caravan and finally a hostel, but always a life on the edge. It was watched by over 12 million viewers and had an enormous and immediate impact. Of course, there were those who claimed that it was totally fictitious and that this kind of thing did not happen in Britain. The *Guardian* reviewer, however disagreed: 'I know by my own observations from the outskirts of social work in a slummy part of London that everything in the early part of the story is a hundred per cent true. I suspect as a fairly regular reader of newspapers that all the rest of it is also true.' He ended the review with a ringing endorsement: 'I rate it in class one – but with a heavy heart because it should not be possible in Harold's Heaven to present such a play without being accused of falsehood. I could see no falsity in it, unfortunately.'

For many, *Cathy Come Home* was a revelation. Millions of viewers had never realized just how bad Britain's housing was, particularly in the private sector and in our larger cities. The play was to have a major impact on politicians, who thereafter promised immediate action to help alleviate problems in the private sector, introducing laws to help protect tenants. They also promised more council house building, although in the end that never really materialized.

Centre Point in London was a skyscraper office block, one of the first in the capital, at the junction of Oxford Street and Tottenham Court Road. It had been built by property tycoon Harry Hyams and was completed in 1966, intended for single-tenant occupancy, such as a company. Hyams, however, was unable to find a suitable tenant at the price he was asking, and as a consequence the building remained empty when thousands in London were either homeless or living in substandard rented accommodation. Hyams could afford to allow the building to remain empty because property prices in London were soaring. As a consequence, Centre Point became something of a *cause célèbre*, with Hyams one of the most reviled men of capitalism. Centre Point epitomized not only the crisis in the property market but of capitalism itself, where a huge building could be left empty and still be worth considerably more year after year. To many, it simply did not make sense. It was little wonder that young people were soon demonstrating outside its doors and threatening to take over the building. Squatting had long been a political activity of some far left groups, as well as those who were genuinely desperate for somewhere to live. Throughout the Sixties, there were takeovers by squatters of small empty properties, mostly in London, though many tended to be brief occupations. The actual takeover of Centre Point may never have materialized until the 1970s, but the whole crisis had been bubbling under the surface since the early Sixties.

By the end of the 1960s, The Beatles had escaped their suburban life and moved into expensive properties, either in London or the south-east countryside – or in some cases both. They were four wealthy young men with all the money they could wish for. They were even able to purchase properties for family members back in Liverpool. They hadn't quite gone full circle, but they had at least escaped the suburban life, so despised by John in particular, and the poverty that Ringo had clearly experienced more than any of them.

For so many others, there would be no escape from suburbia. They would be trapped with eight-to-five jobs, the production line, marriage, children, mortgages, debts and few prospects for escaping. For others with aspirations, it would be an ongoing battle, but at least The Beatles and other groups had shown that there was a way out of suburbia. All you needed were three guitars, a set of drums and a couple of amplifiers. Plus, of course, a lot of talent and luck!

Chapter 8

Top of the Form

Many of the roots of the 1960s revolution can be traced back as far as the 1944 Education Act. The Act was introduced by the wartime government and in particular was the creation of R.A. Butler, then the young President of the Board of Education. Butler's Bill was radical and visionary, although its birth took place in rather bizarre circumstances. The story goes that in March 1943, Butler had spent a weekend at Chequers, the Prime Minister's weekend retreat, with Winston Churchill. After an evening of dining, playing bagatelle and watching Russian Tsarist movies with various others, Butler managed a moment alone with the Prime Minister in his bedroom. Churchill, so Butler later recounted, was in his four-poster bed, wearing his customary nightcap and with a large, fat cat snoozing at the end of the bed. Butler had conceived the idea of his education reforms during the Blitz and wanted to test Churchill's reaction. Butler saw it as a major reform that would herald a new Jerusalem in post-war Britain. Churchill nodded in agreement before finally dozing off. Later, in one of his inimitable radio broadcasts to the nation, Churchill described the Education Act as 'the greatest scheme of improved education that has ever been attempted by a responsible government'.

The concept was simple enough: it would create a tripartite education system, with grammar schools, secondary modern schools and secondary technical schools. Entry to these schools would be via an examination, taken around the age of 11, which in time became known as the eleven-plus. If you passed, then you automatically went to the grammar school. If you failed, then you proceeded to one of the secondary schools. The system would later be criticized for leading students along a certain educational route at such an early age. Only one-third of students went to the grammar schools, whilst two-thirds were subjected to a far less rigorous academic education. Places at a grammar school were also dependent upon the number on offer, which could mean that whilst you were bright enough to pass the exam, you could still miss out, with the benchmark fluctuating from year to year.

But passing the eleven-plus didn't necessarily guarantee working-class pupils would take up their place at grammar school. Shirley Williams, who was the Labour government's Education Secretary between 1976 and 1979, remembered that she had several friends whose parents couldn't afford the uniform. 'They never went to grammar school at all,' she recalled, 'while others who did go had parents who wanted them to come out as quickly as possible and get jobs.'

The system would also unfairly define many people's lives and careers at the age of 11. Jean Birkett in Birkenhead recalls the pressure put on her to pass the eleven-plus:

> 'The eleven-plus was everything, at least it was in our house. I heard about it for years, even from our teachers. That was all you were geared towards and we knew that, the thing that would change our lives. We were relentlessly streamed and ranked. I was in the A class. It was the baby boom years and my classes went down to D, maybe even E and F.'

Failing the eleven-plus, however, could have devastating consequences on self-image, aspirations, motivation and friendships. Jean Birkett adds:

> 'Most of my primary school A class passed the eleven-plus except for my friend and so when she didn't, it was shocking. She ended up going to the secondary modern school, Cavendish Secondary Modern, and I never, ever saw her again. That's the impact of the eleven-plus. Lives diverged so much whether you passed or failed. It did determine quite a bit the rest of the course of your life.'

There was a popular BBC radio programme at the time called *Top of the Form*, in which schools throughout Britain competed against each in a general knowledge quiz. But of course it did not involve all schools; it was just the independent and grammar schools who competed, with the secondary modern schools deemed unsuitable. The programme epitomized the education system of the 1950s and 1960s, and the BBC eventually acknowledged that it was somewhat elitist.

But for all its faults, the grammar school system – as it became known – did offer opportunities for bright, young, working-class children for the first time in history. Prior to this, it was virtually impossible for such children from such a background to conceivably go on to a university education. Under the new scheme, however, many of them did pass the eleven-plus and go on to grammar schools, taking their GCE O-level examination in their final year. Some even stayed on for an extra two years before taking an Advanced GCE examination. Your results here, if good enough, allowed you to progress to a university. Although it was still only a small minority of children who moved into higher education (about 8 per cent at maximum), there were nonetheless some working-class children among those who went to university. Of course, many more middle-class children would go to university, although often the first in their families to ever do so. What it meant was that the nature of British universities began to change. They were still largely elitist institutions and were few in number, but nonetheless they now boasted many more students from a variety of backgrounds. What the new system also did was to offer an escape route from whatever background you came. By doing so, it raised aspirations.

The poet Roger McGough told the writer Paul Morley: 'I had grown up in Liverpool, with a working-class Irish-Catholic background. Men of my father's generation worked on the docks, but I was among the first of that post-war generation for whom education was available – I got a scholarship to go to grammar school and then to a university.'

For girls, it could be even more difficult. Jean Birkett remembers that 'in Birkenhead there were three grammar schools for the boys and also a Catholic grammar school whilst for the girls there was only one grammar school'. The girls were clearly disadvantaged from the start, although this may not have been the case in other local authorities.

Birkett adds:

'Britain was a subservient, compliant society. We didn't realize that at the time. When you look back, we really were. We didn't rebel that much at school. I think we were really programmed. We had a pretty narrow education; we didn't know of other things we could have studied. I was programmed into what I did. I was pretty much being told which subjects I could do, especially at A level.'

Annie O'Malley, who grew up in Wythenshawe in Manchester, recalls that she was one of the lucky few to pass the eleven-plus:

'At my school from about 36 kids, only about 5 or 6 of us passed for a grammar school. As well as pass the 11-plus you also had to sit an entrance exam. I passed and was thrust into grammar school, one of two Catholic girls' schools, Loreto, with a briefcase and tie with homework every night, indoor shoes, outdoor shoes, blazer, boater in the summer and felt hat in the winter. So, it was all a huge change for me. I was the youngest of four children and the first to pass for grammar school, so my parents were really pleased. Girls travelled from the whole of Greater Manchester and beyond, to come to my Catholic convent grammar school.'

Female Catholic schools were generally run by nuns, who instilled a discipline that often exceeded that of their male counterparts. There may not have been as much corporal punishment or sexual abuse as some boys suffered, but there was an intoxicating and stifling rigidity aimed at quashing any idea of individuality.

Christine Parkinson from Newcastle remembers:

'The nuns could be fearsome. We weren't all very good girls – there were some naughty girls. It was pretty strict. It wasn't all nuns. The head teacher was a nun and, in those days, they still wore their long black habits and wimples. We had a mistress of discipline, a nun who used to make us kneel down and if our skirts weren't hovering on the floor, they were too short and she would tie back your hair with string if it was too long. There wasn't corporal punishment but there was the absolute humiliation of having your "note taken" which meant if you had been doing something bad you had your "note taken" and when the whole school gathered every week it was the Reverend Mother, who was the head of the Order of the Sacred Heart, she would attend and in front of the whole school you were called out and had to go down to the front and accept the reverend mother's disappointment at being naughty.'

Annie O'Malley agreed that the nuns were 'incredibly strict':

'I was sent home at 13 to have my hair cut and threatened with expulsion. My hair was on my collar but you couldn't have your hair loose, you had to tie it back or have short hair. And I defied them once by not having it tied back so they sent me home to have it cut. My parents were called in and I was threatened with expulsion. And from that day onwards I resented the restrictions. I thought they were out to make my life really miserable. I was bright but the system failed me and I came out with just two "O" levels, Art and Greek and Roman Literature in Translation.'

Christine Parkinson recalls that school did little to prepare girls for some of the practicalities of life:

'I don't recall being taught anything about birth control or sex. I think in RE we had these boxes where you could put questions in, such as "is it alright to kiss a boy?". The teacher was an older lady, and the answer would be you shouldn't kiss a boy for longer than a couple of seconds! One of my friends got pregnant but she still did her A levels. She wasn't allowed in school; she just came in for the exam. It was all very hushed up. We only knew because she was on the periphery of a circle of friends.'

'Very small numbers of girls in my A class were going to go to university,' says Jean Birkett. 'I think the school controlled the application process. I look back now and I feel that I was very programmed.'

At university, being away from home and being free of all parental constraints was something that could be life-changing. Not only did you have to manage your own life and budget, but you could basically do whatever you pleased. For the first time, sex became a possibility. It was no longer a case of quick sex up some back alley, in a remote part of the park or at someone's party. Instead, for those at university in their own flats or university accommodation, sex was often more readily available, and came with comfort and time.

But it wasn't always the case for everyone, as Jean Birkett remembers:

> 'I ended up in an all girls college in residence that was like being in a boarding school. We had all these rules and curfews. We weren't allowed to live independently. When I moved out and into accommodation in Sheffield it was into an approved billet. The college had to approve it. I was 21 and we still had these curfews, rules and boys would never have been allowed over the doorstep.'

'Moving away from home was something I really wanted to do,' says Christine Parkinson.

> 'My mother had been a widow for a long time, she didn't deal with it very well. My sisters and brothers were older and by 16 they had left home. I felt a lot of responsibility for my mum, so the last couple of years at school I had become a bit of a carer for her. I just wanted to escape it, get away. The first year I went to poly which wasn't good but when I did get to university, yes, it was a wonderful feeling. The excitement that had started in the sixties with the music that was still there, so much going on, we were different, not like those in the past had been. I really enjoyed my time at university.'

In his autobiography, Rolling Stone Keith Richards remembered the frustrations and constraints of the time:

> 'I just felt that I was smart enough, one way or another, to wiggle out of this social net ... My parents were brought up in the Depression, when if you got something, you just kept it and you held it and that was it ... I was a kid and I didn't even know what ambition meant. I just felt the constraints. The society and everything I was growing up in was just too small for me.'

The Beatles themselves were a mix of academic success. John Lennon had passed his eleven-plus examination and gone to Quarry Bank School, a highly rated school that had produced many well-known alumni, including Cabinet Ministers Peter Shore and Bill Rodgers, the actor Derek Nimmo as well as a number of top footballers. But Lennon failed miserably at his O-level examinations, in main because of the tragic death of his mother. But at the age of 16 he did get a place at the Liverpool College of Art.

Paul McCartney also passed his eleven-plus, one of only three students to pass from his primary school. He went on to attend his local grammar school, the Liverpool Institute, where he met George Harrison, who had also passed the eleven-plus. Ringo, however, was not academically successful. After enduring years of illness and hospitalizations, he could barely read or write by the age of 11. He consequently went to Dingle Vale Secondary school and left at 15 to find employment, initially with British Rail, later finding more meaningful and settled work as a machinist. In many ways, the background of the four Beatles epitomized that of many working-class communities. In a later era, three of them – John, Paul and George – would almost certainly have progressed to university, but in the late 1950s, with so few students continuing into higher education, there was little hope that any of The Beatles would follow that path. All that would soon change, though it would not be fully realized until later in the 1960s.

Grammar schools generally tended to be traditional and authoritarian, as Stephen Platt remembered:

'In my own school the teachers wore gowns all the time, we had a play area known as the quad and we had a daily assembly where we sang hymns accompanied by the school orchestra. We also had a school song, *Gaudeamus Igitur*, which we had to sing in Latin. When it came to sport, we only played rugby. Football was unheard of even though one boy, some years ahead of me, played for England schoolboys and later went on to captain Bolton Wanderers in the first division. We also did Latin, though thankfully not Greek as well. Basically, it was trying to style itself on a public school.

'We also had something called "fortnightly marks". Every fortnight all your homework marks were totted up and you were given an overall mark. These would be read out in assembly for all the school to hear. It was nerve-wracking. If your mark fell below 40 per cent you had to go and see the headmaster. The first time he would probably just warn you but if it happened repeatedly, he'd beat you. It was brutal.'

Although you could leave a secondary school at the age of 15, it was rare to leave a grammar school until you were 16, which is when most students left. The majority would leave grammar school with a handful of O-levels and work in offices, banks, local government, the civil services and so on, while those at secondary schools would find either skilled or unskilled jobs, maybe with apprenticeships in factories, shipyards, coalmines or engineering. For those embarking on an apprenticeship, there were technical colleges in most towns and cities, with many employers giving day-release to study for higher qualifications pertinent to their job. Girls could also take courses in hairdressing, home economics and tailoring.

Not many stayed on at school to take their A-levels, as you needed to have passed at least five O-levels. Bob Jones recalled: 'At my school probably no more than 20 stayed on out of a cohort of 100 or so. So that's only 20 per cent. And of those maybe only 10 would go on to university. It wasn't that the education was poor but that opportunities in higher education were severely limited.'

'There were about six classes at GCE O level,' says Jean Birkett.

'I was in the A class but by no means did all my class go on. I would say about half of the A class stayed on. And maybe a quarter of the B class. That makes about 30 out of a cohort of getting on for 200 girls in my year. There were two A level classes but the classes were much smaller. I would say that if you included the colleges of technology, only half a dozen went on to degrees. And maybe only three of them went to an actual university.'

Polytechnics were also springing up in the 1960s. Although a handful had always existed, there was a huge expansion in the early Sixties, allowing students to take a degree in subjects not always taught at a university. Many of these degrees had their roots firmly in industry.

Many secondary school girls left at 15, becoming hairdressers, shop assistants, secretaries, typists, nurses and so on. There wasn't a wealth of choice for those girls without qualifications, and there were barely any apprenticeships for women at that time.

For the grammar school girl, opportunities were little better. Again, the vast majority left at 16 years of age, and of those who stayed on to take A-levels, even fewer than the boys went on to universities. Many of those staying on went to Teacher Training Colleges, while other would look to work in libraries, offices, banks and maybe the civil service.

Also adding to the changing nature of British youth was the ending of conscription. National Service had been introduced following the start of the Second World War in 1939, and was continued after the war. But it was not popular. On their seventeenth birthday or thereabouts, young men would be greeted by an official brown envelope telling them where to report for their eighteen months of National Service. During the Korean War, it was extended to two years. Few looked forward to it, as it meant a total disruption to their lives. Jobs would be left behind, along with family and girlfriends, and futures would be uncertain. In the meantime, you might be sent to a war zone such as Korea or Malaysia, or to some other posting like Germany, Singapore, Hong Kong or any other place where British troops were stationed.

Former Manchester United footballer Wilf McGuiness remembers that he missed National Service through ill-health:

> 'Nobody wanted to go in the army. There wasn't a war on and it just seemed to interfere with your training. David Pegg and I didn't make it. Bobby Charlton, Eddie Colman, Duncan Edwards, Tommy Taylor, and Gordon Clayton all went in. Cos I didn't go in it meant I trained here and I got in the first team before Bobby Charlton, Eddie Colman even though they were older than me.'

Life in the army could be an adventure to some extent, especially if the young conscripts were sent on foreign postings; some, such as Hong Kong, were popular and, for the most part, enjoyable. For many of the young men, it was the first time they had ever been abroad and was something of an adventure. But they were also subjected to rigorous discipline, with cleaning duties, marching and exercising, or 'bullshit' as it became known. If you were sent to a war zone such as Korea, there was the likelihood of front-line action and the possibility of injury or even death. Some 70 per cent of the 100,000 British soldiers who served in Korea were 18–20-year-old lads on National Service. In all, just over 1,000 British soldiers died in Korea, many of them young men. They were subjected to appalling conditions and witnessed the most terrifying sights and experiences.

At the end of their eighteen months' National Service, there were no thanks, no medals and no financial rewards. They were merely told that they had to do reserve training once every few months in case another armed conflict flared up and their services were needed. So it was back to work, or rather to try to find work, and to see if former girlfriends were still interested. In truth, most had been 'dumped' by their girlfriends once they had gone off to some foreign posting.

It was hardly surprising then that when conscription ended in 1957, a whole generation were relieved. A generation was now able to confidently plan its future. It was no longer a case of taking any old job before 'call up' and then finding one with better prospects when you returned to civvy street. Instead, at 16 or 18 if you had stayed on at school, you could look forward to a decent job, brighter prospects, perhaps marriage and children, and buying a home. There was a sense of continuity. And for that generation who followed the ending of conscription, there were suddenly no fears. No worries about being sent to war zones, endless parade ground marching, gruesome sergeant majors or countless hours of polishing your boots. Life in the army, which is where the vast majority of conscripts went, brought with it authoritarianism and discipline. You were not allowed to question, disagree or have any opinions of your own. But with the ending of National Service, a great weight was lifted off a whole generation, among them Chris Prior:

> 'I remember thinking about conscription and doing the calculation whether I'd be called up. My uncle had been in the merchant navy during the war. My Dad had been in the army and they'd talk about the war. You knew there was Korea happening and then Suez as well, I really remember that. But then they stopped conscription and I breathed a sigh of relief.'

So rather than spend two years in the army, grammar school boy Chris Prior went straight to university.

It was another burden gone, a further release from state authoritarianism that suddenly allowed young men in the 1960s to think for themselves instead of having the individualism knocked out of them by squarebashing. Many would go on to blame society's social problems during the 1960s on the ending of conscription. They argued that the army instilled discipline, obedience and maturity into its soldiers, and that once this had gone, young men were free to do as they pleased. It was all too easy to see the ending of conscription as a scapegoat for all the problems that society was facing: Beatniks, The Beatles, long hair, rebellion, it was all the fault of ending conscription. But, of course, that was far from the truth.

Ringo Starr later admitted that he was terrified at the prospect of going into the army. It's hard to imagine any of The Beatles happily answering their call-up papers in the way that Elvis had in America. Paul and George might have grinned and got on with it, and no doubt Ringo would eventually have joked his way through. But John? He would never have been able to accept it. Had conscription still been in operation, The Beatles would never have happened; and the counterculture that they initiated might have taken many more years to emerge.

Chapter 9

Youth On The March

In Britain, the 1960s brought about more fundamental changes in higher education. The university population had doubled since 1939; by the early 1960s some 200,000 18-year-olds were qualified to go to university, but with only 170,000 places available. This left 30,000 qualified students with no option but to go out and look for work. The years immediately following the Second World War had led to a baby boom, with the population of young people rising rapidly. It was expected that there would be some 600,000 18-year-olds by the late Sixties, but with nowhere near enough resources to cope with this bulge. As a result, the Conservative government set up a committee under Lord Robbins in 1961 to examine the future of higher education in the UK. It reported two years later, recommending that in order to be equipped to deal with the rising population, a massive investment was needed in higher education. It also underlined the fact that considerably more students were capable of going to university, but were not being given the opportunity.

Many of Lord Robbins' recommendations had already been realized by the Macmillan government, with a programme to construct a number of new universities having been set in place. Eventually, seven new universities would be built – York, Sussex, East Anglia, Kent, Warwick, Essex and Lancaster. The underlying recommendation of Robbins was that anyone who achieved the necessary qualifications should have the opportunity to attend university. The Robbins Report has since been regarded as one of the most important government initiatives of the 1960s, and would have far-reaching consequences as the government looked to bring the higher educational system into the twentith century and provide opportunities to all those school leavers who had gained the necessary qualifications or were at least capable of achieving them. Labour Prime Minister Harold Wilson later picked up where the Conservatives left off and pledged further funds for higher education, as well as setting up the Open University so that anyone could acquire a degree through evening or part-time study. It was all part of his grand modernizing plan.

The new universities were to be located in non-traditional areas. In the past, Britain's universities had overwhelmingly been in the south-east and in cathedral cities, but many of the new flux of universities were to be situated outside those areas. Instead of old, weathered granite buildings and cold lecture theatres, the new universities offered brand new facilities with architecturally splendid buildings, glass, lakes and greenery. They were outside of city and town centres, with student accommodation, libraries and social activities all on the one campus. It very much followed the American blueprint.

The new universities also took the opportunity to introduce a wider syllabus. Instead of the traditional one-subject syllabus that the old universities boasted, students would be able to study a number of subjects, especially some with more appeal in the modern world. A wider variety of modern languages was introduced, along with American studies, modern European history, politics, economics and of course sociology.

Mike Prior was one of the first students to attend Sussex University:

'It was all new; styled in award-winning red brick, modern, a kind of Oxbridge collegiate without colleges, in a fold of rural downs near the seaside. It was a brilliant representation of a new England. It offered new kinds of degrees like European or American studies, which cut across old classifications such as literature or history. It was staffed, by and large, with clever, leftish young academics and its first students were, by and large, clever, leftish, mostly southern and certainly modern.'

The Robbins Committee did much work in identifying the under-representation of women studying for degrees at universities. In the early 1960s, it was estimated that only 8 per cent of 18-year-olds were going into higher education, with the vast majority of these being male. Just one-in-four students in universities were female, with only 2 per cent of

18-year-old women going into higher education. The under-representation of women was a scandal, but the new expansion of universities began to offer fresh opportunities aimed at women in particular. The former education minister and academic Tessa Blackstone later argued that 'the recommendation to expand the number of places greatly had a direct benefit for women. Many of those who took advantage of the new opportunities to become graduates were women, since the growth of universities coincided with shifts in attitudes about women's roles promoted by the feminist movement in the late 60s and early 70s. Thus Robbins helped to shape the social revolution in the role of women during the last three decades of the 20th century.'

Although this was generally true, many universities still exercised restricted entry requirements. At some universities, admission was not possible unless you had a foreign language qualification at A-level, even if you were not intending to do a language course.

Mike Prior remembered just such a situation:

'Entry to Oxbridge also required a Latin A level, as it did for medicine or dentistry at any number of universities. I also wanted to go to Cambridge because it was the top physics university. Now to go there you had to take entrance exams, apply to a specific college and go for an interview and you had to learn Latin even though you were doing physics. My school didn't teach Latin – that was how a lot of schools differentiated themselves from the others. The entrance exams were in November and as I hadn't done Latin I had to learn it. I had to sit in the library with a Latin textbook doing teach yourself Latin because there was no one who could teach me.'

In the end, Mike failed.

For many working-class families, there was an attitude that universities were 'not for our sort'. It was all about horizons. Nobody in their families had ever been to university, so many working-class children were not encouraged to apply. This was particularly so for girls. The converse argument was that a good apprenticeship or an office job was a prospect better suited to their horizons. Furthermore, it was unusual for a school to encourage a student to go to university if the parents felt otherwise.

'University was only for the best dozen or so students in our school,' recalled Bob Jones. 'And that wasn't me. There simply weren't the places. So rather than waste time, I left and found a job.'

Christine Parkinson, on the other hand, was always encouraged:

'I came from a fairly middle-class family; my father had been a head teacher in a primary school and my mother was a teacher as well. My siblings had also gone to university, so it was assumed that I would as well. I did my A levels, I just knew it was going to happen, why do A levels if you're not going to go on to university? I wasn't particularly academic but it was just an unspoken assumption.'

Going to university or college also offered the chance to escape home, and at the age of 18 most young people were ready to get away from their parents and the restrictions of the towns or cities where they had grown up. The Animals' song 'We Gotta Get Out of This Place' resonated with so many, especially with those bright enough to get their A-levels. This was the Swinging Sixties and everyone wanted a bit of the action. The Beatles had unleashed a drive for independence and excitement. Independence meant being able to go to parties, stay out all night long, have sex, go on demonstrations, do what you wanted and explore the world. Going to university or college was a first step, a way out of the drudgery and dreariness. It offered not only an escape but better pay, more interesting career prospects and so on.

Clare Jenkins agreed:

'Absolutely. I first felt the yearning to escape when we lived in the park in Leicester in the late 50s/early 60s. I used to stand on the bridge beside our house in Leicester and look along the canal, wondering where the water went to, and imagining that it went to America. And thanks to our parents, we knew that the way to do that was through education. My brother was always a zillion times brighter than me, and went to Cambridge and eventually graduated with a PhD.

'Although I later loved living in Birmingham, loved my school, there was a definite sense of "I gotta get out of this place", which my brother and I strongly shared. But then my parents had to leave Birmingham, so Dad had to find another job, with a house attached, which he did in a tiny village in Nottinghamshire, a mile away from the nearest bus stop. I knew I wanted to stay in Birmingham, so I went to live with one of my school friends and her family, before we got a flat together in Moseley, the red-light area! I've always said I effectively grew up at 17, as that's when I unexpectedly got my independence. I flunked my A levels, which meant I couldn't go to university/poly as planned, so, because I'd been working as a library assistant, I got a job at Birmingham's Victorian Reference Library. I was supposed to retake my A levels during that year, but then Birmingham Poly said they'd take me, anyway, so that's where I went. I also had an offer from North London Poly, but – just like Billy Liar – at the last minute I bottled it. I didn't really know anyone in London and it felt like a city too far – plus I was having a great time in Birmingham, with parties, the Windsor pub on a Friday and Saturday nights, boyfriends, pop concerts and so forth.'

In his novel *Room At The Top*, published in 1956, author John Braine struck a chord when his character Joe Lambton is given advice by his friend Charles about leaving his home town: 'There's nothing in Dufton, Joe. Leave it before you become a zombie too ... When you go to Warley, Joe, there'll be no more zombies. Remember that. No more zombies.'

There was also considerable reassessment of the academic curriculum during the Sixties. Although all the traditional subjects – such as English, mathematics, history, geography, science and languages – continued to be taught, the new universities experimented by offering a range of novel subjects, more applicable to the modern era and that might appeal to young people. Almost all these subjects lay in the field of humanities. Among them were sociology, psychology, American studies and social history. The introduction of sociology as a teaching subject was an innovation that was to prove highly popular with young students, particularly the more radical. Sociology was the study of society and the way it functioned, and was almost tailor-made for the Sixties. Although it had been taught in the United States since the late nineteenth century, it did not become a mainstream subject in American universities until the 1950s. By the 1960s, it was beginning to win favour with British academics, and the new universities with their innovative attitudes were an ideal focus for its teaching. Academics were exploring new areas of interest such as alienation, communities, criminology, feminism, race and so forth. Much of it was political and required some understanding of Marxism and the contrasting ways of examining society, again something that appealed to young radicals. Sociologists like Laurie Taylor and Stuart Hall helped popularize the subject, making it both accessible and relevant. Students in their thousands signed up for the new courses, although sociology in particular soon became something of a scapegoat and was blamed by the media and others for the politicization of the young. There were also cutting accusations within some academic institutions that it was not really a 'proper' subject to be taught at a university. With more students attending universities, many of them from working-class and middle-class backgrounds, and with a curriculum that fulfilled their interests, it was inevitable that sooner or later, something would explode.

In March 1968, students at the normally tranquil Université Paris X at Nanterre in the western suburbs of Paris began a protest about conditions and teaching at the university. French universities were traditionally overloaded with students, with lecture theatres often bursting at the seams with hundreds of students, many having to sit on the floor or even stand at the back. Any kind of personal tuition was simply out of the question. In addition, there was a very high dropout rate, particularly after the first year. The protests began within the university, but would over the course of the next few months almost overthrow the French government and lead to similar protests across Europe and America.

The protesting students came out on to the streets and the 22 March Movement was born, with two Daniels (Cohn-Bendit and Bensaid) challenging not just the French educational system but the very authority of the state as epitomized by its monarchical president, Charles de Gaulle. The students went on to set up their own classes and lectures, inviting notable radicals onto their campus. From demanding university reforms, the students soon moved on to something more radical – the need for a change in society. They were soon joined in their call for change by trade unionists and left-wing parties, although there were significant differences of opinion between them all. The communist-led Confédération Générale du Travail (CGT), which was the principal overall body for the trade unions, was totally opposed to the violence and threat of revolution, whereas the students and Trotskyist parties were intent on escalating the rioting until the Establishment had been overthrown.

Strikes broke out throughout the country, with massive demonstrations on the streets of Paris. By May 1968, with the strikes still ongoing, France looked to be on the brink of revolution, with violence breaking out across the leafy boulevards of central Paris. De Gaulle promptly ordered the state's security forces, the Compagnies Républicaines de Sécurité, into battle in the hope that he could cling onto power, but when that appeared unlikely he briefly fled the country before returning to announce that he was not resigning but was dissolving the National Assembly and calling a general election. With the CGT negotiating a massive pay rise for workers and de Gaulle threatening to introduce a state of emergency that would bring the army onto the streets, striking workers returned to their factories and the street protests petered out. France eventually returned to calm.

That same month, an anti-Vietnam War demonstration outside the United States Embassy in Grosvenor Square, London, turned violent. The rally organized by the Vietnam Solidarity Committee mainly comprised young people belonging to left-wing organizations such as the International Marxist Group and the International Socialists. The organization of this and other demonstrations regarding the conflict in Vietnam was to remain in the hands of young people, such as Tariq Ali, rather than the trade unions or more traditional political parties. Indeed, most of the trade unions, who might have been expected to be opposed to the war, deliberately shunned the march, simply because it was not in their control but rather in the hands of young radicals. Tariq Ali, from a wealthy political Pakistani family, was an Oxford graduate and former President of the Oxford Union. He was a charismatic, highly intelligent and accomplished speaker and debater, and a leading member of the International Marxist Group. Also involved in the Vietnam Solidarity Campaign was the ageing but highly respected philosopher and peace campaigner Bertrand Russell. Police on horseback charged the demonstrators as they tried to force their way into the embassy, and the scenes in Grosvenor Square were filmed by Granada Television's *World In Action* team and transmitted in a special half-hour programme the following evening at prime time on ITV. Viewers were aghast at the violence, particularly when the police waded into the demonstrators with batons and boots. It was the largest demonstration in living memory, and certainly the most violent for many years. The police had been ill-equipped, their tactics naïve and their estimation of the numbers likely to be involved far short of those who actually turned up. Nevertheless, it was to be a valuable lesson for them.

Six months later, in October 1968, the Vietnam Solidarity Committee organized a second, similar demonstration. This time even more turned out, again principally young people. They marched through the deserted streets of London, passing shops and buildings boarded up in fear that Britain was about to face the kind of revolt that Parisians had confronted a few months earlier. The media had whipped up a panic. The police, however, were under no illusions this time about the likely turnout, and although they were still not adequately equipped, they were at least better prepared and easily managed to stave off an attempted invasion of the embassy.

Pinpointing the precise start of the student revolution in Britain is always difficult and debatable, but an event at the London School of Economics in June 1965 was clearly the first of its kind on this side of the Atlantic. Writing in his diary, Labour minister Tony Benn noted: 'On Friday night there was the first teach-in at the LSE in London on Vietnam. It was based on the teach-ins that have appeared in the United States and which are an aspect of the non-violent movement. I think they probably will have an influence and I'm told that whenever Harold Wilson's name was mentioned at LSE people booed.' Benn was right; it would have a major influence over the course of events later in the decade.

The art colleges were also a focus for political activity and demonstrations. In general, the colleges tended to attract creative, radical young people who were at the forefront of pushing the artistic boundaries. John Lennon had been at the Liverpool College of Art, along with Stuart Sutcliffe and Thelma McGough, who later became a BAFTA award-winning television producer. There was a major sit-in at Hornsey College of Art, organized by Kim Howells, later to become a minister in the Blair government. Other art colleges followed suit.

In April 1968, readers of *The Times* woke to see a headline that students at Ruskin College, Oxford, were to go on strike on May Day in protest at Enoch Powell's 'Rivers of blood' speech. Ruskin students had last gone on strike in 1909, and there had been no other serious strikes by students in the UK since. Three hundred students from the London School of Economics also marched to Enoch Powell's Belgravia home, only to discover that he was actually in Canada. Thereafter, students began to question what was happening in their own universities as well as in the wider political world.

The real focus for student revolt in the UK, however, was the London School of Economics. In March 1969, the LSE dismissed two of its young lecturers – Robin Blackburn and Nick Bateson. Both had been actively involved in urging students to tear down security gates which had been erected in the school. Ostensibly they were fire gates, but they were seen by the students as a symbol of authoritarianism. The gates were subsequently pulled down by the students. As a result, the university decided not to renew the contracts of Blackburn and Bateson, who were regarded as troublemakers. Blackburn, in particular, was an active Trotskyist and a frequent contributor to *Black Dwarf*, the newspaper of the International Marxist Group. As a result of the sackings, socialist society students at the LSE organized a sit-in. Although they were not successful in having Blackburn and Bateson reinstated, a flame of student discontent at the LSE had been lit. Other disturbances soon followed.

The university had also controversially appointed Dr Walter Adams as its new Director in 1967. Adams was at the time principal of University College Rhodesia, a country that had recently declared unilateral independence from the UK. At the core of this particular dispute was apartheid, and the appointment of Adams was interpreted by many students as being supportive of racism. The LSE also had financial interests in a number of apartheid-linked companies, which again led to a variety of protests. Adams would remain at odds with the student body of the university throughout his tenure, which came to an end in 1974.

So alarmed was the Labour government that Minister of State Shirley Williams called LSE director Walter Adams and Lord Robbins into the Education Department. A secret minute of the meeting reported:

> 'Lord Robbins drew a clear distinction between the ordinary student who, disturbed by world affairs and questioning society's values, felt confused and frustrated and gave expression by demonstration and protest; and a minority of dedicated dissidents [whose] aim was to break the nerve of the Governing Body and academic staff, to create a new university to serve as a revolutionary centre ... They made Union meetings discordant, bitter and obscene. They sought to run the University by huge but unrepresentative mass meetings which they had packed with their followers. The situation was becoming very ugly. The President of the Union (who had resigned) had besought him not to open the school for the time being; the building would be taken over by extremists. These people had a black list of staff who, they had resolved, were not to be allowed to lecture in future.'

Robbins and Walter were so sensationalist that it must have put the fear of God into Shirley Williams and her Cabinet colleagues. Shirley Williams' husband, Professor Bernard Williams, a Professor of Philosophy at Cambridge University, also added to the hysteria. Delivering the Foundation Oration at Birkbeck College in London, he described the aims of LSE students as 'absurd', 'patently insane' and 'childish'.

The LSE had also been a focal point for the October 1968 demonstration against the Vietnam War, with many of its students active in the organization of the march. Radical American activists became frequent visitors and speakers at the university, while the LSE also had on its staff a number of radical lecturers, including Marxist philosopher and activist Ralph Miliband and radical lawyers K.W. Wedderburn and Michael Zander.

Protest was growing everywhere, with young students becoming more politicized and indeed more interested in issues than their own course work. Young student Chris Hitchens remembered: 'As an undergraduate at Balliol College, Oxford, I was already a militant student member of the International Socialist group. That winter of 1967 I doubt that our Oxford branch contained more than a dozen members but ... in a year it had grown to perhaps a hundred, with a periphery of many more and an influence well beyond our size.'

Further student disturbances, for one reason or another, took place at Warwick University, Essex University and the Hornsey College of Art. In February 1970, during a sit-in at Warwick University, one of the new fleet of Sixties universities, a student thumbing through a file on 'Student-University Relations' in an unlocked cabinet, came across a document that revealed the university had been keeping files on the political activities of left-wing students and staff. Copies of the files were made and rapidly circulated to universities around the country. The documents revealed Warwick University's complicity with local manufacturing industries, and in particular its role in assisting major manufacturers in the Midlands to uncover potential industrial troublemakers. The unearthing of the document caused a furore, leading to a major sit-in at the university, which gained support from other universities up and down the country as they too began to question whether their own seats of learning were complicit in similar activities.

Even the elite Oxford University was not immune. In 1969, Oxford students, led principally by some from Ruskin College, stormed the university's Treasury building and began a week-long sit in, demanding access to the university's files, in fear that the university had been keeping similar files on them. In the event, no files were found and after a week the demonstration petered out.

Inspired by the events of 1968, The Beatles offered their own view, recording the song 'Revolution'. Released in August 1968, it was a hit around the world. It was very much Lennon's song, with his lyrics expressing the need for change:

> 'You say you want a revolution
> Well you know
> We all want to change the world
> You tell me that it's evolution
> Well, you know,
> We all want to change the world.'

The other Beatles were hesitant about the lyrics, not wanting to court even more controversy. Despite his bandmates' reservations, Lennon persevered with the song and insisted it be their next single, but the original lyrics were toned down to cast doubt on any violent tactics that were being suggested by the New Left, the burgeoning left-wing radicals:

> 'But when you talk about destruction
> Don't you know that you can count me out.

Ironically, when the recording was released in August 1968, the song was viewed by the New Left as something of a betrayal and a sign that The Beatles were out of step with radical elements of the counterculture.

In 1968, Mick Jagger and The Rolling Stones had also released *Street Fighting Man*, which was a considerably more political song than anything The Beatles had recorded. 'In sleepy London, there's just no place for a street fighting man,' ran the lyrics. But then, Jagger was always more political than Lennon. He had studied at the LSE, was friendly with Tariq Ali and had made a notable appearance on *World In Action* in which he defended modern youth.

The same kind of protests were being repeated throughout Europe. In Germany, the Free University of Berlin was at the centre of protests, with sit-ins and demonstrations. President John F. Kennedy's famous '*Ich bin ein Berliner*' speech in front of the Brandenburg Gate in June 1963 had resonated with an entire generation of young Germans, helping to radicalize them and free them from their recent past. But it was essentially the war in Vietnam which was the focus of their protests. This, coupled with the belief that there remained many state organizations, banks and capitalist enterprises still employing former Nazis, helped fuel their protests in a different direction, making the violence in Germany far more extreme than elsewhere, with bombings and assassinations. Leading student activist Benno Ohnesorg was shot dead by a policeman in West Berlin in 1967 during a demonstration against the Shah of Iran's visit. As a result of his death, some students adopted a more revolutionary approach, setting up the Red Army Faction (also known as the Baader-Meinhof Gang) that sought to answer violence with violence through bombings and murders. Then in April 1968, the leading student spokesman and activist Rudi Dutschke was shot in the head in an assassination attempt. He survived, but never fully recovered and died some years later following an epileptic fit.

Barbara Weber, a young German student at the time, remembers everyone's shock at the death of Ohnesorg in particular, and then the shooting of Dutschke:

> 'We couldn't believe it. We thought we could change everything and to some extent we did change things. I always remember that in our family we never spoke about the Second World War, ever. Then in the sixties, for the first time I can remember us as a family talking about the war. We suddenly had the confidence and the courage to raise the subject and to confront it.'

While radicalism had swept through the universities, it was also winning supporters among more traditional, non-university people. The Campaign for Nuclear Disarmament (CND) was the first radical pressure group to emerge out of the gloom and Cold War politics of post-war Britain.

Before the Second World War, the National Unemployed Workers' Movement had campaigned against unemployment, with marches and protests throughout the 1930s. There had also been a Peace Movement, but CND began in 1957 and had been officially launched in 1958 at a public meeting. The possession of nuclear weapons had become a major issue towards the end of the 1950s. Only three countries possessed a nuclear capability – Britain, the USA and the Soviet Union – but there was clearly the likelihood that other countries such as France and even Israel might soon develop nuclear weapons of their own. But not only was the proliferation of nuclear weapons becoming an issue, but also the very possession of them. Within the Labour Party, it was already a fiercely debated issue, one which would culminate in left-winger Nye Bevan controversially defending the possession of nuclear weapons at the 1957 Labour Party conference. The first Sputnik had also been launched by the Soviet Union in that year, clearly demonstrating their capability in rocket technology and bringing the fear of rocket-launched nuclear warfare a step closer. The Left feared that Britain was being dragged into a nuclear arms race that might have catastrophic consequences.

When CND was formally launched, it immediately drew support from many in respected circles, including leading scientists, politicians, writers and artists such as Betrand Russell, Michael Foot, Peggy Ashcroft, John Arlott, A.J.P. Taylor, Benjamin Britten and Barbara Hepworth. It also pulled a number of other organizations into its structure and acted as a focal point for the protest against nuclear weapons. From then onwards, it organized an annual Easter march from Aldermaston in rural Berkshire, which was the home of the Atomic Weapons Research Establishment, to London, where it would end on Easter Monday with a mass rally in Trafalgar Square.

In April 1960, the writer J.B. Priestley addressed seventy delegates representing student organisations from thirty different countries in a meeting at St Pancras Town Hall in London to debate the threat of nuclear war. The Japanese delegates even brought film of the aftermath of the Hiroshima atomic bomb to show at the conference. Then in 1966, BBC Television commissioned *War Game*, a documentary, produced, directed and written by Peter Watkins, about the consequences of a nuclear attack. The film, however, was deemed by the BBC and government to be so disturbing that it was promptly pulled and not shown on television until twenty years later.

By the early 1960s, more than 150,000 people were marching on the annual Easter pilgrimage from Aldermaston to London. Indeed, the numbers had become so huge that in 1964 it was reduced to a one-day event. The march appealed in particular to young people, with many of them regarding it as something of a festival, it being very much the precursor of the music festivals of the late Sixties and Seventies. Young people from all over the country would assemble in Aldermaston, with rucksacks and guitars on their backs, full of hope and protest. They would camp in fields, cook food over open fires and join in singing protest songs as darkness fell. 'At the edge of a field, surrounded by crowds of teenagers, a jazz band was blaring out some bouncy numbers,' reported the *Guardian in* 1960.

Not everybody sympathized with their ideals and actions. Alan Brien in *The Spectator* colourfully described them as 'weirdies and beardies, colonels and conchies, Communists and Liberals, vegetarians and alcoholics, beauties and beasts'. The esteemed journalist Rene MacColl, writing in the *Daily Express*, was even more damning, calling them 'the sort of hairy horrors, who think it intellectual not to wash more than once every three weeks'.

You could see a theme emerging – The Beatles, students and CND demonstrators, all scruffy and unwashed. The young, of course, just laughed. The *Guardian* reported that there were big student contingents and noted that 'the representation also seems to have become rather broader than it was in several ways. Perhaps 60 per cent of the marchers ... were under 20.'

The Cuban Missile Crisis of 1961 had brought the threat of nuclear war to everyone's doorstep. Suddenly it was a reality. Although General Curtis Le May, during the Korean War, had drawn up plans for a nuclear strike on Chinese and North Korean forces, it was a long way from Britain; and anyhow, his proposals had not been further advanced thanks to British Prime Minister Clement Attlee jumping on a plane to meet with President Truman, threatening to withdraw British support of the war if such an attack did take place. And in Korea, there was really no threat of nuclear retaliation. But with Cuba it was different. There was a genuine fear that if America carried out its threats to attack suspected Soviet nuclear missile sites in Cuba, the Soviet Union might retaliate. The consequences would have been disastrous. For forty-eight hours, everyone held their breath. In the event, a peaceful solution was agreed and the Soviets backed off and took their missiles out of Cuba. But the incident showed how real the threat of nuclear war could be. The following year, even more people marched with CND.

The protests were not confined to the Berkshire countryside. In April 1960, Elizabeth Dales, described as 'a housewife from Gillingham', had led a British contingent to a similar demonstration in Hamburg, taking her 12-year-old daughter, Margaret, with her. CND's influence was growing. 'The campaign has not only shown staying power but has recently gained in momentum and its influence has spread,' reported *The Observer* in the same month.

For any young political hopeful, the Easter CND march was a rite of passage. The CND symbol also became a badge to be worn with pride, although it did not always curry favour with parents, teachers or employers. Young people embroidered it onto their jackets and coats, painted it on walls and guitars, and wore rings and necklaces displaying the symbol. Later in the Sixties, it would be daubed on the helmets of dissident US soldiers in Vietnam. The symbol meant something – chiefly that you were young and wanted peace. The newspapers even referred to CND's supporters as 'peaceniks'.

Mike Prior, who was among those who marched from Aldermaston to Trafalgar Square, remembers the first attempts at a sit-in:

'The first Trafalgar Square sit-down was an odd affair. Beginning in the afternoon, those taking part in the traditional rally, listening to largely inaudible speeches from notables, were invited to sit-down in, as I remember, the southwest part and so break the law.

Evening drew on and the police started to carry away, quite carefully, those lawbreakers.

'It may have had a fairly civilised response from the police, but later sit-ins drew a very different response. As the civil disobedience turned to the nuclear bases like Swaffham, it was rather different. When demonstrators cut through the fences they were roughed up badly and got serious jail-time. The idea that a few ragged idealists could actually block the big birds [the nuclear-capable US bombers at the air base] clearly freaked the authorities.'

There would be demonstrations at nuclear sites all over the country, especially at Holy Loch, near Dunoon in Scotland, where the American Polaris submarines were based. Mike Prior joined the protesters at Dunoon:

'We marched up to the base, legally ... the police moved in fast and hard, throwing people like sacks out of the way ... and as fast as they dragged the bodies and dumped them on the verge, others moved in ... In the end the police had to resort to arrests and so we ended up in cells, six or seven of us together.'

The media loved the idea of disobedience; it made for good photographs and exciting footage in the evening news bulletins.

Watching on television, young people applauded the challenge to authority and agreed with the sentiments of the demonstrators, who were simply demanding a better future, free of war, and in particular free of nuclear war.

Chapter 10

'I Get High With A Little Help From My Friends.'

Drugs have always been about. Even early Egyptian and Greek societies recorded the use of poppy juice as a stimulant. And in the nineteenth century, the poets Thomas De Quincey and Samuel Taylor Coleridge were both known opium users. Indeed, China and Britain waged two wars during the nineteenth century over issues surrounding opium. In China, opium smoking had long been commonplace, with up to 40 million people said to be indulging in the practice shortly after the Second World War. Opium may have been readily available in China, but it was in short supply elsewhere. During the late nineteenth and early twentieth centuries, scientific advances brought about the introduction of new drugs, such as morphine, heroin and amphetamines, meaning that by the 1950s, drugs were becoming more widespread, particularly in the show business world. Even President Kennedy was allegedly a regular amphetamine user. Writers, artists, actors and musicians all flirted with drugs. The difference in the Sixties was that drugs became popular among a much wider range of people, and as the demand increased, so too did the supply.

There is no doubt that the use of drugs by The Beatles and The Rolling Stones gave drug-taking legitimacy among young people. In the early 1960s, amphetamines were beginning to appear on the streets of Liverpool, and The Beatles had certainly encountered them in Hamburg, using pills to keep them awake for all-night band sessions. John Lennon admitted to taking drugs while still a teenager. 'The first drugs I ever took, I was still at art school,' he said. 'With the group – we all took it together – was Benzedrine from the inside of an inhaler.'

These amphetamines, which were basically dexamyl, came in a variety of names and were known commonly as Purple Hearts, French Blues and Black Bombers, though they were neither purple, blue or black. They had been designed in the early 1950s in America to give the taker a lift, as well as extra courage and the ability to remain alert and active for lengthy periods of time. They were initially prescribed to housewives for a variety of problems, and were also said to have been given to American soldiers in the Korean War and the Vietnam War. British Prime Minister Anthony Eden was also prescribed Dexamyl in 1956 at the time of the Suez Crisis to treat the abdominal pain he was suffering. Dexamyl-based pills later became highly fashionable among middle-class Mods, whereas the working-class followers of The Beatles and The Rolling Stones were more likely to be found smoking cannabis.

The Cavern DJ Bob Wooler, however, remembered that in Liverpool in the early Sixties there was very little drug-taking: 'We didn't have a strong drug scene by any means. Originally, it was just Purple Hearts, amphetamines, speed or whatever you want to call it. When The Beatles went down south, they sometimes brought back cannabis and gradually the drug scene developed in Liverpool.'

Bob Jones recalled a similar situation:

'I hardly ever heard much about drugs in the early 60s in Liverpool. But I do remember getting offered some amphetamines in the Legs of Man pub on Lime Street. I also had a good friend who had been in Turkey and had been busted at Dover bringing some hashish back. He was fortunate because the general secretary of the YMCA put in a good word for him and he got off with a fine. In many ways that acted as a warning to us.'

The Rolling Stones' use of drugs was probably even more public than that of The Beatles. Living and playing in London, they were always liable to come into more regular contact with drugs than their Liverpool rivals.

In February 1967, the police famously raided Keith Richards' mansion in West Wittering, where they found various tablets and substances. Mick Jagger and Keith Richards were subsequently arrested and charged with the illegal possession of drugs. The raid became more notorious because

Jagger's girlfriend, the singer Marianne Faithful, was found wearing nothing but a fur coat, which the police said she let slip from time to time. Although Jagger and Richards were initially sentenced to imprisonment, their sentences were considered harsh and later quashed on appeal. The publicity surrounding the case only served to give extra oxygen to the idea of taking drugs. If the Stones and The Beatles were doing drugs, then what was the harm, asked the younger generation. Other well-known people also began to confess to experimenting with drugs, often claiming that they were no more harmful than alcohol. Even Princess Margaret was rumoured to have smoked dope.

Following the court case in July 1967 and the convictions of Jagger and Richards, *The Times* created a major stir with an editorial headlined 'Who breaks a butterfly on a wheel'. It suggested that the arrests of Jagger and Richards on drug offences were more to do with who the defendants were than the severity of the crime. The editorial stated:

> 'There are many people who take a primitive view of the matter, what one might call a pre-legal view of the matter. They consider that Mr Jagger has "got what was coming to him". They resent the anarchic quality of the Rolling Stones performances, dislike their songs, dislike their influence on teenagers and broadly suspect them of decadence ... Has Mr Jagger received the same treatment as he would have received if he had not been a famous figure, with all the criticism his celebrity has aroused? ... It should be the particular quality of British justice to ensure that Mr Jagger is treated exactly the same as anyone else, no better and no worse. There must remain a suspicion in this case that Mr Jagger received a more severe sentence than would have been thought proper for any purely anonymous young man.'

Importantly, the editorial was signed by the editor of *The Times*, William Rees-Mogg. The article seemed to be calling for a little more common sense and reason about drugs. It soon led to a wider public debate. Immediately following the quashing of the court's sentence, Jagger appeared on a famous

World In Action programme made by Granada Television. Jagger had not spoken to the press for three months, but now he arrived by helicopter to be questioned about his views and lifestyle by the very man who had written the editorial in *The Times*, William Rees-Mogg, along with Lord Stowe Hill (formerly Sir Frank Soskice, Attorney General), the Bishop of Woolwich, Dr John Robinson, and Jesuit priest Father Corbishley. It was a case of the Establishment versus the counterculture. Much to the surprise of many viewers, Jagger came over as a highly intelligent person who had clearly thought out his case and responses.

That same year, 1967, Paul McCartney paid for a full-page advertisement in *The Times*. It was signed by a number of academics, politicians and other pop stars and called for a reform of the cannabis laws. A public debate had begun in earnest.

In the early 1960s, drugs were primarily available in the South, particularly London, and used by young middle-class, often well-educated, kids. By the late Sixties, they had infiltrated their way into working-class communities and into the North. But they were still primarily used by young people rather than by those of an older generation. While drugs may have been rare on the streets of northern cities like Liverpool or Manchester in the early 1960s, by the end of the decade all that had changed. Annie O'Malley in Manchester remembers:

> 'Drugs were about and you could get them very easily. We probably started smoking cannabis when I was 16 or 17 so it would be 1968, 1969. My friend had an older brother who was a musician and very hip and knew lots of things. I think the first time we scored we got some dope off him. But we didn't smoke loads. I managed to keep down my job and they kept going to college. It wasn't serious; we'd have a couple of joints at the weekend.'

One LSE student recalled that he had a tutorial one evening in 1968: 'It was a winter's evening, getting dark and my tutor was sitting on his sofa with the lights subdued. And while I sat opposite him reading out my essay he sat there puffing away on a joint. He wasn't young either and I was a bit surprised.'

A Birmingham Polytechnic student also remembered experimenting with drugs:

> 'I went through a period – a year or so, I guess – where I did smoke dope. When we used to go to the Windsor pub in Birmingham city centre, I'm sure there would have been people there offering drugs for sale. I don't know whether I ever bought any myself, but we'd know people who had bought some, and they'd sometimes share it out. If we had an after-pub party, someone would make joints, rolling them up with tobacco from a tin, and would then pass the joint round. Most of the time, it had a very relaxing effect.'

Drug-use was restricted to cannabis and various amphetamines. Heroin and cocaine were rare and generally too expensive. Most young people wanted a bit of fun, something cheap, readily available and that wasn't going to cause any long-term effects. The Birmingham same student added:

> 'When I had a Saturday job at a local Library, there was a young man there, an Oxford Uni drop-out, who was a real hippy – open-toed sandals, long hair and goatee beard, head always in a book. We'd smoke dope together. One particular incident really stands out. We'd gone to a local park one evening, climbed over the railings, smoked, and he took off all his clothes and danced naked round the park in front of me. It was autumn and very cold, so he gave me his fur coat to huddle in while he danced. And then I had a bit of a trip – there were leaves blowing around, which seemed "like ghosts from an enchanter fleeing", and they started to spook me. He calmed me down, and we had to walk round a fair bit to clear my head before going to his parents' house so his father could drive me home. I remember feeling that I had to try to hide the fact I'd been tripping, so I think I was a bit too talkative – his mother certainly looked at me in a slightly odd way.'

Smoking dope was one thing, but heroin and cocaine were a different matter. LSD did become available later in the Sixties, but it was potentially dangerous and frightening, and needed to be taken under some form of supervision. Most people steered clear of it. There were plenty of scare stories in the newspapers about what drugs would do to you – it was said they could cause sterility, brain damage and even early death. You name it, and drugs were the cause.

The Beatles made little or no attempt to hide their drug-taking. John Lennon confessed that he had first taken drugs when he was at art school in Liverpool, taking Benzedrine from the inside of an inhaler. There is no doubt that they were taking stimulants, or 'uppers' as they were sometimes known, in the form of prellies or the German diet drug Preludin to keep them awake during their all-night sessions at the Star Club in Hamburg.

It was said that it was Bob Dylan who first introduced The Beatles to cannabis in a New York hotel in 1964. Thereafter, they became regular cannabis smokers, with both Lennon and Harrison later being arrested for possession. It was also said that they had smoked a joint in Buckingham Palace before they received their MBEs, although George later claimed that it was actually just cigarettes.

Probably of more significance was The Beatles' later use of the hallucinatory drug LSD and its influence on their music, particular the 'Revolver' and 'Sgt Pepper' albums. LSD, or acid as it was better known, had been manufactured in the United States and was a hallucinogenic drug which altered thoughts, feelings and the awareness of one's surroundings. The drug had initially been introduced in the United States by the Central Intelligence Agency as part of a research programme to study ways of reshaping people's minds and thoughts. It came to prominence through the Harvard academic Timothy Leary, a clinical psychologist, who would go on to urge its use as a means to exploring one's own self. Leary gave talks and lectures around America, particularly to university students and young people, whom he encouraged to 'trip', as he called it. It led to President Richard Nixon describing him as the 'most dangerous man in the world'. Leary later struck up a friendship with John Lennon, and appeared with Yoko Ono and others on the recording of 'Give Peace A Chance'.

When The Beatles began experimenting with LSD, it was done without much attempt to hide the fact. They spoke openly about it, what they had experienced and how it had influenced their music and song writing. The BBC took a dim view towards their drug habits and even banned two of their songs, which, they believed, made reference to drug-taking, and a third because it had sexual references. Two tracks from the album 'Sgt Pepper's Lonely Hearts Club Band' were immediately banned after it was released in 1967, and that same year, 'I Am The Walrus' also came under fire from the BBC. 'A Day in the Life' was targeted by the BBC because of the lyrics: 'Found my way upstairs and had a smoke. And somebody spoke and I went into a dream.' 'Lucy in the Sky with Diamonds', meanwhile, was banned as it was believed that it made reference to psychedelic drugs. Ironically, years later, John Lennon said it had nothing to do with drugs whatsoever, but had simply been inspired by a painting his son, Julian, had done at school. Such was the fear The Beatles generated among the Establishment that they would believe anything.

Chapter 11
'Ho. Ho, Ho Chi Minh !'

The war in Vietnam had complex roots, and in time would account for at least 280,000 American lives and many more Vietcong and civilian casualties. There are estimates of a total of at least 1.3 million dead. As the daily number of deaths of US troops escalated, so the war was called into question more and more.

The conflict had originated in the 1950s as a war against French imperialism when Viet Minh forces in the north of Vietnam, under the leadership of Ho Chi Minh and backed by the Soviet Union and China, waged a war against France's presence in the country. In 1954, following a disastrous battle at Dien Bien Phu, where the French suffered a humiliating defeat with significant casualties, they decided to pull out of Vietnam altogether, agreeing a demarcation of the country. To the north of the demarcation line was the Democratic Republic of Vietnam, which had waged the eight-year struggle against the French and was under the full control of the Vietnamese Communist Party, led by Ho Chi Minh, with its own capital of Hanoi. In the South, the French transferred most of their authority to the State of Vietnam, which had its capital at Saigon. An unease in the south continued, with incursions from the north and tensions and outbreaks of violence within South Vietnam itself. Into the vacuum stepped the United States, initially with funding, armaments and training for South Vietnam's government. As disturbances grew, so too did American involvement.

The inauguration of President Kennedy in 1961 might have signalled hopes for an end to the various Cold War standoffs, but actually resulted in the very opposite. Kennedy simply carried on with the policy laid down by previous administrations under Presidents Truman and Eisenhower. In October 1962, as the world faced a nuclear catastrophe over the Cuban Missile Crisis, Kennedy's determination to stand up to communism was only reinforced. Instead of de-escalation, Kennedy increased the number of American troops in a show of strength against the forces of communism. By the time of Kennedy's assassination, there were 16,000 US military operatives in Vietnam.

Kennedy's successor, Lyndon Johnson, turned out to be even more of a hawk on foreign policy, and the number of troops operating in Vietnam continued to escalate so that in 1968 there were some half-a-million US servicemen stationed in the country. By this time, America had run out of professional soldiers, and more and more civilians were being drafted into the US Army. It made for not just an escalation of the conflict in Vietnam, but at home as well as many questioned the morality of the war. There were also growing numbers of casualties, with many soldiers returning home with lost limbs, post-traumatic stress and other severe injuries. Young male civilians lived in dread of being called up to go to Vietnam. Cassius Clay, boxing's heavyweight world champion, led protests when he refused to accept the draft and faced imprisonment. America became a divided nation, between those who genuinely believed that they were fighting a just war to stem the march of communism and those who believed that the Vietnamese should be left to decide their own futures.

For the first time, television pictures of B52 bombers on air raids dropping powerful explosives were beamed around the world, often within hours of their raids taking place. Helicopters spraying napalm and burning down villages were also daily features on the news bulletins in America and around the globe. The television pictures may have looked impressive to the generals and politicians, but they were disastrous PR as many viewers watched in disbelief that their country could be perpetrating such atrocities. There was no censorship and no attempt to control the movement of journalists, meaning reporters were free to roam wherever they chose. It wasn't just American journalists filing their stories, but those from most western media outlets. Photographers also ventured everywhere, snapping some of the most gruesome and telling moments of the war: a young girl running down the road, her body on fire; a member of the Vietcong being shot in the head from close range. These were images that would not go away. It was little wonder that opposition to the war grew and spilt over onto the streets.

By 1964, serious protests were being held at a number of American universities, including in Philadelphia, Minneapolis, Boston and Miami. Draft cards were also being publicly burned. Over the next few years, students throughout the United States, many of them in danger of being drafted, organized anti-war demonstrations and marches. Meanwhile, in other countries, students were taking a similar view of the war. In the spring of 1968, a massive march in London to the American Embassy in Grosvenor Square led to violent clashes as the police struggled to control the demonstrators, resulting in many injuries on both sides as well as over 300 arrests. It was said to be the largest demonstration in Britain in living memory, being filmed by Granada's *World In Action* programme and relayed at length on television screens the following evening. As they marched, the crowd chanted 'Ho, Ho, Ho Chi Minh'. At Hanoi's museum of the war, excerpts from that programme are still shown to this day.

Later that year, a second demonstration involved even more protestors, with shops and buildings boarded up along the route to Grosvenor Square. There were similar huge marches throughout Western Europe, particularly in West Germany, Sweden, France and Italy, as well as in Japan. Students in America occupied university buildings and other government offices. It may have been the young who were affected most by the war as they faced the draft, but their parents and family also lived in fear of having to wave them off to whatever fate they might meet. Public opinion, as well as international opinion, was firmly against US involvement.

While American troops had been fighting in Vietnam, back home, state troops had been waging a war against black activists demonstrating for civil rights. In August 1962, more than 200,000 protestors had marched on Washington to be addressed by leading civil rights campaigner Martin Luther King. A year later, President Johnson signed the Civil Rights Act 1964, but the problem did not go away. The activist Malcolm X was assassinated, and then too was Martin Luther King. Abuses of civil rights continued, with the police themselves regularly accused of unnecessary aggression against the black community. Cities such as Detroit were set on fire as police and rioters clashed. There were similar serious disturbances and fires in Newark, Los Angeles and elsewhere. America, it seemed, was at war not only with communism but with itself.

Out of Detroit's black community at this time came a sound that was to be forever linked with the American civil rights movement – Motown. It was music composed by and sung by black musicians and singers, and was recorded on the black Motown Records label. Nearly all those involved were young people. In 1961 came Motown's first million-seller, 'Shop Around' by Smokey Robinson and the Miracles, and its first chart-topper, 'Please Mr Postman' by teenage girl group The Marvelettes. In the deluge of recordings that followed from the likes of The Supremes, The Temptations, The Four Tops, Marvin Gaye and Stevie Wonder, the label released more than 180 number one hits worldwide. In 1968, Motown had five records in the American Top Ten, as well as hits throughout the world.

The songs may not have been overtly political, but Motown's popularity certainly contributed to the civil rights movement by achieving crossover success. Thanks to its chart hits, African-American songs and faces entered the homes of every American in the country, regardless of race.

American universities were also in revolt. It was not just about Vietnam, but also the teaching curriculum and the right to political activity. In some universities, political expression by students was banned. Leafleting was not allowed and outside speakers were vetted. It wasn't that the university administrators necessarily objected to dissent; they simply did not want trouble. They also wanted to control the traditional curriculum, which in many universities did not allow for liberal subjects such as sociology, social history, Marxist philosophy and so forth.

Much of the revolt was centred around two universities – the University of Michigan and the University of California at Berkley. At Michigan, Students for a Democratic Society (SDS), led by Tom Hayden, quickly became the national rallying force, taking their case to universities across the country. There were occupations, marches and meetings. At the Democratic convention in Chicago in 1968, Hayden and the SDS were involved in serious rioting as the Democratic Party met to decide its candidate for the 1968 Presidential election campaign. Hayden and four others were convicted of crossing state lines to incite a riot, but the charges were later dropped.

Writing in the *New Yorker* many years later, journalist and academic Louis Menand summed up their campaign:

> 'Although it helped mobilise opinion on issues like civil rights, urban poverty, the arms race and the war, the New Left never had its hands on political power. But it changed left wing politics. It made individual freedom and authenticity the goals of political action, and it inspired young people who cared about social justice and inequality to reject the existing system of power relations, and to begin anew.'

If there was one person who symbolized the radicalism of the 1960s, it was the Argentinean revolutionary Che Guevara. His image – head held high, roguish beard and piercing eyes – from a photograph by Alberto Korda appeared as a poster of one kind or another on almost every student's wall, and was always certain to be seen on a flag or banner at any demonstration, whether in Washington, London, Paris or Rome.

Ernesto ('Che') Guevara, born in Rosario, Argentina, in June 1928 into a middle-class Leftist family, studied medicine at the University of Buenos Aires before training as a doctor. It was a later motorcycle journey through Latin America, where he witnessed at first hand the poverty and inequalities of the people, which really forged his radicalism. Convinced that the inequalities in society could only be overcome through some form of social and political revolution, he left Argentina to join a band of rebels headed by Fidel Castro who were planning a revolt in Cuba. Guevara was said to be the brains behind the revolution, and in January 1959 he marched triumphantly into Havana alongside his friend and colleague Castro.

Then in 1965, he vanished from public life, and the myth of Guevara began. Much of what happened over the next few years remains a mystery, but he is known to have been active in the Congo. However, Africa was not ready for his radicalism, and with the American CIA already monitoring his movements, he went in search of more fertile territory. This eventually took him back to Latin America, a continent then in the grip of right-wing military dictatorships, most of whom were in collusion with the United States. In particular, Guevara homed in on the small mountainous country of Bolivia, one of the poorest in Latin America and consequently ripe for revolution.

Over the next year, Guevara and his band of loyal revolutionaries marched through the Bolivian countryside attempting to drum up support, but it was not as easy as it had been in Cuba. Conditions in the Bolivian jungle and forests were particularly difficult, and he and his supporters suffered from illness and fatigue. The CIA was also hot on their trail, and in October 1967 Guevara was finally captured by Bolivian troops. A few days later, he was executed and the myth of Che Guevara was perpetuated.

Guevara cut an impressive figure. He was an intellectual and an orator, his writings on revolution being extensively read even before his death. After his death, they would become his legacy as textbooks for revolutionary thinkers and activists.

Guevara, however, was hardly a cult figure among the British working classes. The trade unions, many under the influence of the old Communist Party, regarded him as something of a dreamer, remembering that he had been highly critical of the Soviet Union. He had little relevance to modern industrial society, with its complex network of trade unions, wage negotiating bodies and political parties. Although few young people in Britain were much aware of Guevara before his death, that would soon be remedied. He had a messianic appeal, and of course there was that unforgettable image.

Ho Chi Minh was, like Guevara, seen as a true revolutionary engaged in a long and bitter struggle. As leader of the North Vietnamese Communist Party, he was the public face of the Vietcong. As the Vietnam War raged, Ho Chi Minh was regarded as a revolutionary, attempting to unite his nation in a struggle against initially French imperialism, and later American imperialism. On Vietnam demonstrations, the face of Ho Chi Minh loomed large on posters and banners, while chants of 'Ho, Ho, Ho Chi Minh' could be heard echoing around the streets and piazzas of Europe.

Woolton Parish Church

Garden Fete

and

Crowning of Rose Queen

Saturday, July 6th, 1957

To be opened at 3p.m. by Dr. Thelwall Jones

PROCESSION AT 2p.m.

LIVERPOOL POLICE DOGS DISPLAY
FANCY DRESS PARADE
SIDESHOWS   REFRESHMENTS
BAND OF THE CHESHIRE YEOMANRY
THE QUARRY MEN SKIFFLE GROUP

ADULTS 6d., CHILDREN 3d.   OR BY PROGRAMME

GRAND DANCE

at 8p.m. in the Church Hall
GEORGE EDWARDS' BAND
THE QUARRY MEN SKIFFLE GROUP
Tickets 2/-

The Beatles, then known as the Quarry Men Skiffle Group, play their first ever gig in Woolton, Liverpool.

Mathew Street, Liverpool where it all began.

The Beatles' statues on Liverpool's waterfront

The original entrance to the Cavern Club.

A moody John Lennon looks across to the Cavern.

Mathew Street, Liverpool. Four Lad Who Shook The World.

Cilla Black, another Brian Epstein protege. (*Wikimedia Commons*)

Chuck Berry's rhythm and blues music inspired a generation of Mersey Beat fans, including the Beatles. (*Wikimedia Commons*)

The Cavern Club as it is today.

The Star Club in Hamburg where
the Beatles perfected their act.
(*Wikimedia Commons*)

Cavern membership card. A prized possession for any Liverpool teenager.

Granada Television's 'Coronation Street' introduced northern accents and northern life to southerners. (*Wikimedia Commons*)

The Everyman theatre in Liverpool pioneered new writing and innovative productions as well as popular weekly poetry evenings. (*Wikimedia Commons*)

Brian Epstein, sophisticated and entrepreneurial, the man who made the Beatles. (*Wikimedia Commons*)

The Rolling Stones, the Beatles' biggest rivals. (*Wikimedia Commons*)

Bob Dylan and Joan Baez, the voices of American youth. (*Wikimedia Commons*)

The 1963 civil rights march on Washington, one of the biggest demonstrations in American history. (*Wikimedia Commons*)

The CND badge became a symbol of protest and adorned the jackets and sweaters of many young people. (*Wikimedia Commons*)

The Beatles appearance on the Ed Sullivan show took America by storm with a record-breaking television audience of over 70 million. The Beatles had conquered the world. (*Wikimedia Commons*)

Sit-ins and street rioting in May 1968 almost brought the French government down. (*Wikimedia Commons*)

In August 1968, a Czech uprising, led mainly by young people, was brutally put down by the invading Soviet army. (*Wikimedia Commons*)

Daniel Cohn-Bendt. The French political activist was at the forefront of the May 1968 demonstrations in Paris. (*Wikimedia Commons*)

The German sociologist and activist Rudi Dutschke, was seriously injured in an assassination attempt in 1968. (*Wikimedia Commons*)

The Maharishi Mahesh Yogi, spiritual mentor to the Beatles and many other young people. (*Wikimedia Commons*)

Marjorie Proops' weekly advice column delved into areas not previously tackled by Agony Aunts. (*Wikimedia Commons*)

The Park Hill flats in Sheffield introduced a new concept in city-centre living. (*Wikimedia Commons*)

The University of Sussex, one of many new universities created in the 1960s with courses designed to be more appealing to young students. (*Wikimedia Commons*)

The Profumo affair rocked the British establishment, led to salacious tabloid headlines and made Christine Keeler a household name. (*Wikimedia Commons*)

Muhammad Ali's refusal to fight in Vietnam won him few supporters in America. (*Wikimedia Commons*)

The Cuban revolutionary Che Guevara, whose poster appeared on every young student's wall. (*Wikimedia Commons*)

Prime Minister Harold Macmillan, an aristocratic Conservative. (*Wikimedia Commons*)

Harold Wilson brought a breath of fresh air and youth to British politics. (*Wikimedia Commons*)

The Black Power salute during their medal ceremony at the 1968 Olympics by American athletes, Tommie Smith and John Carlos, caused a furore back home. (*Wikimedia Commons*)

London's Carnaby Street, centre of 1960s fashion. (*Wikimedia Commons*)

Designer Mary Quant revolutionised 1960s fashion with her miniskirt. (*Wikimedia Commons*)

Another image that could be spotted on most marches or demonstrations was that of Mao Tse Tung. The Chinese leader, however, had neither the youth nor the glamour and charisma of Guevara. Mao had led the Long March through China during the 1940s, finally seizing control and declaring the People's Republic of China in 1949. Over the next twenty years, Mao would insist that everyone in China wear his uniform and carry his Red Book, copies of which sold in their millions around the world. In China itself, he also forced what was termed a Great Leap Forward, the Cultural Revolution and an agrarian revolution that resulted in millions dying of famine. Given China's international isolation, the precise details of their repercussions did not become known until many years later, and even now much is calculated guesswork. What Mao offered to his followers was yet another so-called 'socialist' philosophy associated with revolution.

Inspired by Guevara, and to a much lesser extent Mao, the 1960s would spawn a wide variety of revolutionary political organizations. Not only was there the traditional Communist Party of Great Britain, still Stalinist and pro-Soviet in its outlook, but there was also a range of Trotskyist and Maoist groups beginning to burst onto the scene. Chief among the Trotskyist groups were the Socialist Labour League, the Socialist Party of Great Britain, the Workers Revolutionary Party, the International Marxist Group, the International Socialists and the Militant Tendency, each with its own brand of Trotskyist philosophy. Mostly, they had splintered from one another. Then there were the Maoists, with the Communist Party of Britain (Marxist Leninist) and the Communist Federation of Britain (Marxist Leninist).

Most of these Trotskyist and Maoist groups were small in number and had little political influence, certainly in Parliamentary terms. Neither did they have much sway in the trade union movement, but on the streets they were always active in organizing demonstrations and campaigns, as well as showing up with their banners wherever there was a march, making their presence felt way beyond their actual numbers and influence.

As the Sixties progressed, young people had become more disillusioned with the Labour Party. When it was elected in 1964, there had been a wave of optimism. It was the first Labour government since that of 1945–51, and with a youthful Harold Wilson as Prime Minister it seemed that anything was possible. But as the decade wore on, the party seemed to struggle in office, burdened by one problem after another. Above all, it had given complicit support to American action in Vietnam, although in truth, Wilson's refusal to send British troops – even though under pressure from American politicians – was one of his most commendable battles. By the late Sixties, the Labour Party seemed old and tired. The youthfulness that inspired its election victory and early years had dissipated. The economy had foundered, jobs were not so plentiful and a sterling crisis had only underlined the problems of capitalism. The Utopia that Labour promised simply was not there.

If young people were looking for a left-wing alternative, it was certainly not in the direction of the Communist Party, which offered little or no appeal to young people. It was Stalinist and intolerant, and consequently failed to attract a young membership. Young people remained suspicious of its centralist control and total adherence to the Soviet Union. Hundreds, maybe more, had resigned from the Communist Party in 1956 following the Hungarian uprising. Many of these were academics, so their desertion left the party struggling to find an intellectual argument to justify its position. The invasion of Czechoslovakia in August 1968 would deal a further blow to the Communist Party, with young people simply saying, 'we told you so'. The party had lost its academic base, and during the 1960s this was to prove disastrous. Some of them edged their way eventually into the Labour Party, while others joined up with the far-left Trotskyist organizations.

The Communist Party, at the time, had also became more deeply rooted in the trade union movement, where it saw more fertile ground for mobilization, but as most young people were not union members, they were not persuaded to join up.

Women were also looking for some political outlet, having felt let down by the traditional parliamentary parties and trade unions.

Young people were desperate for some form of intellectual debate about politics and the way forward for society, and the Communist Party did not fulfil this desire. It had little sympathy with students, who were regarded as elite and middle class. Their long hair and scruffy dress were also an anathema. Nor did it have much sympathy with their tactics, which often verged on the side of violence, as at Grosvenor Square in March and October 1968.

Into this gap, the Trotskyist parties began to emerge and thrive. As one prominent Trotskyist, Tariq Ali, put it: 'Two of the British Trotskyist groups of the 1960s, the International Socialists and the International Marxist Group (IMG), were very much more open to the so-called counterculture. They didn't frown on kids with long hair who smoked dope. They waved their own Vietcong flags. They shifted farther and faster on gay liberation and women's rights.'

In the main, however, it was the International Socialists who benefitted most from the student population, signing up many recruits to their cause, including the journalists Paul Foot and Christopher Hitchens.

Many of the disenchanted former Communist Party academics began to feel a need for some form of publication where all the polemical issues surrounding Marxism and the Left could be debated. As a result, immediately after the Hungarian uprising, the historians E.P. Thompson and John Saville established *The Reasoner* magazine. A few years later, this became the *New Reasoner*. Also around at the time was *Universities and Left Review*. In 1960, both these journals merged to form the *New Left Review*.

In February 2010, on its fiftieth anniversary, Stefan Collini, writing in the *Guardian*, summed up the importance of *New Left Review*. He wrote that it had been 'especially strong in universities', had 'repudiated the reformism of the Labour party' and 'provided a rallying ground for those communists and ex-communists who, post-1956, disowned orthodox Stalinism. New Left clubs were formed around the country, and the Campaign for Nuclear Disarmament provided a mobilising and unifying focus.'

The disturbances of the 1960s by students around Europe threw up a number of prominent spokesmen, all of them young, and all identifying with youth and far-left politics. In France, the riots at Nanterre University in Paris in 1968 had been led by Daniel Cohn-Bendit, an articulate young sociology student of French-German parentage who became known in the French press as *Danny le Rouge*. Also of prominence was the French philosopher Regis Debray, who had been a young professor of philosophy at Havana University during the early Sixties. He later left Cuba to join Guevara's revolution in Bolivia, but was captured by Bolivian forces and sentenced to thirty years in prison. Debray's book *Revolution in the Revolution* became something of a textbook on guerrilla warfare. He was eventually released from imprisonment in 1970 following an international campaign, headed by some of France's most prominent writers and academics.

In Germany, students rallied around another young sociologist, Rudi Dutschke. He had been a student at the Free University of Berlin and became a leading activist and spokesman in student politics, organizing demonstrations against the war in Vietnam. In 1968, Dutschke was wounded in an assassination attempt which shocked many in Germany and had hallmarks of the murders of prominent socialist politicians Rosa Luxembourg and Karl Liebknecht in 1919. Although Dutschke survived, he was seriously injured and his days as a political activist drew to an abrupt end.

The New Left, as it became universally known, was basically always a student movement, both in Europe and in America. It had, perhaps unwittingly, rejected the traditional parties of opposition. It was always a counterculture, but in being so it had borrowed from the counterculture espoused by The Beatles. The students who demonstrated in American universities were the same teenagers who had screamed and danced at Shea Stadium and elsewhere.

In America, the folk singer Bob Dylan was setting the tone for young people with recordings such as 'The Times They Are a Changin'' and 'With God on Our Side'. His music soon began to resonate with teenagers on both sides of the Atlantic. The Beatles seized upon his music and soon befriended him. But while Dylan sung of protest and opposed war, he was careful not to become labelled as a political activist. His folk-singer girlfriend at the time, Joan Baez, implored him to join her on anti-Vietnam marches, but Dylan preferred to stand on the sidelines as an observer rather than a direct participant. He may have been opposed to the Vietnam

War, but he didn't want to trumpet his opposition. His relationship with Baez soon faded.

In 1971, Marvin Gaye released his ground-breaking album 'What's Going On', though only after a seven-month power struggle with Motown's founder, Berry Gordy. The album explored the issues of racial discrimination, poverty, urban decay, environmental destruction, police brutality, drug abuse, political corruption and the devastating effects of the Vietnam War. In the song 'What's Happening Brother', Gaye drew on the experience of his brother Frankie, who had served in Vietnam, and the disillusionment at war of veterans returning to Nixon's America and inevitable unemployment.

John Lennon was always the most political and radical of the four Beatles. He even composed a song, 'Give Peace a Chance', which became a hit in both America and Britain. Essentially an anti-Vietnam War song, it could equally have been about any conflict anywhere. He recorded it in June 1969 with the Yoko Ono's Plastic Ono Band. Neither Paul, George nor Ringo featured on the recording. Instead, Lennon recorded it with a group of friends who included his girlfriend Yoko Ono, Timothy Leary and Petula Clark.

John explained the reasoning behind the song: 'What we're really doing is sending out a message to the world, mainly to the youth, especially the youth or anybody, really, that's interested in protesting for peace or protesting against any forms of violence.' 'There's many ways of protest,' Lennon told journalists gathered as he and Yoko stretched out on their bed-in for peace in room 1742 of the Queen Elizabeth Hotel in Montreal, 'and this is one of them.'

He told people:

'Protest against peace but peacefully, because we think that peace is only got by peaceful methods, and to fight the establishment with their own weapons is no good, because they always win, and they have been winning for thousands of years. They know how to play the game violence, and it's easier for them when they can recognize you and shoot you.'

By October 1969, 'Give Peace a Chance' had become a universal song at anti-Vietnam War demonstrations and among counterculture movements generally. On 15 November that year, during a peace rally in Washington, D.C., the legendary folk singer Pete Seeger led nearly half-a-million demonstrators in singing it at the Washington Monument. Seeger interspersed phrases like 'Are you listening, Nixon?' and 'Are you listening, Agnew?' (Spiro Agnew was Nixon's Vice-President) between the choruses of protesters singing 'All we are saying ... is give peace a chance'. Asked what he thought about that day, Lennon later remarked: 'I saw pictures of that Washington demonstration on British TV, with all those people singing it, forever and not stopping. It was one of the biggest moments of my life.'

A few years later, in 1972, following a peace agreement with North Vietnam, American President Richard Nixon announced that the United States was pulling out of the war. The conflict was over, but at an enormous cost, not just in casualties but in international prestige. Ironically, the ending of the war left behind a united Vietnam but a divided America.

Chapter 12

With God on Our Side

As the Sixties progressed, both the Church of England and the Catholic Church found themselves coming under increasing pressure in Britain. Not only were congregation numbers tumbling, but the institutions and all that they stood for were being questioned. The Church, be it Catholic or C of E, was no longer the authority that it had long been, as people lost respect and interest, with many simply regarding their views as outdated and out of touch. The world was changing, and churches seemed unable to meet the challenge.

In 1960, 71 per cent of people questioned in a poll claimed to have attended a Catholic church service in the last seven days. That was an astonishing and impressively high number. By the end of the decade, however, the percentage had fallen dramatically to just 57 per cent. For a church so rigid in its disciplines, it was a catastrophic decline. Figures for the Church of England were similar, with a fall from 44 to 37 per cent. Both churches were in serious trouble.

Even in the United States, there was a sharp fall in the popularity of religion. Whereas parents and the elderly continued to attend church on a regular basis and in numbers, the fall-off among the young was remarkable. A Gallup opinion poll showed that in 1960, church attendance in the last seven days among those between 21 and 29 years of age was 38 per cent. Ten years later, it had fallen to less than 30 per cent. A similar story was reflected in another Gallup poll which asked: 'How important is religion to your own life?' In 1960, 68 per cent of people said 'very important', but by 1970 this was down to just 55 per cent.

Evangelism, however, was on the increase. The American evangelist Billy Graham had first visited the UK in 1954, preaching at the Haringey Arena in north London for a couple of weeks before preaching to massive crowds in Hyde Park and the Royal Albert Hall. He rounded off his tour with a huge rally of 120,000 people at Wembley Stadium and another 67,000 at the White City Stadium. Graham revisited England in 1961, preaching at Manchester City's football ground, Maine Road, before enormous crowds for several evenings. He proved so popular that he was invited back to London in June 1966, where it was claimed a million people attended his meetings throughout the month, again culminating in a service at Wembley before 100,000. Graham's firebrand version of religion was appealing to many, though in most cases those who claimed to have been 'saved' soon lost their initial enthusiasm.

In February 1966, journalist Maureen Cleave interviewed each of The Beatles separately about their views on life. The interview with Lennon was published in the *London Evening Standard* a few weeks later. It portrayed Lennon as a restless soul in search of a greater meaning in life. 'Christianity will go,' he claimed, 'it will vanish and shrink. I needn't argue about that; I'm right and I'll be proved right. We're more popular than Jesus now; I don't know which will go first – rock 'n' roll or Christianity.'

At the time there was little or no reaction to what had been said, with the rest of the British press ignoring it. In America, both *Newsweek* magazine and the *New York Times* made reference to the interviews, but again provoked no reaction. With a forthcoming Beatles tour of America pending, their press officer decided to offer the interviews to a publication called *Datebook*, which was known to have the similar liberal values to The Beatles. The interviews were subsequently published prominently in the magazine in late July 1966. *Datebook* editor Art Unger also sent copies of the interviews to a number of radio stations and publications in the American South, including a radio station in Birmingham, Alabama. That was when the storm truly broke. The station's DJs regarded Lennon's views as sacrilegious and began an on-air campaign against The Beatles, banning and threatening to burn their records. They invited viewers to phone in with their views and the response was overwhelmingly anti-Beatles. With right-wing religious groups also getting steamed up, the story suddenly escalated and bounced back to New York, where it now received even more prominent coverage.

The controversy quickly spread beyond the United States. South Africa and Spain banned The Beatles' music on national radio stations, while the Vatican denounced Lennon's comments, saying: 'Some subjects must not be dealt with profanely, not even in the world of beatniks.' Such was the reaction that the share price of The Beatles' Northern Songs publishing company fell sharply on the London Stock Exchange.

When The Beatles arrived in America in August, they were immediately besieged by the American press, who wanted to know if Lennon really thought that the band was bigger than Jesus Christ. He tried to explain his views and apologized if anyone was offended: 'I suppose if I had said television was more popular than Jesus, I would have got away with it. I'm sorry I opened my mouth. I'm not anti-God, anti-Christ, or anti-religion. I was not knocking it. I was not saying we are greater or better.'

Although the American press were now less damning of them, the damage had been done. The tour was not an overwhelming success. There were demonstrations outside some venues where they performed, with bonfires of records burned and attempts to stop performances, and even members of the Ku Klux Klan turning up. Lennon was deeply upset by the whole affair and at the pressure put on him by the band's management to apologize, and was said to be in tears about it at one point. It all made The Beatles suddenly fear that one day, someone, somewhere might take a gun to them

Both McCartney and Harrison had been baptized in the Roman Catholic Church, but neither of them followed Christianity. In his interview with Cleave, Harrison was also outspoken about organized religion, as well as the Vietnam War and authority figures in general, whether 'religious or secular'. But it was Lennon who came in for most criticism.

In 1966, George Harrison, always in search of new musical innovations, had met the Indian sitar player Ravi Shankar and became interested in his music and playing skills. Shankar would team up with The Beatles on a number of recordings, including 'Within You, Without You', which George had written. John and George were always exploring new philosophies, and their interest in Indian music led them to transcendental meditation, which seemed a less rigid, more personal spiritualism.

In 1968, the four Beatles travelled to India to join the Maharishi Mahesh Yogi for a period of reflection. The Beatles had met the Maharishi previously, spending time with him in meditation in North Wales. Indeed, they were with him when they learnt of Brian Epstein's death in August 1967. The visit to India, however, was not an overwhelming success. Ringo, never one to be swept up with such fancy ideas, left after only ten days. Paul remained for a month, but George and John spent six weeks with the Maharishi before they too decided to leave, amidst reported squabbles about money and sexual impropriety. Despite any subsequent reservations, The Beatles' relationship with transcendental meditation and a fascination with all things Indian appealed to many young people. As a result, interest in more spiritual and non-institutional religions became a feature of the late Sixties. Young people packed their bags and took the overland trip to India in search of peace and reflection. Garlands, loose garments and brightly coloured clothes became popular, whether in India, Illinois or Ilkley. It was almost wholly The Beatles who influenced this interest.

The orthodox churches came under increasing pressure as they faced new social questions. In particular, both the Church of England and the Catholic Church were forced to face up to such issues as premarital sex, contraception, homosexuality, marriage, abortion, divorce, single mothers, race, liberalism on television, the cinema and theatre, drugs and the war in Vietnam. It was an age like no other age in history, when so many and such a wide and varying range of issues confronted the clergy.

In particular, the Catholic Church faced serious questions. For too long, it had taken a rigid approach around sexuality. The Church's teachings on sex were severe. Annie O'Malley recalled her Catholic school in Manchester:

'At my school there were very rigid disciplines laid down. A good catholic girl won't do this and won't do that. Some of the rules they gave us at school were hilarious. We were told that if you were at a party and somebody turned off the light you had to jump up quickly turn on the light and shout "I'm a catholic!" That was supposed to solve everything. And if a boy asked you to sit on his knee you had to put a telephone directory on his thighs and then you sat on top of the telephone directory. We were told that you had to wear underskirts because if you had polished shoes on – which you were supposed to – then you would see your underwear reflected on the shoes.'

The use of contraception was strictly forbidden by the Catholic Church, and if sexual intercourse resulted in pregnancy, then so be it. Sexual intercourse for anyone unmarried was also regarded as a sin. Sex was for procreation within the family and little else. The only forms of contraception were the withdrawal method or the rhythm method and its use of complicated charts. If it resulted in huge families and ensuing poverty, then again, so be it – that was God's wish. And if you were single and became pregnant, then either you should marry or consider a Catholic home for unmarried mothers. Clare Jenkins remembered:

'Growing up as a Catholic, contraception and abortion were forbidden. The only contraception allowed was "the rhythm method" which resulted in quite a few unplanned pregnancies. Abortion was absolutely forbidden throughout the UK, not just for Catholics. And contraception wasn't easy to obtain for women. A friend who was not a Catholic, had to show her engagement ring before she was allowed the Pill at the birth control clinic. So we were pretty chary of sex, as lots of people were, whatever their religion, in the 60s.'

In 1968, there were 172 known homes for mothers and babies, mostly run by religious institutions. Premarital pregnancy was heavily stigmatized and families lived in fear of being ostracised by church, family, neighbours and friends. The shame was appalling. As a result, young pregnant girls were sent to homes where they could spend their remaining days of pregnancy, give birth and then hand their child over for adoption, before returning to their parental homes, telling all outsiders that they had been working away.

Young girls who had to live with their family until it was time to go to the unmarried mothers' home stayed indoors, and wore loose-fitting clothes and a duffle coat when they ventured outdoors. More often than not, the homes would be in a different locality so that the family could claim that their daughter had gone away to work in another city. It was a process encouraged by the churches, the Catholic Church in particular, with local priests and social workers complicit in the process. In 1968, the number of adoption orders reached an all-time high of 16,164, reflecting the number of children available for adoption.

During their weeks in the homes, the women did cleaning, washing and cooking chores, and in the religious homes were forced to attend church services, especially on a Sunday, where they were expected to show repentance. In Ireland, the situation was even more barbaric. It was little wonder that young women began to rebel against the Church and all that it stood for.

The other, almost unthinkable, option to an unwanted pregnancy was a backstreet abortion. Even there, you had to know where to go and had to be able to pay for it.

Annie O'Malley recounted:

'I was becoming more politically aware. I kicked [back] against the school. I thought it was an unfair school, they had all these rules and regulations that seemed to be about making your life grim. Laughing and having fun was really not on the agenda at all. It's about a catholic upbringing where life is very, very serious and the sooner you realize it the easier it will be for you. You shouldn't take life with a light touch, you are made to suffer, life is hard, all this kind of stuff. I always thought you should enjoy life.

'I stopped going to church when I was 15 or 16. I used to stay at my friend's house on the Saturday evening and come home on the Sunday afternoon and used to tell my mother I'd been to church on the Sunday morning. I used to tell quite a few lies about that. My parents did go to church every Sunday and I was their last hope as the rest of the family had all given up.'

To counter the upheaval which was visibly taking place in churches throughout Europe and America, the Catholic Church established a council, known as Vatican II, which was assigned the task of considering reforms and stances on the various issues confronting the Church and society. The council conferred between 1962 and 1965, much of it in Latin, though ironically, at the end of its deliberations, it came out in favour of a more accessible approach to religious services, with much of the Latin liturgy disposed of. Catholics, who had been bidden historically to eat only fish on a Friday, were also told that they were now free to eat meat if they so wished. The most significant changes were made to the Mass service; changes that did not go down well with everyone. Whilst the new service might have endeared some younger people to the Catholic Church, many older people stopped attending.

A further papal encyclical, issued in 1968, known as the *Humanae Vitae*, reaffirmed the pre-Vatican II prohibition against birth control by any means other than abstinence, and also reaffirmed the prohibition against abortion and sterilization. It left many Catholics disillusioned and sad that the Church, whilst appearing to move with the times, had in fact made only artificial changes at the edges rather than at the core. Many Catholics were anyhow practicing contraception of one kind or another and simply continued, whilst those who were more orthodox continued to obey the ruling, though often under the most difficult circumstances of larger families and resulting social deprivation.

If the Catholic Church was forced into re-examining itself, so too was the Church of England. In 1963, the Bishop of Woolwich, John Robinson, published his book *Honest to God*, which proved to be a religious bestseller. The book caused an immediate controversy, especially as it was written by a leading bishop. In essence, the book challenged the notion that there was in fact a god 'up there' and that we needed to rethink our image of God. It was a breath of fresh air with church liberals, who applauded its courage of tackling what they saw as outdated concepts. But there were those in the C of E, in particular the Archbishop of Canterbury himself, who strongly disagreed. Nevertheless, the book did at least open up a debate which suggested that there were some in the Church of England who understood the need for answers. For many, faith alone was not enough.

Perhaps at the root of so many of the Church's problems was that its authority was being challenged. The Church had long been a fundamental pillar of society, setting standards, educating and acting as a social bond, particularly in poor communities. But now, people were not only staying away from churches, they had also lost respect. Social issues such as contraception, abortion and sex posed difficult problems. Young people were pulling in one direction whilst the Church was seen to be pulling in the opposite direction, or if not pulling then certainly digging its heels in. Science was providing answers to many social problems in the form of a contraceptive pill, safe abortions and so on. As such, people wanted science to help them; science was overtaking the Church in being able to provide solutions.

Theology was also being challenged. Whereas hardly anyone had previously questioned the existence of a god, or that a god ruled from some place on high, modern society – with all its advances in science – was now seeking more specific answers. In particular, the Church of England was buckling under the pressures of modern society, whilst the Catholic Church simply retained its rigidity. It was rather like the battle between capitalism and Soviet communism; one prepared to bend a little, whilst the other hardened its position in order to retain its authority. It would remain a feature of society throughout the twentieth century.

The Beatles and their interest in meditation, along with their various trips to India, resulted in thousands of young people jumping into camper vans and making the long trek across Europe and into India to experience for themselves this new spiritual practice. It was in a large part a rejection of the conventional religions of Britain and Europe. Christianity seemed, to many young people, unable to offer answers to the questions they asked. The Church of England and the Catholic Church appeared too rigid, controlling and authoritarian. Young people wanted something different, something they could relate to, something that was more individual than statist.

When it came to the war in Vietnam, Bob Dylan questioned the validity of using religion as a tool; where all nations in any conflict believed that they had God on their side, and equipped with their God, they could justify any war. 'You don't count the dead when God's on your side,' he sang.

Chapter 13

Social Changes

Beatles manager Brian Epstein kept his homosexuality quiet. That was the way it was at the beginning of the 1960s. The Beatles guessed early on that he was gay, and although they may have made some disparaging remarks to one another, they were always careful not to embarrass him. They always respected him, and at times could be very protective. Epstein, recognizing that they were simply four testosterone-packed young lads with only girls on their mind, simply tolerated any hurtful remarks. But The Beatles were not concerned by Epstein's homosexuality, which soon melted into the background of their lives. Epstein never flaunted his gayness with the group. He kept it to himself, and although there have been rumours of a brief fling with John Lennon, this remains a matter of conjecture.

Like many homosexuals at the time, Epstein was leading a double life: happy and successful in public, but lonely and confused in private. It would lead to his eventual death through an accidental overdose of drugs and alcohol in August 1967, just one a month after the legalization of homosexuality became law. Nowhere in his obituaries was it mentioned that Epstein was gay.

Epstein had been arrested in April 1957 for 'persistent importuning' by a police provocateur in a Swiss Cottage toilet in North London. He was devastated, and wrote at the time: 'The damage, the lying criminal methods of the police in importuning me and consequently capturing me leaves me cold, stunned and finished.'

In his document for his defence, he wrote that he 'believed that my own will-power was the best thing with which to overcome my homosexuality'. At the same time, it gave him a wider understanding of what it was to be an outcast: 'I feel deeply because I have always felt deeply for the persecuted, the Jews, the coloured people, for the old and society's misfits.' Fortunately, Epstein did not receive a prison sentence.

At the dawn of the Sixties, homosexuality was still a serious criminal offence, with anyone caught indulging in the practice likely to be prosecuted, fined and possibly even imprisoned. Even in the early 1960s, Epstein kept a flat in the centre of Liverpool, where he could conduct his private life as he wished, away from his family home in Queens Drive, Childwall.

Male homosexuality had been illegal in England since the Buggery Act of 1533, with some acts even punishable by death. In 1885, the law became considerably stricter in many areas, with the Criminal Law Amendment Act classifying all homosexual activity, whether public or private, as illegal. Perhaps the most famous prosecution had been that of the writer Oscar Wilde in 1895. There was, however, no mention of women in any of the Acts, meaning lesbianism was effectively legal, although strongly disapproved of by society. In truth, however, few had any concept of what it meant.

Under the existing law, a homosexual act could incur a penalty of anything from a £5 fine to life imprisonment. At the end of 1954, in England and Wales, it was estimated that there were 1,069 men in prison for homosexual acts.

Alan Turing, the esteemed mathematician at Manchester University who had played a decisive part in the deciphering of the enigma code at Bletchley Park during the Second World War and was working on developing the world's first computer, was charged in Manchester in 1952 with gross indecency. Rather than face imprisonment, Turing, who was desperate to continue his research, pleaded guilty and accepted a programme of medical reform, which chiefly involved taking a number of drugs. Two years later, Turing committed suicide. Apart from drugs, other homosexuals were subjected to electric shock aversion therapy or physcoanalysis as part of a programme of reform.

Tom Driberg, the well-known Labour Member of Parliament, was also regularly in trouble with the authorities. He was charged with indecent assault on at least one occasion, although numerous times he managed to use his position as an MP or Government minister to escape being charged. He once asked a policeman who had caught him if he was a Labour voter. When the policeman said he was, Driberg warned him that if he was charged it would almost certainly lead to him losing his seat and the demise of the Labour government, which was hanging on by the narrowest of margins. The policeman duly gave him a warning and let him go. There were many other gay MPs and peers in Parliament, most of whom kept their sexuality very private. It was the same with other professions, such as law, medicine, academia and journalism. It was clear that there was a social issue, and the number of imprisonments for homosexuality was something of an embarrassment. As a result, it was necessary for the government to examine the situation.

The distinguished Shakespearean actor Sir John Gielgud was arrested in a public toilet and charged with indecency in 1953, shortly after having been knighted. Gielgud was fined £10, but what was worse for him was that he was recognized in court and publicly exposed by the newspapers, causing him much anguish and to even contemplate suicide.

During the 1950s, Conservative MP Bob Boothby was a prominent advocate of decriminalizing homosexual acts between men. Boothby, who had a long-standing affair with Harold Macmillan's wife, was also a homosexual, although, like others, this was kept quiet. Indeed, his affair with Dorothy Macmillan was more widely known in political circles than his homosexuality. Fleet Street was well aware of Boothby's less-than-discreet private life, but chose not to expose it. In his memoirs, he wrote that he was determined to 'do something practical to remove the fear and misery in which many of our most gifted citizens were then compelled to live'.

In December 1953, Boothby sent a memorandum to David Maxwell Fyfe, the Home Secretary, calling for the establishment of a departmental inquiry into homosexuality. In it, he said:

'By attaching so fearful a stigma to homosexuality as such, you put a very large number of otherwise law-abiding and useful citizens on the other side of the fence which divides the good citizen from the bad. By making them feel that, instead of unfortunates they are social pariahs, you drive them into squalor – perhaps into crime; and produce that very "underground" which it is so clearly in the public interest to eradicate.'

Boothby premised his argument for law reform, claiming that it was the role of the state 'not to punish psychological disorders – rather to try and cure them'. He argued in the House of Commons that the law as it was did not 'achieve the objective of all of us, which is to limit the incidence of homosexuality and to mitigate its evil effects'.

Epstein and The Beatles may not have directly contributed to a change in the law, but as the writer Jon Savage commented in the *Guardian*, 'Although it did not directly contribute to the changing of the law, the saturation of 60s pop in androgyny and homosexuality contributed to a more liberal climate.'

In March 1954, at the Winchester Assizes, three men were found guilty of gross indecency and sentenced to prison. The defendants were Lord Montagu of Beaulieu, his cousin and the *Daily Mail*'s diplomatic correspondent. The trial had attracted a large crowd of press and public, many of whom had gathered outside the court house. The police, worried about the men's safety, kept them locked in their cells for two hours, hoping that people would disperse. But they didn't, and when the men finally emerged from the court on their way to prison, they were greeted, not with jeers and boos, but instead with claps and cheers. The public reaction suggested that the law was well out of tune with public opinion. It was another reason why the law needed to be re-examined.

In 1961, the British actor Dirk Bogarde – who was himself gay, although he never admitted it until much later in life – starred in the film *Victim*, playing a London barrister who represented a young man with whom he had an emotional and loving relationship and who was being blackmailed. In exposing the blackmailers, Bogarde's character risks his reputation and marriage in order to see that justice is done. *Victim* was a film well ahead of its time, the first English-language film to use the word 'homosexual'. The film proved to be highly controversial and was initially banned in the United States, but its sympathetic approach to the subject and readiness to put the issue on the big screen helped contribute to liberalization regarding homosexuality.

In 1954, the Conservative government appointed a committee of twelve men and three women, under the chairmanship of John Wolfenden, to examine the legislation surrounding homosexuality and prostitution. The Committee on Homosexual Activities and Prostitution met for sixty-two days, interviewing a variety of witnesses, including police and probation officers, psychiatrists and religious leaders who had been affected by the legislation of the time. The committee, however, unfortunately had enormous difficulty in finding gay men prepared to testify. It was a sign of the times and the fear under which so many then lived. The committee even considered advertising in the press, but in the end succeeded in finding three men willing to be interviewed. In a further indication of the culture of the time, Wolfenden famously suggested that, for 'the sake of the ladies' on the committee, they should use the words Huntley & Palmers (a make of biscuits) instead of the terms 'homosexuals' and 'prostitutes'.

After three years of deliberation, the committee's 155-page report recommended that homosexual behaviour between consenting adults in private should no longer be a criminal offence. All but one member of the committee was in favour. It further found that, importantly, 'homosexuality cannot legitimately be regarded as a disease'. The report added:

> 'The law's function is to preserve public order and decency, to protect the citizen from what is offensive or injurious, and to provide sufficient safeguards against exploitation and corruption of others ... It is not, in our view, the function of the law to intervene in the private life of citizens, or to seek to enforce any particular pattern of behaviour.'

The recommended age of consent was to be the age of majority, at that time 21 years of age. The report, however, did not in any way sanction homosexuality; it merely accepted that it should be decriminalized. At least it was a step in the right direction.

The report was greeted with a mixture of reactions, ranging from a sense of relief among the gay community to outrage from some Church leaders, although the Archbishop of Canterbury did welcome its findings. War hero Viscount Montgomery of Alamein told the papers that he favoured the age of homosexual consent being fixed at 80, whilst the Chief Scout complained about England going the way of Ancient Greece. Such was the controversy caused by the report, and the antipathy within the Conservative government, that it was shelved until a new Labour administration had been elected. Even then, only after it had increased its majority at the 1966 general election, was it able to consider implementing its recommendations. Inside Wilson's Cabinet there were mixed views, with the older, working-class members generally opposed to decriminalization, while the younger, well-educated ones were in favour.

Public-school educated Labour Cabinet Minister Richard Crossman was not impressed. He wrote in his diary in July 1967:

> 'Frankly, it's an unpleasant Bill and I myself didn't like it. It may well be twenty years ahead of public opinion; certainly, working class people in the north jeer at their members at the weekend and ask them why they're looking after the buggers at Westminster instead of looking after the unemployed at home.'

Interestingly, Crossman later confessed to having had a same-sex relationship while a student at Oxford.

Crossman may himself have been well educated, but it was Home Secretary Roy Jenkins who was the more liberal and who was able to carry the vote. It led to the Sexual Offences Act 1967, which decriminalized homosexual acts in private. Homosexuality was only legalized in Scotland in 1980, Northern Ireland in 1982 and the Isle of Man in 1992.

The Wolfenden Report and its deliberations were far more muddled when it came to lesbianism. It was almost as if they didn't understand or even recognize it. The report also discussed the rise in street prostitution, which it associated with 'community instability' and a 'weakening of the family'. As a result, there was a police crackdown on street prostitution following the report's publication.

Just as important was that the report shifted perceptions about the role of the law in enforcing sexual morality. It generated an immediate debate about whether the state had the right to intervene in private morality.

Following the Act there was, somewhat surprisingly, a police clampdown on homosexuality, and the number of men charged with offences trebled between 1966 and 1970. It was almost as if the police regarded the new law as an anathema that they would have no truck with.

Nevertheless, a major step forward had undoubtedly been taken by the decriminalization of homosexuality. To be a known homosexual became more acceptable. Through various books, Brian Epstein's homosexuality became more publicly discussed, while artists like David Hockney and writers such as Joe Orton made no attempt to disguise their sexuality. But it would not be until October 1970, when the Gay Liberation Front was formed by students and others at the London School of Economics, that homosexuality would begin to make marked progress in reforms and acceptability.

The 1960s brought about other major social reforms. Abortion is discussed elsewhere in this book, but also of importance was a major change to the law surrounding capital punishment. During the 1950s, the number of executions each year had fallen from around fifteen to four or five, reflecting the various changes that had been made by the Conservative government to the range of criminal acts that warranted the death penalty. Yet even though some reforms had been implemented, there remained considerable disquiet and debate among the general public about the justification of hanging. Particularly among older people, there was strong support for continuing with the death penalty, but within Parliament and in the legal system there was undoubtedly a shift of opinion and a growing move, markedly among young people, for its abolition. But whilst the Conservative government remained in office, there was little chance that Parliament would consider any further reforms. It would take a change of administration to seriously consider taking the major step of abolishing hanging altogether.

In July 1955, Ruth Ellis, a young mother, was hanged for the murder of her unfaithful lover. She would be the last woman to be hanged in Britain. There were also question marks against a number of other convictions during the period, particularly that of Derek Bentley, who was hanged for the murder of a policeman during an armed robbery. The murder had actually been committed by Christopher Craig, but as he was just 16 at the time of the shooting, he escaped the gallows. His accomplice, Bentley, however, was 18 and as such was sentenced to death, even though he had not actually committed the murder and was judged to have the mental age of a child.

Chief among the backbench abolitionists was the Labour MP Sydney Silverman, who had campaigned vigorously for its end since the 1950s. In 1965, Silverman persuaded Home Secretary Frank Soskise to provide time for a free vote on the issue. The well-known broadcaster and investigative journalist Ludovic Kennedy had also campaigned persuasively for the death penalty's abolition and had written several books questioning a number of convictions. One of the cases he investigated concerned Timothy Evans, who had been hung in 1950 for the murder of his baby daughter. Kennedy argued that Evans was innocent, and that the murders of his wife and baby had instead been committed by serial killer John Christie. Kennedy's case proved to be overwhelming and Christie was hanged three years after the hanging of Evans, following the discovery of six more bodies at 10 Rillington Place, none of which could be ascribed to Evans. Indeed, two of the skeletons found at the house dated back to the Second World War – long before Evans and his family had moved in. After a long campaign, Evans was posthumously pardoned in 1966. The realization that there had been a severe miscarriage of justice shocked the nation and certainly contributed to growing demands for the abolition of the death penalty in the UK. Following the free vote in the House of Commons in October 1965, it was suspended for a period of five years, except for cases of treason. It was finally abolished in 1969 by Home Secretary James Callaghan.

The *Daily Mirror*, which had long campaigned for its abolition, wrote at the time: 'It must always be the duty of Parliament to lead if there is ever to be any progress in penal reform. The lead has been given. It is clear-cut. It is humane. This agonising controversy can now be buried with the hangman's noose.'

The Guardian sounded a similar note in an editorial: 'The Home Secretary has backed the argument with a powerful case. That the Commons should have reached the decision they did is common sense.'

The abolition of the death penalty was one of many major social reforms in the Sixties, which included new divorce procedures, the decriminalization of homosexuality and changes to abortion laws and to the Obscene Publications Act. Support for the abolition of the death penalty came largely from young people, whereas older members of the public favoured its retention as a means of controlling crime, particularly violent crime. It was all part of the authoritarian nature of pre-war Britain that still lingered but was now being challenged openly by young people, and it was slowly crumbling.

Chapter 14

The Ticking Time Bomb

Yoko Ono cuts a controversial figure in the history of The Beatles. Often denigrated as the woman who broke up the Fab Four, she nonetheless was an artist in her own right. Whether or not she did cause their breakup is a matter of ongoing debate, but what is undeniable is that she was a major influence on the political radicalization of John, and in particular his feminist outlook. It could be said that Yoko brought feminism to The Beatles, and in doing so gave credence to the feminist movement for many female Beatles' fans. As an activist, she demonstrated against the Vietnam War, campaigned for peace and produced what she called 'feminist art'. John supported her wholeheartedly; the rest of The Beatles a little less so.

It has been said that she personified everything that non-hippies hated about hippies. She was American, her art was obscure, she was called an art-witch and she was Asian.

There has long been a degree of misogyny about Yoko Ono, although in recent years it has lessened. In the 1960s, however, when she entered John's life she was not only blamed for The Beatles' breakup but also cast as the villain; a conniving, publicity-grabbing, interfering woman. In the days when the *Sun* newspaper displayed half-naked women on page three and Miss World contests were a part of the entertainment calendar, it was hardly surprising that she got a bad press.

In 1960, the roles available for young women were severely limited. Their chances of higher education beyond the age of 18 were almost non-existent, particularly if they were from a working-class background. A mere 4 per cent of the total female population went onto a university education, with many of those ending up in teaching rather than other professions such as law, medicine, architecture or industry. Any woman pursuing education until 18 who had not acquired the requisite qualifications to enter university would, more often than not, move on to a teacher training college, with the intention of joining the teaching profession. But for the vast majority of women who left school at 16, the future meant some kind of unskilled occupation, depending on how much you had achieved academically. Those who had a passed a handful of GCEs might go into nursing, where there was always a demand, but for those who had done poorly at GCE or had not gone to a grammar school, the outlook was bleak. They would tend towards the retail sector, working in shops, or the office sector that was beginning to boom, with jobs as secretaries on the increase. Other women went to work in local factories, sometimes in canteens or on the production line.

Clare Jenkins remembers:

'The comics and magazines we read gave us information about those jobs, with glamorous-looking photos of secretaries in short skirts and painted nails. You could also borrow books from the library that detailed what certain jobs entailed – again, making basic clerical work sound glamorous.

'I actually wanted to be an air hostess from around the age of 14 – though my French teacher was pretty scathing about it, saying it was just "a waitress in the sky". One of my schoolmates did become a BA stewardess, though, and rose through the ranks.'

For the vast majority of women, any kind of job was regarded as only a short respite before marriage and a family. Once they were married, women were not expected to work, although this outdated view was slowly beginning to change. Once they were pregnant, they would certainly be expected to leave work as soon as possible. Indeed, in some occupations, women would be sacked as soon as they became pregnant. There was also a reluctance by employers to either train, promote or even employ young women, as they would be anticipating that their working careers would be short-lived and that they would soon be married and pregnant. In the vast majority of cases, women did not return to full employment, and if they did it was not until much later in life. Instead, they were expected to devote their time to raising a family and looking after their husband.

Veronica Palmer remembers getting married towards end of the 1950s:

> 'I stopped work when I got married. Married women never worked. If a woman did work it didn't look good. When we had three children and we didn't have a lot of money, I said I'd go back to work but John [her husband] said, "No don't go back to work, 'cos it'll look like I can't keep you. It'll look bad."'

And so she didn't go back. Veronica's experience was typical.

Clare Jenkins did not get much from her convent school in the way of career guidance:

> '[That] could be part of the reason why three of my four closest friends became schoolteachers, and the other one eventually became a college lecturer. Our careers teacher was also my English teacher, and I was very good at English. But that didn't stop her from smiling rather dismissively when I said I wanted to work for the BBC, and giving me the distinct impression that girls from my background didn't end up doing such things. I've always said it was that impression that put iron in my soul, and made me determined to do just that, and work for the BBC.
>
> 'When I went back to interview women I'd been at school with when we were in our mid-30s, I did find that most girls had gone into teaching, secretarial work, nursing, and so forth and we were all in the A stream, not the B or C stream. One girl had left at 16 and joined the Gas Board, and moved up the ranks in management; one of my closest friends eventually became a primary school headteacher, as did at least one other girl in our class, but at that stage, mid-30s, none of us had become university lecturers or doctors or anthropologists – or archaeologists. So yes, I think our expectations were limited – though not as limited as for those who failed their 11-plus and went to secondary modern schools rather than grammars.'

Pay was also appalling for women. Apart from teaching, where pay anyhow was less for a woman than a man, salary levels were poor. An article in *The Observer* in March 1968 blew the lid on the role of women in employment. It revealed that a three-year survey into women in the workplace had been secretly hidden by the Labour government. The report (Women's Employment Survey, March 1968 [LAB 8/3388]) was scheduled to have been published in the spring of 1967, but so devastating were its findings that it was quietly shunted to one side. *The Observer* newspaper, however, had managed to get hold of a copy, and its conclusions were shattering.

It painted an appalling picture of women at work. More than half of Britain's working women were earning less that 5 shillings an hour. For a forty-hour week, they would be earning perhaps £10, which was roughly half of what any man would be earning in the lowest-paid occupations. The report concluded that 4 million working women were being used virtually as slave labour. The report also pinpointed the lack of training for women and lack of child care and nursery facilities, and sounded an alarm that unless the government and local authorities took action soon, there would be a grave crisis in child care facilities over the next ten years. It was a prediction that turned out to be accurate.

In Liverpool, Thelma McGough remembers that girls 'weren't listened to':

'I didn't have the courage to say I don't want to go to grammar school, either to my Headmaster or my mother. So I didn't answer any questions on the eleven plus paper. I just sat there. When the results came out, the Head called me into his office. He said, "you didn't answer any of the questions, what happened, were you not well?" I said, "No, I don't want to go to grammar school, I want to go to the art school." He was raging, his face was puce. I told him, "I've heard about art school and I can't go until I'm 13." He said, "what do you think you want to be?" I said, "an artist." He replied, "Get your head out of the clouds. Girls can't be artists, particularly where you come from [a working-class council estate].'"

Most women were also working in what was described as 'low-level' jobs, such as clerical, typists, shop assistants and so forth. Only one woman in twenty had any kind of managerial position, whilst in some industries it was as bad as one in 100. Most women were also dissatisfied with their employment, believing that they could do better, and were actively seeking an improved job.

The report suggested that the Ministry of Labour was doing nothing to encourage employers to improve the position of women in the workplace. The situation was appalling. Instead of seeing women as a vital part of the economy, the government seemed to regard them as a hindrance, always nagging on about equal pay, training and childcare. It was a grim picture, and it was little surprise that the government should try to censor the report.

The report, which had interviewed 8,000 women, also concluded that men were doing nothing in the house apart from the occasional washing-up. 'Dad would occasionally wash up but he never did the cooking, washing, ironing or cleaning. He'd do odd DIY jobs about the house and look after the car but never anything else. He just assumed that because Mum was at home all day, that was her job,' noted one respondent.

Thelma McGough recalls:

'Any aspiration I had was squashed or attempts were made to squash ideas above my station. I knew that when I was 13 I wanted to go to art school. Because of instability at home, my behaviour was bad, and I was dubbed wilful. I joined a boys' gang. There was such a huge difference between being a boy or a girl. When my brother was born it was, "ooh we've got a boy at last". He was the youngest and wasn't expected to lift a finger, so I always envied boys. I didn't want to do anything domestic. I just wanted to paint and be free. Boys had freedom so I joined this boys' gang. Ultimately, it was being wilful that helped me pass the exam for art school at 13 and then I got into the art college at 16.'

The trade unions offered little help, with some unions – particularly the manual work-based or the smaller craft unions – actively discouraging female membership. Most other unions did little or nothing to encourage female participation or deal with issues that affected women, such as equal pay, child care provision, training and advancement at the workplace. Even the student revolutionaries of the 1960s failed to grasp or understand the plight of women. Search through the policy documents of the Trotskyist and communist organizations and there is scant attention paid to the role of women. It was little wonder that women ultimately shunned the male-dominated organizations and formed their own groups, although this was not until the early 1970s.

For women, there were also other issues, chief among them being the business of changing your name when married. Young women who had been to university and started a career under one name could see no logic in changing their names once they had married, but many men hung on to the old principle that a woman should take her husband's name. There was also the question of living with a boyfriend. Generally, this was frowned upon. Educated women living away from home had much more freedom than those who stayed at home and were more inclined to move in with their boyfriends, particularly if it was a serious relationship where marriage was on the horizon. If young couples did share a flat, then it was often without their parents' knowledge or a case of parents turning a blind eye though never admitting it to any friends or relations. It was rare for it happen in the same town or city. Andi Thomas recalls:

> 'There was an unwritten rule that you had to live at least one hundred miles away. Boyfriends visiting their girlfriend's parents for a weekend did not find themselves being offered the same bed as their girlfriend. We might have lived together for a year or so but it was always the couch downstairs until we were married and then it was fine, we could share the same bed.'

All these issues were suddenly tackled in a proliferation of advice columns, chief among them being Marjorie Proops, the *Daily Mirror*'s 'Agony Aunt'.

When she began her column, the issues were somewhat tame, generally from young girls wanting to know how they could attract a boyfriend or wanting to know how they could win his affection back. By the late 1960s, Proops found that the letters in her mailbag were changing, with more girls raising questions about sexual matters such as illegitimacy, the pill, orgasms, divorce and abortion. The *Mirror* was initially not too keen on Proops tackling these issues. However, it wasn't long before the 'Dear Marje' column confronted them head-on, and in doing so attracted a new range of readership, something her *Mirror* editors obviously liked. It wasn't only young women who were reading her column with enthusiasm, but older women and men too. For the latter, it was something of an eye-opener, and certainly educational.

There was also the question of property rights. At this time, women had few property rights, and as the divorce rate rose sharply, many more women found themselves destitute. In 1965, there were 2.8 divorces per 1,000 married adults. By 1976, this figure had risen to 9.6, giving Britain one of the highest divorce rates in Europe. Women may have been recognized as equal partners in marriage, but it was not until 1970 – when a further law was introduced to require women's work inside and outside the home to be taken into account in all divorce settlements – that women began to receive proper and adequate settlements. It meant, however, that women were more likely to suffer financially after divorce than men. Despite their legal rights to property and maintenance, women heading single-parent households had lower incomes than their ex-husbands. Widespread social disapproval of divorce persisted and was, more often than not, directed at women rather than men. It meant that rather than seek a divorce, many women continued to tolerate appalling behaviour. Abuse was prevalent in many marriages, as was male drunkenness, and many wives were given minimal financial 'housekeeping' to maintain a family. It meant that women often scrimped or went without in order to feed and clothe their families, while the men would spend freely in the pub as well as smoke or bet on the horses. The Sixties was very much a man's world, but young women were beginning to realize the inequities, and as educational opportunities began to open up, with more women attending universities, so their aspirations and questioning of this male-dominated society began to take effect. The feminist movement was still in its infancy, with Germaine Greer's seminal work *The Female Eunuch* not being published until 1970.

Divorce had been permissible since the introduction of the 1857 Matrimonial Act, but it was a hugely expensive business, requiring the proof of fault on someone's part. In most cases, this involved adultery and required necessary proof. This meant private detectives, confessions and so forth. It was an enormously expensive business, making it an option only for those with money and able to finance the evidence to prove 'fault'. Over the next hundred years or so, there had been some minor revisions, but the major change to divorce law came in 1969 with the Divorce Reform Act. This allowed for divorce after a couple had been separated for a period of two years, plus it was no longer necessary to prove fault on behalf of one of the partners. The Act still favoured men, but it was a huge step forward for women and inevitably led to a massive increase in the number of divorces.

Nevertheless, divorce remained an option limited only to those who could afford it for much of the 1960s. It still carried a stigma as well. The Church remained opposed to divorce, with no divorcee allowed to remarry in a church. In the 1950s, even Princess Margaret had been persuaded not to marry the man she loved because he was divorced. While divorce might have been more common in certain socialite circles, it remained almost unheard of among the working classes. Divorce was also a risk, with any case involving adultery likely to lead to salacious newspaper headlines, particularly if the people involved were well-known public figures or members of the aristocracy. Typical at the time was the Duke and Duchess of Argyll's divorce proceedings in 1963, which produced front-page headlines about many affairs of the Duchess. In court, the Duke had produced a list of eighty-eight men who were alleged to have had affairs with his wife. Also produced was a polaroid photograph of the Duchess – wearing only a string of pearls – performing a sexual act on a man, but without his head showing so that it was impossible to identify him. Indeed, it led to considerable speculation in the newspapers.

During the case, the judge commented that the Duchess had indulged in 'disgusting sexual activities.'

Almost every week, Sunday newspapers like the *News of the World* or *The People* would carry scandalous details of divorce cases, all of which in their own way helped expose the nation's socialites as hypocritical and degenerate. It was ironic that the Argylls's divorce proceedings were taking place at exactly the same time as the Profumo affair was hitting the headlines, reinforcing the belief that society was falling apart and that the nation was at a crossroads.

At the end of the 1960s, the *Sun* newspaper began to feature page three girls. Initially they were scantily clad, with nudity not appearing until 1970. But for a few more years it would not attract too much attention. The Miss World competition, however, continued attracting massive television audiences, and it was not until 1970 that it was disrupted by female protestors with flour bombs and water pistols. The American magazine *Playboy*, with its explicit nudity, flourished during the 1960s, recording sales of over 5 million copies across the world. The Playboy clubs, where scantily clad women in ridiculous bunny costumes would serve drinks and food, opened up, not just in America, but in 1966 in London as well. The Park Lane club attracted little or no protest during the Sixties.

Women faced sexism at work almost on a daily basis. Even in a prestigious organization like a bank, there were problems. Annie O'Malley, who worked in a bank in Manchester, remembered Christmas parties with horror:

> 'There was a deputy manager who chased me downstairs trying to get a Christmas kiss off me. He was in his late forties. That was very, very creepy. What was strange at the time was that you would never have stood your ground and said "no". As a female and with him having a position of power you just had to run faster than he did, back up the stairs in the hope that he didn't catch you. One of the tellers went out with another young girl who started when I did as well. He was married and everybody in the bank knew. He was

in his late thirties and she was 16 or 17. I remember thinking that was really weird but again nobody ever said anything.'

Fear of pregnancy could impact on a woman's career aspirations. The vast majority of women married early, usually before the age of 23, and immediately took on the task of setting up a home and raising a family. The man was the breadwinner; the woman the homemaker. Any notion of a long-term career for a woman was simply out of the question, as a pregnancy would swiftly lead to the curtailment of employment. Employers were not sympathetic and didn't like the idea of pregnant women about the office or factory floor, and certainly did not hold positions open for women once a child had been born. Women had few employment rights and there was no maternity leave. Indeed, in some occupations such as teaching you were promptly dismissed once you were pregnant. For most women, it was then back to the home, a life of drudgery and caring for husband and children.

If there was one single event or action that was to revolutionize the lives of women in the 1960s, it was the introduction of the oral contraceptive pill. It was claimed that the pill, if taken every day, was 99 per cent effective against pregnancy. The pill had first been available in the United States during the late 1950s, arriving in the UK in 1961, when it was announced by Minister of Health Enoch Powell that an agreement had been reached for it to be prescribed on the National Health Service. He did not, however, make it clear whether it would be readily available to both married and single women. There seemed to be an assumption that it would only be married women who would want it. Indeed, it was not until 1967 that GPs were formally allowed to prescribe the pill to single women. Nonetheless, in those intervening years it was generally not too difficult to find a friendly General Practitioner who would be prepared to prescribe it if you were single, usually citing that there were good medical reasons why you should have the pill. The pill was also known to regulate periods and lessen period pains and other difficulties, making it comparatively easy for young women to persuade sympathetic doctors of their need. With many other more conservative GPs, however, it was necessary for young women to borrow a wedding ring in order to 'prove' that they were indeed married and eligible for the pill.

Although the pill had some known and worrying side-effects, they did not seem to discourage women from taking it. Within a year, 50,000 women had been prescribed it; by the end of the 1960s, more than a million women in the UK were on the pill. Not all young women jumped at the opportunity, and there is also plenty of evidence to suggest that the vast majority of women taking the pill were in long-standing relationships. Nonetheless, one young reader of the *Sheffield Star* felt concerned enough to write to her local paper in September 1966 protesting about the potential increase in promiscuity:

> 'I feel I must protest at the proposed institution of a "sex clinic" in Sheffield. The doctors say that their desire is to prevent the birth of unwanted children, but surely they must realise that by the widespread issue of contraceptives they are removing the only natural barrier to illicit sex – the fear of conception – and encouraging a moral delinquency which is already woefully out of hand.'

What the pill did was to take the responsibility of contraception away from the man and put it in the hands of women. Prior to the introduction of the pill, women largely had to rely on men to take precautions, usually by wearing a condom. This was a simple rubber sheath, available in most barber's shops. 'Anything else for the weekend?' was the question most barbers would ask with a knowing smile. If you answered 'yes', the condom would be discreetly passed to you. Condoms could also be purchased in some chemist shops. Boots the chemist started selling them in 1965, but it had to be bought over the counter as there were no condom vending machines in those days. This inevitably led to some embarrassment for the person purchasing them, particularly if the shop assistant was a woman. Although the condom was the most popular form of contraception, it was nonetheless notoriously unreliable, with the sheaths either ripping, being put on incorrectly or simply coming off. The onus was on the man to put it on correctly, so women had to be confident not only that he would carry a condom but also that he knew how to apply it. It wasn't easy to practice putting on a condom, and when it came to the real thing, pulling them on in the dark, fumbling under the sheets or in the park was always liable to not only 'spoil' the moment but lead to disaster. Often they did not work, resulting in an unwanted pregnancy. Some women did take the precaution of carrying a condom in their handbag in case the man did not have one. Most lads, however, adopted the method known as *coitus interruptus*, or 'withdrawal'.

Sex education was appalling, being virtually non-existent on the school curriculum. Parents assumed that schools told their teenage children all about sex, while schools assumed that it was up to the parents. In the end, nobody usually told anyone about anything. Mostly, you learnt from your friends. Annie O'Malley recounted what happened at her Catholic girls' school:

> 'We had a talk on sex – it must have been 1964 – and it was all about the birds and bees and sex was never mentioned. Somehow you were supposed to fathom it all out. They talked about the "act" and she was saying if two people love each other, they get married and then they do the act. I remember one girl innocently putting her hand up and asking "Mother, what is the act." And being told she should go home and ask her parents. And then she said if you're very fortunate when you've done the act then nine months later you will have a baby. We all left that lesson more confused than when we started because they never called a spade a spade.'

Jean Birkett was no better informed at school about sexual matters:

> 'We had no sex education at school and I was doing A level biology! We were learning all the reproductive methods of frogs but there was never any mention of how humans reproduce. And at home occasionally there was a dire warning when I got to the age of 16, a dire warning from my father – "remember boys only want one

thing". But he didn't tell me what the one thing was. He was basically maligning his whole sex. "And if you give in it will ruin your life."'

Another woman, Jenny (not her real name), had similar memories:

'As we were Catholics, we were doubly discouraged from going anywhere near sex – because contraception for girls, women, wasn't available, and because it was actively forbidden by the Catholic Church. But that didn't stop one of my school friends from getting pregnant. So there was a shotgun wedding and she was sent to Ireland to have the baby in order to avoid neighbourhood shame, though of course everyone knew. That was the usual course of action – and, if the man wouldn't marry the woman, then she'd be sent back to Ireland and have to give the baby up for adoption. All very sad.'

Jean Birkett remembered a situation that happened when she was in the sixth form:

'My best friend who I was supposed to be going to college with that autumn wrote to me. I had a summer job in Scarborough working in an hotel. She said that she was pregnant and getting married. I was flabbergasted. But where would you have gone to get the pill, or to have sex for that matter. There weren't many options. I was very scared.'

Coitus interruptus, while a common approach, was nororiously unreliable and certainly spoilt the pleasure. Women had to be sure that the man would pull out, and more importantly, know when to pull out. Rubber protections, known as diaphragms or caps were available for women, but these were cumbersome, equally unreliable and required a considerable degree of foresight and planning. They usually had to be fitted by a doctor or nurse to ensure that it was the correct size. This may have been alright for married women, but single women would never contemplate visiting their doctor regarding such matters, and anyhow most doctors would refuse advice to a single woman. They were also not the kind of thing to be left in bedroom drawers, where parents, brothers or sisters might rummage and discover them. Women could also calculate when in their cycle they were least likely to conceive, but this was a notoriously inaccurate and dangerous method of contraception.

The result of this lack of effective contraception was an increasing numbers of unwanted pregnancies. It placed numerous constraints on women, forcing many of them into unsuitable marriages as well as further restricting their employment opportunities and lifestyles. Once the pill had been introduced, women knew that they had some control over their bodies and their sexual activities. The feminist writer Julie Birchall, however, has pointed out that 'the freedom that women were supposed to have found in the 1960s largely boiled down to easy contraception and abortion; things to make life easier for men'.

Jane Brown remembered when her teenage sister became pregnant:

> 'My parents were devastated. But there was no talk of an abortion. We were a good catholic family. So, she had to get married. Amazingly she's still married to the same guy 40 years on. Things weren't spoken about in those days. There was so much you didn't know about sex. You didn't really get much from school and parents were too embarrassed. You fumbled your way, talked to your friends who were just as innocent as you and didn't know much either. Every boy I met also didn't know much.'

Writing in *The Observer* in April 1962, Marghanita Laski talked of 54,000 illegal abortions in the UK each year. What really angered her was the lack of discussion about the problem.

The pill made no difference whatsoever to most Catholic families, with the Catholic Church continuing to be vehemently opposed to the very idea of contraception. This was made blatantly clear in Pope Paul's encyclical, *Humanae Vitae*, published in July 1968, which threated excommunication for any woman using any form of contraception. The result was that many Catholic women continued to suffer repeated pregnancies and multiple child births. This often led to social deprivation, overwork and long-term illness. But for some Catholic women, the pill was a blessing. It may have been against their religion, but many Catholic women secretly resorted to the pill in order to alleviate further pregnancies and more children, often without even telling their husbands. The constant fear of pregnancy hung like a dark shadow over most married and single women, whether they were Catholic or not. An unplanned pregnancy meant an unplanned family.

Growing up as a Catholic, contraception and abortion were forbidden, remembers Clare Jenkins:

> 'The only contraception allowed was "the rhythm method" – which resulted in quite a few unplanned pregnancies. Abortion was absolutely forbidden – throughout the UK, not just for Catholics. And contraception wasn't easy to obtain for women – a friend, not Catholic, had to show her engagement ring before she was allowed the Pill at the birth control clinic. So we were pretty chary of sex, as lots of people were, whatever their religion, in the 60s. One of my Catholic friends had to get married and I knew of other Catholic girls in England who were sent back to family in Ireland to have the baby, which may then have been given up for adoption or as I know of in at least one case adopted by a family member and brought up as their child, causing great distress later in life when they realised everyone knew apart from them. When I interviewed other Catholic women in our mid-30s, there were some very funny stories about sex – like one girl who said her mother had told her that, if she did anything with a boy, she would immediately know. And another girl, who was convinced her guardian angel was watching everything she did, which was a bit of an arousal-buster. The important thing was to be a "good girl".'

An unplanned pregnancy usually meant a quick marriage, tying both husband and wife to a long-term partnership that may have not been planned or really wanted. However, any idea of a woman bringing up a child on her own was an anathema and stigma on her character. If the couple married quickly, everyone would knowingly shake their heads or give a quiet chuckle. But for the woman to remain single and walk around pregnant without a partner was considered shameful. There was also the financial consideration of bringing up a child on your own. The likelihood was that the man would not contribute anything financially, making life doubly difficult for the woman, who would often find herself without work, without money and dependent on her parents for financial help and even somewhere to live. There was also the stigma of being an unmarried mother.

Of course, any couple finding themselves with an unwanted pregnancy could simply get married, and many who had a longstanding relationship would simply accelerate the date of their wedding. But few people were fooled, and many was the bride who walked down the aisle with a bulging lump in front of her. In many working class communities, it was expected that if you got a woman pregnant then you did the honourable thing and married her as soon as possible. The result was that many couples, marrying in haste, repented at leisure. A sudden pregnancy and a short relationship were hardly a solid foundation for marriage.

The alternative, however, was not to be welcomed. The problems for any woman having a child out of wedlock were considerable, particularly in Catholic communities. A woman might be ostracized, there would be whispers in the street and the newly born child would not be greeted with universal enthusiasm, perhaps for years. Indeed, in some families the pregnant woman would be thrown out of the family home for having brought disgrace on everyone. They would be made homeless, and in time would have to quit their jobs in order to have and to care for the child.

The introduction of the pill may not have brought all this to an end, but it certainly made a radical difference. Hairdresser Gavin Hodge remembered it vividly:

'There were two phases to the 1960s: pre-pill and post-pill. My sister, who was growing up in the late 1950s, didn't have half the freedom: if you got into trouble back then, you had to get married or you ended up down a back street with a coat hanger. Then the pill came along – it gave women the freedom to be the equal of their boyfriends. There was a lot of moral debate at the time but, as far as I could gather, most girls couldn't care less about that: they just wanted to get their hands on it. We smoked a bit of dope, did a bit of acid, but the major drug of the 1960s was the pill.'

Whether or not the pill did lead to a rise in promiscuity is much debated. Probably in rural areas and church-going households, it had little effect. But among a strata of young people, particularly students, the story was different.

'Sex was everywhere – The Wednesday Play, Play for Today, both of which my Mum fought hard for us not to watch, books by Alan Sillitoe, Stan Barstow, *Up the Junction* by Nell Dunn, *Women in Love*, other films, other books,' recalled Clare Jenkins.

In his book *The Swinging Sixties*, Brian Masters had little doubt that the pill had an impact on promiscuity: 'People copulated on the slightest pretext after an acquaintance of some minutes. Sexual partners were snapped up and discarded without ceremony, provided that they had the newly available contraceptive pill in their pocket or handbag.'

Manchester-born Annie O'Malley recalled:

'I spent a lot of time fighting to keep my virginity. I was frightened of getting pregnant and even though we knew there was a pill it was about having the confidence at 16 or 17 to go and get one. And at that age I didn't have the confidence. I was still living in my parents' house, so it probably wasn't until I left home that I had a bit more confidence. There were no family planning clinics and even though your doctor wouldn't have told your parents it was still the same doctor that your parents went to.'

During the 1960s, the number of births outside of marriage continued to rise, from 5.8 per cent of all births in 1961 to 8.43 per cent in 1971. Although many of these births were unplanned, just as many were planned. Couples were now living together in a married state and having families.

Many of them would not get married until later in life, if ever, although they continued to live together as a couple.

The term 'family planning' came into common currency in the Sixties, whereby women and their husbands started to plan how many children they would have. This in turn would lead to a planned economic life, bringing with it the benefits of better homes, cars and social goods.

The alternative to pregnancy was an abortion. Although there are no official figures to verify it, there is little doubt that the number of illegal abortions taking place in Britain during the 1950s and early 1960s was at an all-time high. It was an appalling situation, and although the figures of deaths following botched abortions had declined since the 1950s, much of this was reckoned to be due to improvements in sterilized equipment and medical care. Although the number of deaths had fallen, there is no evidence on the actual numbers of abortions taking place. One estimate put the number of private abortions carried out in Harley Street at 10,000 per year, while around 35,000 women each year were admitted to NHS hospitals to deal with problems arising from botched abortions. Andrew Marr, in *A History of Modern Britain*, has guessed that the number of illegal abortions per year was probably between 100,000 and 250,000. Whatever the true figure, it was unspeakably high.

Legal abortions were in fact allowed in Britain following the acquittal in 1938 of Dr Alex Bourne, who had performed an abortion on a suicidal 14-year-old gang rape victim. In court, Bourne successfully argued that as a result of her rape, the victim's mental health was at risk and that an abortion had therefore been necessary. The case paved the way for abortion in such circumstances, but required the permission of two psychiatrists who could verify that the woman's mental condition was in jeopardy. It immediately turned abortion into a class issue as well as a moral issue. The ruling meant that any woman contemplating an abortion would need not only to know of and then consult a number of psychiatrists, but would also have to pay a professional price for an abortion. No working-class woman would even know of any psychiatrists, let alone be able to afford their prices before having to pay for the abortion itself. And there was hardly likely to be any psychiatrists in places such as Gateshead, Accrington or Walsall. One woman, recalling her own legal abortion in 1964, spoke of it costing about £150 at a time when the average weekly wage was no more than £15. On top of this would be consultancy fees with the psychiatrists and an overnight stay in a clinic. If any abortion was agreed to, it was invariably carried out at a Harley Street clinic, with its Harley Street prices. Consulting psychiatrists, arranging clinical appointments and so forth also took time, when time was of the essence. Any delays and an abortion would further endanger the health of the woman involved.

Bob Jones remembered what happened to a girl he knew:

'She had got pregnant when she was about fifteen and had been asked to leave school. Her parents then sent her to the opposite end of the country where they had relations while she had the baby. Once it was born, the baby was then offered for adoption. She then suddenly reappeared at the youth club one evening as if nothing had happened. There were suspicions about it all because one of the other girls in our gang was at the same school and everyone just put two and two together. It must have been appalling for her in later life to have this memory, and to wonder what had happened to the child. Would she tell her future husband, children?'

Jones also recalled another girl in their gang who had became pregnant when she was 15:

'She got married to the guy when she was 16, was having an affair at 17 and divorced at 19. That's the way it was then. Until the pill came along there was no safe form of contraception. And, as with this girl, she married the guy but it was a disaster from the start.

'And there was another girl in our gang who had gone off to Teacher Training College. She got pregnant as well and had to get married though she was about 21 by then. I'd forgotten how many there were who finished up pregnant.'

Nor was it just single women who faced difficulties when pregnant. In the early 1960s, there was no such thing as maternity leave or maternity rights. Many married women, particularly those who already had as many as three, four or even five children, found themselves facing financial and domestic difficulties with the prospect of an additional child. Living in a two-bedroom house or small flat with even more children on the way was a daunting prospect, to say nothing of the increased financial burden. It was little wonder that given all these pressures, many women opted for illegal abortions. It was not an easy decision. It was an appalling moral dilemma in a society that was far more moralistic and religious than that of today.

As the Fifties and then the Sixties grew increasingly liberal, with more and more couples engaging in pre-marital sex, so the demand for abortions increased. But while those with money and contacts could afford a professional abortionist, those without were forced to resort to the 'backstreet' abortionist. On council estates and in apartment blocks and communities of terraced streets, someone always knew someone who would be prepared to perform an abortion. The price would be a fraction of what a Harley Street clinic would charge, plus there would be no need for psychiatrists and it would be carried out in a neighbour's house within days and in secret. But there were obvious dangers.

Former midwife Jennifer Worth recalls going to meetings at the time in Women's Institutes up and down the country to promote her book, *Call The Midwife*:

> 'At nearly every meeting at least one woman will relate a horrifying story of a distant relative who tried a do-it-yourself abortion. Knitting needles, crochet hooks, scissors, paper knives, pickle forks and other implements have all been pushed into the uterus by desperate women who preferred anything to the continued pregnancy.'

The going rate for an illegal abortion was a couple of pounds, and of course there was no overnight stay and no aftercare. Worth continues:

'Chronic ill health frequently followed a backstreet abortion, [with] infections, anaemia, scar tissue or adhesions, continuous pain, cystitis or nephritis, incontinence, a torn cervix or perforated colon. I remember a girl of 19 who developed renal failure due to damage to the bladder. Her kidneys packed up, but amazingly she survived.'

In her novel *Up The Junction*, published in 1963, Nell Dunn wrote for the first time about the horrific reality of illegal abortions:

'You see I can't keep it …' Rube began.
    'Don't try and explain, love. How can you ever explain anything? It's the most bloody impossible thing in the world. How much money have you got?'
    'Four pounds.'
    'Give it over. You don't look more than seventeen.'
    'I'm eighteen next month.'
    'Come on upstairs, then your friend can wait for you down here.'
    When I came back from ringing, Rube was shrieking, a long, high, animal shriek. The baby was born alive, five months old. It moved, it breathed, its heart beat. Rube lay back white and relieved, across the bed and her mum lifted the eiderdown and peered at the tiny baby still joined by the cord. 'You can see it breathing, look.'
    … Finally the ambulance arrived. They took Rube away, but they left behind the baby, which had now grown cold. Later Sylvie took him, wrapped him in the *Daily Mirror*, and threw him down the toilet.'

Having an illegal abortion was a risk, but for many women, in particular teenagers and older women already struggling with a large family, it was a necessity and a risk worth taking. At least there was a code among the women to maintain secrecy and respect.

Nonetheless, many of the women carrying out these abortions were unqualified; others were retired midwives or nurses, or even struck-off doctors. You could also find carefully worded adverts in some newspapers offering help to women with 'menstrual blockages'. Some professional doctors or foreign doctors who were not registered with the NHS also performed abortions in private, and consequently made money. The result of all these illegal abortions was that many women died, were infected or even traumatized for life. Much of it was due to using poor or inadequately sterilized equipment and second-rate medical care. Society had turned a blind eye to the problem, although the success of the BBC's Wednesday play and Ken Loach's subsequent film *Up the Junction* helped raise the question of abortion to a new level. It was clearly an issue that needed to be confronted.

The Royal College of Obstetricians and Gynaecologists estimated that there were 14,600 illegal abortions per year taking place during the mid-1960s. Other organizations suggested that the figure was as much as ten times higher. It will never be known exactly how many illegal abortions were taking place, as the debate was so controversial and accurate figures are impossible to come by. Although the number of illegal abortions was undoubtedly in the thousands, the number of prosecutions remained small. The police would only become involved if there was a resulting death.

As the debate about abortion intensified, a young Liberal Member of Parliament, David Steel, introduced a Private Members' Bill to the House of Commons in 1967 aimed at legalizing abortion. Steel was just 29 years of age when he introduced the Bill and had been one of the youngest elected MPs when he entered the House of Commons in 1965. He was commonly known as the 'the boy David'. Steel brought with him young ideas and a new, fresh attitude to an otherwise staid, middle-aged, male-dominated Parliament. He had been moved by the stories that had emerged around *Up The Junction*, and as a young person knew the kind of pressures that other young people were experiencing. He even watched an abortion taking place as part of his inquiry into the issue. Steel was fortunate in that the Labour government had, in Roy Jenkins, a Home Secretary with an equally liberal outlook on domestic issues. Thanks to Jenkins and the Labour government, Steel was able to muster support for his Bill.

'Back to the Commons where I voted for the Abortion Bill,' wrote Labour Minister Tony Benn in his diary on Friday, 22 July 1966, 'which was carried by 223 votes to 29 – a notable victory.'

Interestingly, Prime Minister Harold Wilson makes no mention whatsoever of the subsequent Abortion Act 1967 in his history of the 1964–70 Labour government, nor even of Labour's contribution to what was to be one of the major social reforms of the era. Indeed, his Cabinet colleague Richard Crossman notes in his diary that in private conversations, Wilson had confided to him that he was 'against the legal reforms to deal with homosexuality or abortion'.

Many, however, particularly on the Conservative benches and in the Catholic Church (although the Church of England was just as hostile), remained vehemently opposed to any idea of abortion. There was much discussion throughout the country, particularly in the media, but after considerable Parliamentary debate, the Bill was passed, and with Government backing, became law in April 1968. The new Act now allowed for legal abortions up to twenty-eight weeks of the pregnancy.

The effect of the new Act was immediate and dramatic, with Government figures showing a remarkable increase in the number of legal abortions, from 23,000 in 1968, to 54,000 a year later and 86,000 in 1970. The figures would continue to increase, levelling out at around 200,000 by the late 1970s.

The result of the new Abortion Act was that young women's lives and attitudes would be changed forever. Britain was changing, and much of these changes were focused around women. Of all the social reforms of the 1960s, the Abortion Act is the one which still causes concerns and deep rifts. Even David Steel was said to have been shocked by the number of terminations that resulted from his Private Members' Bill. Whereas many of the social reforms of the Sixties, such as the changes to the Obscene Publications Act and homosexuality laws, became accepted in an era of enlightenment, the same could not always be said of the Abortion Act. Time and again it has been revisited, and the likelihood is that this will continue.

Andrew Marr has paid respect to the Liberal Party's role in these social reforms: 'Liberals, though unimportant politically ... were particularly influential – not only Steel on abortion and Ludovic Kennedy on the death penalty, but through the parliamentary enthusiasm of their leader Jo Grimmond.' Marr also spotted a generally unrecognized influence: 'The left-wingers and intellectuals around *Tribune*, who were being elbowed aside by Wilson, also had a real influence on these non-economic issues.'

Pinpointing exactly when the feminist movement was born is difficult, but there is no doubt that the National Women's Liberation conference at Ruskin College, Oxford, in February 1970 was pivotal in the development and widening of the women's movement. The organizers, Sally Alexander and Arielle Aberson, were both students at Ruskin College. They took over the college for the weekend and expected about 300 women to attend, but instead more than 500 turned up. Mostly they were young female students, though a few men did attend and ran a crèche. At the final session, the conference issued a number of demands: equal pay, equal educational and job opportunities, free contraception and abortion on demand, and finally free twenty-four-hour nurseries.

Prior to the Ruskin conference, however, there were distinct signs of a female lobby fermenting. There had been debates at the London School of Economics and other universities, but there was little encouragement from the organizations that might have been expected to lend support, such as the Labour Party and trade unions. Instead, most of the campaigns were focused on the universities and their students.

Later that year, the publication of Germaine Greer's *The Female Eunuch* was ground-breaking. It received mixed reviews when published, but within a year it had sold out and would in time become a best seller. In a *Guardian* interview, the journalist Rosie Boycott remembered the impact it had on her:

'I was 19 when the book came out and she bowled me over. I was stunned by her extraordinary beauty and her daring, her openness about sex, her obvious pleasure in taking on men, her extreme cleverness which combined with her wicked sense of humour. In

1970, women couldn't get a mortgage, or even buy a car, unless their husband or father countersigned the documents. Horizons were low – maybe a little job in that enticing gap between education and motherhood. Germaine burst into this stifling and limiting life like a whirlwind. Get a life, she said, think beyond your social conditioning. She challenged the accepted concepts of marriage, the nuclear family and the obligation to breed, exhorting us instead to be doctors and lawyers and businesswomen.'

It was to signal a major shift in the perceived role of women in society.

Chapter 15

Beatniks and Biba

Sub-cultures among young people had long existed and were hardly something new to British youth culture. They had always been there, principally in major urban areas and large industrial cities. Turf wars had raged across London throughout much of the twentieth century. Young people living in North London rarely ventured south across the river, and especially not down to the East End, where they were likely to encounter even more threatening looks. It was a similar situation in cities like Manchester, Liverpool, Newcastle and especially Glasgow, which had the added mix of religious strife.

After the Second World War, Teddy Boy gangs emerged on a national and local level. They differed in that they wore clothes that identified them as being Teddy Boys. The term was derived from the style of dress they adopted, which was said to reflect that of the Edwardian era. In fact, it bore only a passing resemblance. They always wore suits, often pale blue in colour, along with tight trousers, known as drainpipes. Their jackets were hip-length and sported black velvet lapels. Along with that they would wear a shirt and bootlace tie. Their shoes were also of a particular fashion, usually crepe-soled and black. It was a distinctive outfit and certainly set them apart from other young people. Teddy Boys attracted a female following, with the girls also wearing a unique style of clothing, generally flowing dresses with underskirts, high heels and tight sweaters.

Teddy Boys, however, did not have a good reputation. They were working-class lads, often doing dreary jobs, who liked rock 'n' roll music, loved to jive and were known to enjoy a fight, usually because it added a bit of daring and excitement to their lives. Football special trains were regularly wrecked by gangs of Teddy Boys who had been following their team to away matches.

On the other side of the youth cultural divide were the Beatniks, who espoused beat culture, in particular the beat literature of the United States, favouring writers such as Allen Ginsberg, Jack Kerouac and the Beat poets. They wore dark clothes and were usually middle-class, artistic, university students with a love of poetry, books and music. They rejected the norms of society, were anti-authoritarian and instead advocated rebellion. Ginsberg himself vigorously opposed militarism, economic materialism and sexual repression. Beatniks wore their hair long and dressed casually, were often bare-footed or wearing sandals, and also wore sunglasses irrespective of whether it was sunny or not. They were originally centred around New York's Greenwich Village, but by the 1960s the culture had taken root across Europe, particularly in London and Paris. Beatniks were also more likely to dabble in drugs than Teddy Boys.

In Britain, many of the Beatniks flocked to the seaside resorts, in particular Newquay, where they could live cheaply during the summer. Journalist Alan Whicker on the *Tonight* programme visited them there but struggled to find many locals who were outraged by them. One councillor complained that they didn't wash and as a result were smelly. The Beatniks themselves said that they enjoyed the freedoms to do what they wished. 'I just like to play the guitar,' said one of them.

John Lennon epitomized the Beatnik. He was artistic, had attended art school, loved the poetry of Dylan Thomas and even dabbled in poetry himself. Stuart Sutcliffe, a founding member of The Beatles and close friend and fellow student of John, was later acknowledged an accomplished artist. Both John and Stuart wore black polo-necked sweaters, black corduroy trousers and black Chelsea boots, and adopted the rebellious nature of the Beatnik. They were outspoken, assertive and moody.

By the early Sixties, the Teddy Boys had morphed into Rockers. The latter were almost wholly working class, with a love of motorbikes, speed and leather. The term 'Rocker' referred not to rock'n'roll but to the rocker head on a motorbike. Nonetheless, Rockers also had a love of rock'n'roll music, in particular the leather-clad Gene Vincent and Elvis Presley. Other heroes were the actors Marlon Brando, who also had a love of motorbikes, and Rebel Without a Cause star James Dean, who had been killed in 1955 whilst driving his Porsche Spyder car at over 80mph.

British motorbikes were their preference, because they were noisier and could be easily adapted so that they sounded even louder. Italian bikes tended to have a more soothing sound. Rockers wore tight leather trousers and leather jackets which were usually covered in badges, but rarely wore crash helmets (which at the time were not obligatory). They also had long white socks carefully folded over the top of their leather riding boots. Their hair was swept back with sideburns, in the style of 1950s rockers like Elvis, Jerry Lee Lewis and Johnny Cash. Their principal objective as a Rocker was to 'hit a ton' on the motorbike, though in truth few of the bikes could actually achieve that speed; even if the speedometer did clock 100mph, it was usually wrong and more like 85mph.

Rockers hung out in roadside cafes, where they could meet fellow Rockers and compare bikes, leathers and so forth. They would race up and down a stretch of road, demonstrating the acceleration of their bike and an ability to hit a certain speed in a certain time. In particular, they liked a quiet stretch of road with as many hairpin bends as possible. They also had names; one group in Nottingham called themselves the Aces. Sometimes they would congregate in other venues such as clubs, but dancing was not a major part of their culture. There were girls, but on a limited basis. Few girls actually owned their own bikes, instead preferring to ride pillion behind their boyfriends.

But if the Rockers did not attract too many girls, the opposite was true of the Mods, who became a phenomenon of the later Sixties. Mods were more salubrious. They wore suits, white shirts, slim ties, trilby hats and parker jackets, usually with a fur collar. They had shorter hair and were stylish in a way that Rockers were not. They went for the continental look and usually rode scooters, mainly the Vespa and Lambretta, with an abundance of wing mirrors. Whereas the girls might have been a little afraid of driving or being pillion on a Rocker's motorbike, they held no such fears for a scooter, which was quieter, slower, less dangerous and did not necessitate special clothing to keep the wind and rain out: a parker would suffice. The result was that numerous Rockers deserted their former ranks in favour of the Mods, solely in search of girls. It was generally the boys who owned and drove the scooters, with girls always a mere accompaniment.

The Mods also loved their music, but rock 'n' roll was not their choice. Instead, they opted for a post-Beatles style, in particular The Small Faces, The Who and The Kinks, all of whom wore the same style of clothing. Rhythm and blues, soul and ska were all very popular with Mods. But unlike the Rockers, Mods loved to dance. They frequented clubs, invented their own dance styles and even indulged in drugs, mainly amphetamines in order to keep themselves awake. Chief among these were Purple Hearts, an amphetamine which had originally been concocted in the United States to help American servicemen stay awake. They soon found their way to Britain, and were cheap, not illegal and effective. The Mods devised an entire culture. They were working class but with aspirations, more likely to be from a grammar school than a secondary modern.

It was probably inevitable that the Mods and Rockers would clash, but it is now acknowledged that such clashes were more to do with media interest and hype than with any natural antipathy. The first clashes began at Clacton on the Easter weekend of 1964, but were magnified out of proportion by the newspapers. There had been some trouble between the two groups over the years, but never anything more than minor skirmishes, and it had never really escalated into anything serious until the press began to take an interest. That interest seemed to signal a war, and on Whitsun bank holiday in late May, hundreds turned up at south-coast resorts like Clacton, Margate, Hastings and Brighton.

'They were like Medieval knights on chargers,' recalled one witness as the Mods and Rockers rode into town in their dozens on their scooters and motorbikes. The police were out in force, adding to the tension. Inevitably, clashes developed – 'Terror on the Beach', ran the headline in Brighton's *Evening Argus*.

The clashes were certainly a culture shock for both local residents and visitors, who had expected to enjoy the sunshine, beach and ice cream. Instead, they found violence and rampaging hordes charging across the beach at each other, with the police caught somewhere in between. More than a thousand were said to have been involved in Brighton. Even the police had been caught unawares and had little inkling on how to deal with it. Policemen raced heavy-footed across the sands, clinging onto their helmets, stumbling and outnumbered by the marauding 'armies'.

The battles produced acres of headlines and opinion. Beneath a headline of 'Wildest Ones Yet', the *Daily Sketch* reported that 'the wild ones of Whitsun went even wilder yesterday. Out came the knives at Margate and three men were stabbed.'

Parents watched aghast at the BBC news as they saw the violent scenes. Britain's youth seemed suddenly out of control. While that was an exaggeration, what was certainly true was that young people were increasingly out of parental control. Newspaper editorials helped fan the flames of hysteria. Typical was the *Birmingham Post* editorial in May 1964, which warned that Mods and Rockers were 'internal enemies' in the UK who would 'bring about disintegration of a nation's character'. The *Daily Mirror* dubbed them the 'Whitsun wild ones'. Accompanying a photograph of a Mod kicking in a Rocker's head was the headline 'Living for Kicks'.

The magazine *Police Review* was even more hysterical, arguing that the rivals' lack of respect for law and order might cause violence to 'surge and flame like a forest fire'. It seemed to some as if the nation was about to slip into some kind of catastrophic civil war among young people. There were calls for the reinstatement of conscription, the birch and other harsher punishments. In all, more than 100 were arrested and the courts handed down severe sentences. Four were jailed, half-a-dozen others were sent to detention centres and fines totalled well over £1,000. One youngster, when fined by the court, astonished everyone by whipping out his cheque book and writing out a cheque. It wasn't just the effrontery, more the fact that he could afford it. Britain was changing, led by British youth.

In truth, the Rockers and Mods were not that diametrically opposed. Indeed, they had much in common: they were both overwhelmingly working class, both in search of new horizons (though one more so than the other), both with a means of independent transportation and both adopted a style and dress code of their own. They were trailblazers for a new kind of generation.

Hire purchase was at the root of much of Britain's growing affluence, but in particular it was a boon to the normally impoverished British youth. Young people in post-war Britain had no wealth at all, with spare cash at a premium. There may have been jobs, but many of them were apprenticeships and as a result were poorly paid. It was only the older skilled workers who received anything that could be considered a decent salary. Hire purchase, or the 'never-never' as it was colloquially known, allowed young people to make purchases that would have been beyond their means.

The Beatles themselves and most of the other pop groups on Merseyside had been fortunate enough to be able to purchase their guitars, drums and amplifiers from Frank Hessy's music shop on Whitechapel on the 'never-never'. It was the only music shop in the whole of Liverpool and Merseyside prepared to give credit to young people. As a consequence, it was a magnet for them. In 1957, John Lennon had paid £17 for his first guitar from the shop. When Brian Epstein took over management of The Beatles, the first thing he did was to walk across the road from his own NEMS store to Hessy's shop and pay off the remaining credit owed on the band's instruments. Others who took advantage of Hessy's credit facilities included Gerry and the Pacemakers, The Searchers, The Big Three and The Undertakers. Without that facility, there would almost certainly have been no Beatles, no Merseybeat music and maybe even no youth revolution.

Just as you could purchase a musical instruments and potential ticket to fame at Hessy's, similarly you could obtain a motorbike or scooter on the 'never-never' elsewhere. Hire purchase was a passport to aspiration. You might pay over the odds in the long run for whatever you were buying, but at least you could have it there and then, simply paying off a certain amount each week or month. For those buying guitars and drums it was an investment, as it meant they could form a group, get bookings and pay off their dues with the earnings they made from playing at the Cavern or elsewhere.

Credit for young people also stretched into fashion, allowing boys and girls to buy suits, shoes, dresses and so forth that they would not normally have been able to afford. It would lead to a fashion revolution, and was also a boost to the car industry.

The 1950s had been the era of the white consumer good. Washing machines, fridges, electric irons, televisions, radiograms and much else had all flowed into the shops and were being snapped up by households suddenly able to afford more luxuries, as full employment and a bubbling economy left them with surplus cash. But if the Fifties were about white goods in the high street shop windows, the Sixties would be about fashion.

For young people, fashion, style and music were set to become a statement about who and what you were. It was about being different and being seen to be different, being young and being seen to be young, being inventive and being seen to be inventive. There may have been Teddy Boys in the past, but they were always a minority, often frowned upon by their contemporaries. But that was about to change.

It was undoubtedly The Beatles who kicked it all off for fashion. Before Brian Epstein had taken control of them and their stage attire, The Beatles were inclined to wear black polo-neck jumpers, tight corduroy trousers and Chelsea boots. It was the Beatnik look, probably best espoused by John Lennon. But all that changed under Epstein's management. Out went the casual stage attire and in came fancy matching suits buttoning up to the collar. Lennon, years later in a *Rolling Stone* magazine interview, confessed that he had hated it and that they were being 'marketed'. But at least Epstein didn't seem to mind what they wore off-stage. He allowed them to keep their long hair, although by today's standards it hardly seemed long. At the time, however, with short back and sides the norm, The Beatles' hair was considered outrageous. Once The Beatles had shot to fame, longer hair became the custom among Britain's teenagers. Everyone wanted a Beatles haircut. If you didn't have long hair, then you were immediately identifiable as someone who wasn't quite 'with it'. Parents hated it, employers cringed and schools banned it altogether. But for Britain's youth, long hair meant 'rebel' and was a sign of non-conformity.

Parents and teachers hated the new style. Boys at Clark's Grammar School in Guildford faced the threat of suspension unless they got rid of their Beatles haircuts. The headmaster, John Weightman, told *The Times* that 'this ridiculous style brings out the worst in boys physically. It makes them look like morons.' The boys, naturally enough, didn't agree. One senior boy said that 'the ban will not go down well with most of the boys. The Beatles are great and I see nothing wrong with their style of haircut.'

At another school, Mandeville Secondary in Aylesbury, a similar ban was enforced, with two boys having to spend three weeks separated from the rest of the school and forced to sit in a dining hall instead of in lessons until they got their hair cut.

It was even worse in America, as Keith Richards remembered regarding one of The Rolling Stones' early tours: 'In America if you had long hair you were a faggot as well as a freak. They would shout across the street, "hey fairies!"' And on television, Dean Martin introduced them as 'these long-haired wonders from England, The Rolling Stones ... They're backstage picking the fleas off each other.'

Generally, The Rolling Stones took matters a step further. Whereas The Beatles wore suits on stage, the Stones just looked plain 'scruffy'. Their hair was even longer, their clothes hardly uniform like The Beatles, and they had an attitude that matched their dress sense. They almost made The Beatles look tame. When they made an early appearance on Granada Television's evening magazine programme *Scene At Six Thirty*, they created mayhem backstage, leading the company's Director of Programmes, David Plowright, outraged and vowing never to allow them on Granada TV again. But as their fame increased, he soon relented, with Granada conducting a lengthy interview with Jagger on *World In Action* as well as making a hugely successful recording of the Stones' concert in Hyde Park.

Keith Richards also remembers how they took a deliberate decision not to ape The Beatles' mode of dress: 'The thing is not to regurgitate the Beatles. So we're going to have to be the anti-Beatles. We're not going to be the Fab Four, all wearing the same shit.'

Clothing styles for women had long been dictated by the Paris and Rome fashion houses, until a young fashion designer in London called Mary Quant decided otherwise. Quant had first opened a shop called Bazaar in Chelsea's King's Road in the mid-1950s. But it wasn't until the early 1960s that Quant became a household name when she turned her attention to young people and began to produces styles that were both affordable to the young and also appealing. Although hemlines had gradually been getting higher since the mid-Fifties, it was Quant who slashed them on her skirts and dresses so that in some cases they were thigh-high. The media loved it, and countless stars and young women featured on the front pages in ever-shorter skirts – now termed miniskirts – showing off their long, slim legs. A fashion revolution was underway. Cathy McGowan, presenter of television's *Ready, Steady, Go*, was one of the first to buy into the Quant revolution, wearing her short skirts and dresses on her weekly show, adding credibility and fuel to the new trend. If you couldn't afford the new fashion, then you simply got out the scissors and cotton and cut the length of your old wardrobe, or even created your own new fashion.

Quant later said: 'It was the girls on the King's Road who invented the mini. I was making easy, youthful, simple clothes, in which you could move, in which you could run and jump and we would make them the length the customer wanted. I wore them very short and the customers would say, "Shorter, shorter".' Quant even gave the miniskirt its name, claiming that it was named after her favourite make of car, the Mini. It was to be one of the, if not *the*, defining fashions of the 1960s. And again it was young people at the forefront. Quant was just 26 years old when the Sixties began. Just as long hair on boys had parents up in arms, so too did the girls wearing miniskirt. Hoards of young girls give testament to leaving the house with their skirts just above the knees, only to be hitched up another 8 inches as soon as they were down the street and out of their parents' view.

Annie O'Malley in Manchester remembered Cathy McGowan: 'We used to watch Cathy McGowan on *Ready, Steady, Go*, and that was a big thing. All you ever talked about when you went into school or work on the Monday morning was who was on, who did you see, who did you like, what was she wearing.'

If there was one female face that epitomised the Sixties, it was that of Twiggy, the London-based model. Born Lesley Hornby in 1949 in Neasden, London, she shot to fame as a model during the mid-1960s.

She was as thin as a rake, and as such was nicknamed Twiggy, which rocketed her to international fame. With her skinny figure, short blonde hair, large eyes and long eyelashes, she was unmistakable on the catwalk and in the magazines. The press initially joked about her scrawniness, at a time when most models were far more voluptuous. But Twiggy, with her mischievous nature and Cockney accent, soon became a media star. She was the girl next-door and, like *Ready, Steady, Go* presenter Cathy McGowan, helped set fashion standards for all young girls.

Christine Parkinson remembered:

> 'We took a lot of care about what we wore. I had a Sandie Shaw dress which was black velvet, a short mini dress with a lacy collar. I had long hair as well and loads of Twiggy type make up; black eye liners and sometimes we used to draw eyelashes on the bottom lid. We thought we looked amazing, sometimes shimmery eye makeup on our eyes as well.'

Annie O'Malley added:

> 'Twiggy was the epitome, and I suppose as a young teenager I preferred Twiggy because she was very doll-like, very innocent and sweet. Also there was Patty Boyd who was George Harrison's girlfriend. She had that same doll-like look of Twiggy; she was very girly as well, rather than womanly. Sandie Shaw was pretty cool because she didn't wear shoes and that was getting into the hippy thing. I would also put rags in my hair so that I had a more tousled look.'

The other female face of the 1960s was Jean Shrimpton. Known as 'the Shrimp', she was more in keeping with the image of a traditional model than Twiggy. She too was young, a party-goer, girlfriend of celebrity photographer David Bailey, and helped popularize the miniskirt, causing an outrage when she attended the Melbourne Cup race meeting in Australia sporting a hemline 3 inches above her knees. Shrimpton and

Twiggy were fashion icons of the 1960s, featuring on the front covers of countless glossy magazines around the world.

It wasn't long before Mary Quant-style clothes hit the high streets around Britain. Another young designer, Ossie Clark, also began to make an impact with his more daring, adventurous lines. The high street was changing, with a new range of shops including Biba and Miss Selfridge, while London's Carnaby Street became the focus of young shoppers. In particular, the Lord John shop attracted male customers.

The young girls of the Sixties were the baby boomers, born immediately after the Second World War. There were half-a-million more teenage girls in the Sixties than there had been in the Fifties. The vast majority of them had jobs and money to spend, and what better way to spend it than on the latest fashion, be it for work or a Saturday night out. Biba founder Barbara Hulanicki remembered how 'they poured into London to their office jobs, earning £9 a week. They spent £3 on rent for their bedsit, £3 on food and the remaining £3 on clothes.' It was to make her fortune.

'We used to wear Biba which was popular and Miss Selfridge as well,' recalled Manchester-born Annie O'Malley. 'We used to shop at a place near Piccadilly bus station for the short skirts and you could buy Biba clothes at a shop near where Mark and Spencer's is now.' Manchester United footballer and style idol George Best also got in on the act, opening up his own boutique in Sale and later in the centre of Manchester.

Chart-topping Liverpool singer Cilla Black also wore Biba, in doing so giving a seal of approval to their styles. Biba was soon producing new lines every week at affordable prices. It was high street fashion for everyone. The newspapers and television soon picked up on the craze, featuring attractive teenagers in the latest styles. It was cool, cute clothing for skinny, teenage girls.

During the 1960s, a whole new range of magazines for young women and girls hit the market, including *Jackie, Teen Life, Twist, Mirabelle* and *Teen Beat*. They all catered for the new teenage girl, with articles and photographs about pop music, clothes, fashion and work. They also openly discussed the questions young girls were asking, and very much took the place of those staid magazines which had been aimed at women for decades, such as *Woman's Weekly*, *Woman's Own*, *Family Circle* and *Tatler*.

'My boyfriend and I are both 17. We are always having rows and he says it's my fault. Should I break with him?' was typical of the kind of letter that appeared in the magazines during the early 1960s. But as the Sixties progressed, the letters and advice took on a new form: 'My boyfriend just seems to look at me as a sex machine. You can be shocked if you like, but it's the truth and I'm desperate.'

Jackie was perhaps the best-known of the magazines. Launched in 1964, it dominated the market for almost twenty years, with weekly sales of 451,000 before ceasing publication in 1993. *Mirabelle* was also hugely popular, selling just over a half a million copies of each issue in the mid-1960s, but dropping to 175,000 by 1968.

Clare Jenkins was also reading the popular girls' magazines: 'At the time, I'd be reading *Jackie* magazine, and looking at all the groovy chicks in there, like Twiggy, and the cool boys, like The Small Faces, and mooning over the comic strip stories, and reading Cathy & Claire's advice to girls like me, usually about boys.'

In the 1950s, many women had made their own clothes, simply because they could not afford to shop at the high street fashion shops. Inevitably, there were girls in the 1960s who also could not afford to buy clothes; many of them were students. Consequently, they began to create their own fashions, rummaging around in Mum's or even Grandma's wardrobe as well as hitting the second-hand clothes shops, putting together contrasts of old and new and different types of material, from suede to velvet.

However, the new styles didn't always go down well at home, as Jean Birkett recalled:

'We had so many arguments at home about what I wore. I remember my dad disapproved of anything that resembled the Beatles' fashion. Any boys with long hair, or who wore black or leather and there would be derisive comments. I remember he was outraged by me making my own black leather miniskirt. I taught myself how to sew as I couldn't afford to go out and buy new clothes. I would copy

Biba fashions and another line called Dolly Rockers. And of course there was creatively modifying your school uniform – rolling up your skirt to make it as short as possible, as soon as you left the school. You'd hitch your skirt up and spend hours in the toilet backcombing your hair.'

Clare Jenkins also remembers making her own clothes:

'My sister and I made quite a few of our own clothes – the dresses at least, usually from Simplicity patterns. We both wore miniskirts – and, on our way to school, we'd roll up our pleated green skirts to make them shorter, then make them longer again once we were there. We wore shift dresses, I had a red one with a zip up the front and a matching hat, which I loved. It would have been the early 70s, I guess, when we started wearing maxi-dresses and long skirts. And I grew my hair quite long to go with the hippy vibe, wore dangly earrings, and so on.'

Annie O'Malley recounted the excitement she felt at the new fashions:

'There was a sort of antiques shop just under where George Best's shop was, and you could go down there and buy second hand clothes. I remember having a second hand beautiful suit that looked like satin. It wasn't but it was a long skirt with leg of mutton sleeves on it with lots of buttons down the sleeve and the jacket was like something Victorian that came in at the waist with 30 or 40 buttons down the front and a big bow on the back.

'We would wear mid-thigh skirts and also mid-shin skirts because maxi dresses were in. I remember when I was about 16 buying an orange suede coat which I thought was the bee's knees. I thought it was absolutely fabulous. And also we started wearing cloaks, floor-length cloaks with hoods. My friend had one of crushed velvet; mine was the same material as a blanket and I remember getting off the bus once and the driver saying, "see you got up late this morning." I also used to wear a poncho a lot, it was a bit like a blanket with the middle taken out. I loved my poncho and I wore it with pride. At the bank you had to be smart, we wore short dresses or midi. They didn't mind us having the hemline above the knees because that was the fashion, it was not a problem. My parents were ok about miniskirts although they did object to an Afghan coat which I had bought and stunk to high heaven. We used to leave our coats in a wardrobe in the hall and my Mum asking nicely if I wouldn't mind hanging it elsewhere as everything in the wardrobe was beginning to smell like the Afghan. We used to wear Afghan coats and loons, the bell bottomed canvas trousers and sandals. In winter you'd put on your fur coat or your Afghan coat and a pair of sandals and people were saying "are you not cold?" and we saying "no, no" when we were absolutely freezing.'

It wasn't just clothes that were radically changing; it was hairstyles too. Twiggy and Mary Quant were at the forefront, with young girls copying their styles, while a range of fashionable hairdressers such as Vidal Sassoon hit the high street, with salons dedicated to young styles and young people. Out went the rollers and in came the straight look.

Annie O'Malley recalled how important it was have to follow the latest look with your hair:

'Hairstyles were very, very important, and everybody fell in love with their hairdressers. We'd save up our Saturday money and go and have a haircut and dream over this guy who cut my hair. We had lots of fantasies. I remember having my hair cut like Julie Driscoll with a very short fringe and I also had, in 1967, a Vidal Sassoon haircut. It came over one side and you had a V and a V at the back and it puffed out and came down. And then there was Mary Quant of course; her style and cut. Before that everybody used to have to put rollers in their hair to get a style. I remember sleeping in these really hard plastic rollers, trying to get this hairstyle. It was really painful and as soon as you went outside the wind blew it away. But hairstyles were very, very fashionable. Eye makeup was really important. You'd have a line just above the eyelashes on your lid, and then you'd have a line just in the crease of your eyelid and then you'd have a line between the crease in your eyelid and your eyebrows and then you'd draw on little eyelashes at the bottom so that it gave your eyes this huge childhood look.'

Changes in men's fashion were also underway. In the 1950s and early 1960s, men's fashion was severely limited. Male office workers generally wore a suit, often with a waistcoat, and if they went out at weekends, even to the pub, men would usually wear something smart, most likely a suit. For casual wear, they'd probably wear grey trousers, known as slacks, and a smart jacket. But there were changes in the air.

If a man wanted new clothes, then he would go along to the local tailor, as Bob Jones remembered:

'I first started working in the early 1960s in an office job, so my father took me to the local tailors to get a hand measured suit. That was what you did in those days and they were expensive. First you chose the material and they took all your measurements. A couple of weeks later we went back and they had the suit all pinned up. So I had to try it on and they made adjustments here and there. Then I went back a couple more weeks later and the suit was finished. I'd try it on and if it was necessary to change anything they would. But generally it would be okay. This was the way it was done then. There were, to my knowledge, no off the peg suits although they would arrive within the next few years.'

Off-the-peg suits became the norm as the Sixties progressed and proved to be highly popular, mainly because they were considerably cheaper than a made-to-measure suit. They may not have lasted anywhere near as long, but it did allow for fashion changes. Lapels became narrower, there were flaps on the suit breast pocket, no flaps on the side pockets, no turn-ups, tighter trousers and no waistcoats.

It was the look of The Beatles, or rather their offstage look, which really took hold. Like The Beatles, most of the other pop groups wore suits on stage, along with white shirts and ties. But offstage it was a different matter. The Beatles would be seen wearing black polo-neck sweaters, tight trousers, Chelsea boots and leather jackets or coats – and always with a cigarette. It was the 'cool' look and was that image which really struck a chord with Britain's youth.

Teenage boys also began to experiment with fashion, though often with the connivance of their mothers. 'I had some corduroy trousers and I got my Mum to make them a tighter fit so that they would be more fashionable. I really loved those trousers,' remembered Bob Jones.

At the hub of the fashion revolution was Carnaby Street in London's West End. Prior to 1960, it had been little more than another narrow street in Soho, with the odd jazz club and a couple of small independent boutiques selling clothes. Just around the corner in Wardour Street was the Marquee Club, where The Rolling Stones played many of their early gigs. In 1958, fashion designer John Stephen had opened a boutique in Carnaby Street, and that was soon followed by other iconic shops such as Mr Fish, Ben Sherman and I Was Lord Kitchener's Valet. Innovative designers like Mary Quant also opened shops, and within a couple of years Carnaby Street became known as the best place to find trendy but inexpensive clothes. With fashionable clubs such as The Roaring Twenties and the Marquee Club nearby, it was inevitable that bands like The Beatles, The Rolling Stones and The Who would end up in Carnaby Street, rummaging through the clothes racks. By the mid-1960s, virtually every shop in Carnaby Street was selling clothes.

The pop group Small Faces were also crucial in the changing market of fashion. Known as Britain's best-dressed band, they had initially been paid in clothes rather than money. They were aspirational, working-class lads from the South, who began to adapt smart fashion to their own styles, introducing shorter-length trousers and lace-up boots. They were regular visitors to Carnaby Street, particularly to the Lord John boutique, and helped promote the image of Swinging London. Another group that shopped in Carnaby Street was The Kinks, who even had a major hit with their song 'A Dedicated Follower of Fashion'. As a result, Carnaby Street soon became synonymous with the Mod fashion phenomenon, with young working-class men flocking to its shops in search of sharp suits, followed by Hippies and party girls attracted by its new boutiques selling mini-dresses, kaftans and tee-shirts emblazoned with counterculture slogans.

Boutiques also sprouted up outside of Carnaby Street and London, particularly in the big cities. Even footballer George Best got in on the act, opening up a boutique of his own in Manchester. Annie O'Malley remembered:

> 'For a short time there was a shop around the back of George Best's called White Rabbit and we knew the people who ran it. My friend and I made shirts for it. We used to go to their house in Wythenshawe where they had about eight sewing machines. We'd stop for a coffee and a cannabis break! We used to have this grass in a jam jar next to the coffee!'

In April 1966, the American magazine *Time* proclaimed on its front cover: 'London, the Swinging City'. Inside, Carnaby Street was described as its 'epicentre'. No matter what you thought about The Beatles, or The Rolling Stones for that matter, there was no doubt that they had brought about a revolution in dress styles. Out went conformity and in came individuality.

Later in life, John Lennon was somewhat scathing of The Beatles' onstage dress code. 'We were the best rock and roll band in the world,' he claimed, 'until we were dressed in those fucking suits.' He would have preferred the black polo-neck sweaters, corduroy trousers and Chelsea boots that had been part of their style in their days at the Cavern, when they looked existentialist and enigmatic.

Chapter 16

A Shared Culture

When The Beatles jetted into New York's JFK Airport for their first American tour in February 1964, they were quizzed by the waiting press about their strange English accents. 'That's not English we're speaking,' replied George Harrison, 'it's Liverpudlian.' The Americans could perhaps be forgiven for thinking that they had strange accents. After all, accents from Liverpool, or for that matter any kind of regional accent, were not commonly heard on a national stage, be it radio or television. Wilfred Pickles, George Formby and Arthur Askey were about the only likely Northern accents to be heard over the airways. The perceived English accent was a BBC accent. But with the arrival of The Beatles, all that was set to change.

Television was already beginning to have an impact on people's lives by 1960. Although it had been transmitting for some years, it did not really begin to take off until the 1953 Coronation. That single event led to many people going out and either purchasing or renting a set. By 1960, the number of household television sets had soared. During the early 1950s, TV viewing had been restricted to the BBC, but then ITV launched as a commercial station in 1955. ITV was a breath of fresh air, introducing a mix of comedy, drama and sport, and above all a regional identity. Suddenly, television was taken out of the metropolis and the Home Counties and into the North, the Midlands, Wales and Scotland. The new franchises for ITV had been deliberately structured on a regional basis, with the headquarters of the new companies based in their regional cities. ITV, with its regional structure, might have been about making television commercial, but it was also about the democratization of television. Into play came regional accents, regional news and regional issues.

Leading the attack was Granada Television, set up in 1956 by Sidney Bernstein, a Jewish Labour Party-supporting businessman who already owned a chain of cinemas. Granada was to be so identified with the north-west of England that the region became known as Granadaland and boasted an array of Northern accents. And then in December 1960 along came *Coronation Street*.

Coronation Street was television's first soap opera based in the North. Ostensibly grounded in Manchester or Salford, it could be almost anywhere 'up North'. It was full of regional accents, regional characters and regional two-up, two-down houses in terraced streets. It also reflected the mood of the times. Principal character Ken Barlow was a young university student, the first of his generation or locality to go to university. He was typically full of himself; his learning and radicalism at odds with those of his parents. He tried to explain his ideas and hopes to them, but with little success, and wandered back to university for another term. Inevitably, he became a teacher, but ironically finished up returning to Coronation Street and a local school.

In time, Ken's rebelliousness would subside and his politics become a lighter shade of red. But for much of the Sixties, he was your typical teenage kid. Elsie Tanner also had a young son, Dennis Tanner, perhaps more rebellious than Ken Barlow, but with no education and no shaped political opinions. Barlow was the grammar school boy; Tanner the secondary modern kid.

Coronation Street initially began transmitting for a series of twelve programmes, but its immediate and surprising – especially to Granada executives – success led to its continuing transmission. What's more, it was broadcast nationally, not just regionally, so that the entire country suddenly became more aware of regional accents, attitudes and culture. 'Granada was at the vanguard of a new idea of the north that emerged in the early 1960s after more than a decade of Tory rule, promising a new vigour and vitality in place of a stale, southern Establishment,' wrote Joe Moran, Professor of Cultural History at Liverpool John Moores University, in his book *Armchair Nation*.

Granada took a pride in its region, which initially was the whole of the north of England, including Yorkshire and Tyne Tees, as well as the north-west. But in 1968, the other areas were hived off to new companies, leaving Granada with a more compact area stretching from the Lake District in the north to Crewe in the south, Derbyshire in the east and Liverpool in the west — and with 13 million potential viewers.

Granada was not producing just regional programmes. Apart from *Coronation Street*, a whole raft of programmes were being transmitted nationally, with *World In Action* leading the way in which current affairs programmes were made. There was no longer a deference being shown to politicians, and social issues such as the contraceptive pill, abortion and homosexuality were being raised for the first time on our screens. In a 1967 *World In Action* episode following his brief imprisonment for a drug conviction, a shy but confident Mick Jagger of The Rolling Stones was interviewed by four Establishment figures — William Rees-Mogg, editor of *The Times*; John Robinson, the Bishop of Woolwich; a leading Jesuit, Father Thomas Corbishley; and Lord Stowe-Hill, a former Home Secretary. In truth, his inquisitors looked like bewildered fathers trying painfully to understand what the hell was the matter with British youth. In what today looks a bizarre interview, they even refer to the Stones frontman as 'Mr' Jagger. With his long hair and kaftan coat, Jagger cut a very different figure to his bespoke-suited Establishment interviewers. 'Like most young people we just want to have as good a time as possible,' he tried to explain. And no, he hadn't sought to become a spokesman for his generation. The LSE-educated Jagger proved more than a match for his interviewers. If ever there was a contrast and a fitting portrait of what youth in Britain was about, this was it.

It was Granada which became aware of The Beatles before any other broadcaster. Leslie Woodhead, a young researcher with the company, had seen The Beatles at the Cavern, and although he was not from Liverpool, he was soon aware of their popularity. In October 1962, Woodhead persuaded Granada to do an item about them and made a short film at the Cavern, but due to a union problem the film was never shown until a year later, by which time The Beatles had topped the charts. It was the only footage ever made of The Beatles performing at the Cavern. In between, however, The Beatles visited Granada studios a number of times to do live performances. On one occasion, it was intended to film them preforming live in the Granada car park, but hundreds of fans descended, climbing over the wall and forcing The Beatles and the camera crews to retreat back into the building and the quieter surrounds of Studio 2.

Janice Finch remembered it vividly:

'My sister was with me and my friend was with me, and there were the Beatles in the car park setting up to do this live transmission of "Twist and Shout". They were there in their black polo-neck sweaters and suddenly they looked up and saw this horde of women running after them and had to run for it. The performance outdoors was abandoned and they had to do it inside in the studio.'

Elsewhere, Yorkshire Television and Tyne Tees as well as Border TV were doing much the same, although the majority of their programmes tended to be regional rather than made for the national network. The BBC was also becoming aware of regionalism and youth.

In 1960, the BBC was still a conservative, Establishment-led institution, presented and run by a clique of elderly, southern-accented males. Much was taboo; shots of pregnant women were not allowed and sex was a no-go area. Interviewers were deferential, never challenging their guests, never insisting on answers and most certainly never aggressive. Politicians especially were given an easy ride. It was equally true that interviewees were appallingly naïve, often honest with their answers and never evasive. There was a master/servant relationship, and the politician was the master. It hardly made for entertaining viewing. The only challenge to this style came from former Labour Minister John Freeman, who had begun to adopt a new style of interviewing with his BBC series *Face to Face*, where he interviewed a succession of prominent people. The programme began in February 1959 and continued until March 1962. Among those interviewed were the journalist Gilbert Harding, comedian Tony Hancock, artist Augustus John, philosopher Bertrand Russell and pop star Adam Faith. What was different about Freeman was not so much that he was aggressive or challenging with his interviewer, but that he ventured into their personal life with questions hitherto regarded as no-go areas for a television interview. It was territory where no other interviewer had ever dared venture, and it caused a furore. 'Why must the Prime Minister, the Foreign Secretary and other important persons of the day be constantly badgered ... to give interviews at a moment's notice on rave issues?' asked future Tory MP John Stokes.

But if television had long been beholden to the politician and celebrity, all that was to change in 1962 when David Frost and *That Was The Week That Was* hit the screen.

The show was devised and fronted by a group of young Cambridge graduates, including Frost, Peter Cook and John Bird, and was an intriguing mix of satire, comedy, music and current affairs. The presenter, Frost, was certainly no gritty, Northern, working-class lad; he was of Kentish stock, the son of a Methodist minister. But Frost was young, a recent graduate and full of the enthusiasm and fearlessness of youth. He was brash, and there was an arrogance of youth about him. Frost was as young as anyone appearing on British television at that time. In effect, Frost and company were taking satire from the subversive comedy clubs of London and placing it at the forefront of public life. Ned Sherrin produced the show, with John Cleese, Richard Ingrams, Gerald Kaufman, Frank Muir and Denis Norden all contributing scripts. Millicent Martin and Lance Percival sang the songs, Bernard Levin delivered the weekly essay, while Cook, Bird, Roy Kinnear, Frankie Howerd and Willie Rushton provided much of the comedy.

The roots of British satire could be traced back to the 1950s, with productions by the Cambridge Footlights and the Oxford Revue. Both companies, whilst producing mainstream comedy, had also experimented with satire in the late 1950s. In the summer of 1960, Robert Ponsonby, the artistic director of the Edinburgh International Festival, brought together members of both companies to put on a production of satirical and musical sketches to be called *Beyond the Fringe*. It opened in August of that year at the Royal Lyceum Theatre in Edinburgh as part of the Festival, before transferring to the Fortune Theatre in London. In between, it toured provincial theatres but failed to raise the pulses of any critics. Among those taking part were a number of actors and comedians who had recently graduated from Oxford and Cambridge, where they had performed with the Footlights and the Revue. They were all young, in their early twenties. Some, such as Jonathan Miller, had already embarked on totally different careers; Miller was training to be a doctor. Others participants included the pianist and comedian Dudley Moore, the writer Alan Bennett and comedian Peter Cook. The show was an immediate hit in London, partly ascribed to a glowing review in the *Observer* by the critic Kenneth Tynan.

Beyond The Fringe – like *That Was The Week That Was*, which was first broadcast in late 1962 – very much took a stab at the Establishment, lampooning politicians, the army and the Church. Violet Bonham Carter recorded in her diary in May 1961 that she 'shook and writhed and shrieked and shouted with amusement for two hours ... it was brilliant ... the targets were Macmillan, the church, philosophers and there were very good musical parodies.'

The Establishment was not amused. In particular, a sketch on *That Was The Week That Was* that suggested British soldiers had been war fodder during the First World War was greeted with incredulity by the armed services. Harold Macmillan, who had fought in the Great War, was also not amused, nor indeed were any members of the Conservative Party, which had been painted as aristocratic and out of touch. Yet despite not being particularly amused, Macmillan was shrewd enough to realize that any attempts to ban or censor the programme would lead to an outcry. Instead, he wrote to the Postmaster General, who controlled affairs at the BBC: 'I hope you will not, repeat not, take any action about "*That Was The Week That Was*" without consulting me. It is a good thing to be laughed at. It is better than to be ignored.'

Conservative MP Sir Norman Hulbert even raised a matter of possible breach of privilege in the House of Commons after the programme had named thirteen MPs who may not have properly carried out their Parliamentary duties. He was outraged, as were most of his fellow Conservative MPs. A *Daily Telegraph* leader added some highly critical comments about the programme.

But young people were thrilled at its anti-authoritarian attitude and its courage to have a poke at the Establishment. Even *The Times* gave it a reasonable review, recognizing the quality of its satire and presenter, though suggesting that 'it should be refined'.

Attitudes were changing, and *Beyond the Fringe* not only encapsulated those changes but also helped encourage and spread them. It was groundbreaking. Satire had been born, and although the show had been restricted to London audiences, there was clearly an appetite for wider viewing.

That Was The Week That Was was first broadcast on a Saturday evening in November 1962 and ran until the end of 1963, causing a sensation. It soon became compulsive Saturday evening viewing, each week viciously lampooning some politician or other. The producers could not have wished for a better moment for their first show, with the Profumo affair providing its writers with a wealth of material. It set the standard. The chief target for much of its run was Prime Minister Harold Macmillan, who epitomized everything they despised, most notably the aristocracy. Other targets included the majority of Conservative politicians, aged businessmen and crooks like the confidence trickster Emil Savundra. Important to the show's success was its informality, a stark change from the usual studio production. Cameras were often in shot, while footage of autocue and the waving of scripts emphasized the live nature of the programme. Performers would stumble over lines and miss cues, not to mention the fact the show often overran. Each edition was both hard-hitting and humorous, and regularly became the talking point in pubs, factory floors and common rooms for much of the following week. Young people anticipated the programme with glee, eager to see who might be the next candidate for lampooning.

After two successful runs, however, the BBC, typically for the time, decided not to screen a series in 1964 as it was election year and they did not wish to upset the politicians any further, or indeed show any bias; such were the stringent conditions that surrounded election programming at the time. By then, the show had upset so many Establishment figures with its no-holds-barred satire and stinging interviews that things would never be the same again. But the show also broke ground in style. It took place in front of an audience, was live and cameras were seen in shot as they wheeled around the studio. Movement on the set took place within full view, whilst there were a number of unrehearsed moments such as Bernard Levin being physically attacked by a member of the audience for a particularly critical review he had written.

TW3, as it became known, was as much a part of the swinging sixties as *Ready, Steady, Go* or Carnaby Street. After TW3 disappeared from our screens, it was replaced after the general election by a number of hybrid satire shows, generally employing the same cast and writers, but none were ever as successful as the first ground-breaking series of TW3.

Perhaps the most important aspect of television in the 1960s was that it had become a shared culture. By the end of the decade, virtually every home had a TV set, and television viewing had become the most popular leisure activity. Evenings were spent in front of the television. Like music and film, it was shared by the general population. Every morning, women at the school gates or men in factories would discuss the previous evening's viewing, be it *Coronation Street, Hancock's Half Hour, Beat the Clock* or *Sunday Night at the London Palladium*. These programmes were watched by millions. *Coronation Street*, at the top of the viewing charts, was regularly watched in 10 million homes twice a week, and sometimes as many as 14 million, meaning that at least 25 million individuals were watching each episode. Little wonder it was the talking point next day.

The influence of television was astonishing, with the boundaries constantly being pushed to new limits. For a large part of the decade there were only two channels to watch (BBC2 did not begin until April 1964, and was seen as a minority arts channel), concentrating viewing even more. ITV was always the most viewed channel, with its schedule of more popular and commercial programmes. As youth took over the Sixties and became rebellious, there was a search for a scapegoat. Not surprisingly, it turned out to be television, and perhaps with some justification. After all, its programmes did reach into almost every household every evening.

Leading the attack on television was Mary Whitehouse, a former teacher, Christian and member of Moral Re-Armament, who held no truck with the decline in the nation's moral standards. She argued that excessive sex, violence and bad language were leading the nation into moral decay, and it was all the fault of television. There was little she could do about ITV and the commercial sector, so the focus of her attention became the BBC and its Director General, Sir Hugh Carleton Greene. Whitehouse quickly became a figure of fun to British youth, as she represented everything they were rebelling against. Whitehouse, however, was not without her supporters. She set up a Clean TV Campaign (later to be the National Viewers' and Listeners' Association) and submitted a petition to the BBC with 500,000 signatures attached. But Greene, to his credit, stoutly defended the BBC against what he perceived as censorship. Comedians such as Benny Hill and Dave Allen, drama such as *The Singing Detective*, sitcoms like *Til Death Us Do Part*, pop music by the likes of Alice Cooper and Chuck Berry's *My Ding-a-ling*, and even the teatime favourite *Dr Who* came in for her disapproval. Whitehouse, despite being a joke figure to many, campaigned long and hard, annoying most people in the business, but in the end with hardly any success, apart from self-aggrandizement.

Television executive Michael Grade, who was on the wrong end of a number of Whitehouse's waspish criticisms, had doubts about her influence. Some years later, he told the *Independent* newspaper:

> 'I don't think she has had any effect at all. She never sees things in context. She will see something in an exploitation video and condemn it in the same breath as she will condemn a Dennis Potter classic. I respect her fortitude in fighting the battles over the years, trying to get her point of view across, but it is a point of view which would have totally destroyed British television if it had become the set of values by which we had commissioned programmes.'

Nevertheless, there is no doubt that television, both BBC and the independent sector, were pushing the boundaries in the Sixties. There was more violence and more bad language on the small screen than ever before, but there has never been any substantial evidence to show that this has had any effect in shaping our social lives.

On the morning of Saturday, 28 March 1964, Britain woke up to a new sound. It was the sound of pop music over the airwaves, only it wasn't from the BBC. BBC radio played virtually no pop music whatsoever, their only contribution being *Saturday Club*, hosted by Brian Matthew, which was broadcast every Saturday morning for two hours on the Light Programme. It was a show listened to by most young people, and over the years featured many of the major British stars, plus numerous American artistes, including Eddie Cochran, Gene Vincent, Duane Eddy and The Everly Brothers. It had even given The Beatles their first hearing over the airwaves when the group appeared on the show in January 1963, just a couple of weeks after *Please, Please Me* had been released. They would go on to make ten appearances on the show over the next few years.

But apart from *Saturday Club*, the BBC featured little other pop music. If Britain's youth wanted to listen to their kind of music on the radio, then they had to tune into Radio Luxembourg, which transmitted from a station based in the Grand Duchy of Luxembourg.

Rolling Stone Keith Richards remembered:

'[Radio Luxembourg was] notoriously difficult to keep on station. I had a little aerial and walked round the room, holding the radio up to my ear and twisting the aerial. Trying to keep it down because I'd wake Mum and Dad up. If I could get the signal right, I could take the radio under the blankets on the bed.'

Tuning into Radio Luxembourg was never easy, and the sound quality was often poor; it would fade, then rush back, and there was always a crackling in the background. Radio Luxembourg also had deals with some of the major record labels, so anything released on other labels simply did not get play-time. Britain's youth was thus starved of pop music.

Then a young music promoter called Ronan O'Rahilly stepped into the breach. O'Rahilly was the manager of Georgie Fame and his Blue Flames, but had found trouble in promoting his records. There were virtually no opportunities on the BBC, and Radio Luxembourg refused to play the record because Fame was not recording on one of the labels with whom they had deals. So O'Rahilly came up with the novel idea of purchasing a small ship, installing a radio station on board, along with a transmitter, and anchoring the vessel outside of British territorial waters, where it could legally transmit pop music. He called it Radio Caroline and chose to anchor it off Felixstowe, outside of the 3-mile limit, where in 1964 it began to transmit pop music throughout the evening. He did so with a succession of young DJs, including Simon Dee, Emperor Rosko, Tony Blackburn and Tommy Vance. The DJs were based on board the ship, where they would live and broadcast for a couple of weeks before having a week back onshore. The young DJs introduced a wacky style of broadcasting that had never been heard in the UK before. It was a mixture of chat, information and humour, aimed at appealing to British youth. It was also anti-authoritarian, irreverent and inventive. Within weeks, most of Britain's youth was tuning in. Radio Caroline proved to be so popular that a number of other pirate radio stations took to the waves, such as Radio London, Radio Atlanta and Radio Jackie.

Bob Jones had fond memories of the impact of early pirate radio:

> 'I remember going to see my mate one Saturday morning, and he said that the BBC had reported about this pirate radio station called Radio Caroline. He'd managed to tune in and he was raving about it, so we both went into his house and spent the next few hours listening. It was terrific.'

The pirate radio stations had begun life under a Conservative government, which turned out to be far more amenable to the idea than the Labour government that succeeded it. The Tories, many of whom were opposed to the BBC's monopoly, seemed happy to let the commercial pirate stations get on with it. But once Labour came into office in October 1964, there was a new approach. The Labour government was outraged at the temerity of anyone daring to challenge the BBC's monopoly over radio broadcasting. The debate went on for some time, with the BBC employing all sorts of dirty tricks to persuade Labour to take a tougher line. Eventually, in 1966, the Postmaster General, Anthony Wedgwood Benn, introduced a law to make pirate radio illegal. An Act of Parliament, known as the Marine Offences Act, came into force in August 1967 but initially had little effect, with Radio Caroline and its young DJs continuing to broadcast from international waters. One of the measures introduced under the Act had made it an offence for any British ships to leave British ports to supply any pirate radio station with food, mail and other supplies. This meant that the daily boat out of Harwich came to an abrupt end, but Ronan O'Rahilly sidestepped the Act by making arrangements for Caroline to bring in supplies from Holland instead. More effective, however, was the ruling to make it a criminal offence for any company to advertise on a pirate radio station. It was enough to frighten off all prospective advertisers, meaning Caroline's principal source of revenue was soon under threat.

Initially, the station operators thought they could get around the law if they were staffed, supplied and funded by non-British citizens, but this proved impractical. Eventually, unable to pay their bills, Radio Caroline and the other pirate radio stations reluctantly went off the air in 1968.

Nevertheless, they left behind a legacy. The BBC had been outraged at the pirate radio stations and had pressured the government to take action. But in the end, they bowed to the inevitable and sensibly decided to set up pop music stations of their own. It was almost certainly part of a deal conjured up with Labour. The BBC therefore restructured radio, launching Radio 1 as an exclusive pop station, and actually began to employ some of the disc jockeys who had made Caroline and other pirate stations so popular, including Tony Blackburn, Ed 'Stewpot' Stewart, Kenny Everett, John Peel and Johnnie Walker.

It had been a victory for the Establishment over young people who simply wanted to listen to popular music on their radios. But the demise of pirate radio did not go down well with young people, almost certainly losing the Labour Party votes in the 1970 general election and perhaps even costing them victory. Prime Minister Harold Wilson records in his history of the Labour government how he regularly faced hostile young demonstrators up and down the country, demanding freedom for the pirate stations. British youth did not forget. In the early and mid-1960s, Wilson had seemed to be on their side – to almost be one of them – but by the end of the decade he was a tarnished Prime Minister, just another Establishment figure, another figure of authority trying to stop them having a good time.

Oddly enough, television seemed at times to be more in tune with Britain's youth. BBC Television had begun transmitting *Six-Five Special* every Saturday evening at five minutes past six. It started in February 1957 and ended in December 1958. The show, produced by Jack Good, was filmed live from a studio and was a mixture of pop music and chat, featuring the likes of Lonnie Donegan, Marty Wilde, Tommy Steele, Jim Dale and Terry Dene, with disc jockey Pete Murray and Josephine Douglas as presenters. Unfortunately, the BBC – never that keen on pop music – wanted more chat and less music. Jack Good wanted the opposite – more music and less chat. It was clear what the viewers wanted, but that wasn't enough for the BBC. Inevitably, Good upped sticks and left, and not long afterwards the BBC axed the show. Good instead took his prototype to ITV, where he produced a half-hour live pop show called *Oh Boy*. It was similar in many ways to *Six-Five Special* and featured most major British pop stars, especially Cliff Richard, The Shadows, Marty Wilde and skiffle king Lonnie Donegan, plus a smattering of American artistes.

BBC Television's answer was to come up with *Juke Box Jury*, in which a panel of four judges and presenter David Jacobs would listen to and discuss the week's new releases and give them a score, before deciding whether they would be a hit or a flop. Although the programme had none of the vibrancy of *Oh Boy* or *Six-Five Special*, it was nonetheless popular, not just with young people but with their parents as well. All four Beatles appeared as the panel on one show, attracting a mammoth audience of 23 million. The Rolling Stones were also panelists one week, trashing every single record they heard. Keith Richards remembered it vividly: 'This was one of those landmark moments that completely escaped us while it was happening. But in the media later it was seen as a declaration of generational war, the cause of outrage, fear and loathing.' It was a good example of the different public images of the Stones and The Beatles.

The programme also got into trouble for playing a number of records that contained references to drugs. Generally, however, it was a harmless show, more a mix of chat and humour than anything else, although record promoters were always desperately keen to get their new record played on the show.

In 1964, BBC Television finally got back to live pop music with *Top of the Pops*, presented initially from Manchester. The programme was a rundown of the week's charts, with groups performing in the studio, although for many years they mimed their songs rather than actually singing them. The first show was presented by DJs Jimmy Savile and Alan Freeman and proved to be a huge success. Over the years, it featured all the major British and American pop stars and introduced a plethora of new DJs to British youth.

Ready, Steady, Go on ITV was the successor to Jack Good's hugely popular *Oh Boy*. Presented by Cathy McGowan, the show became a major hit. It was the usual mix of studio, chat and live music, with an audience dancing and looking as if they were enjoying themselves at some disco. Cathy McGowan added another important ingredient to the world of TV pop music – fashion. McGowan was just 19 years old and had been a secretary at *Woman's Own* magazine when she began presenting the show. She was stylish and a trendsetter. She wore miniskirts well above her knees, two-tone dresses, shifts and flared trousers, and soon became known as the 'Queen of the Mods'.

The author Dominic Sandbrook wrote:

'The show's most celebrated presenter, McGowan was the same age as the national audience; she wore all the latest trendy shifts and mini-dresses; and she spoke with an earnest, ceaseless barrage of teenage slang, praising whatever was "fab" or "smashing", and damning all that was "square" or "out". The atmosphere ... was like a King's Road party where all the performers themselves had only just chanced to drop by.'

At the time, McGowan reflected on how things had been for her when she worked for *Woman's Own*:

'It was horrid. These people of 40 used to water all my ideas down, because they never quite believed me. They looked at me as though I'd taken a turn ... now, on television, everybody takes notice of me.

It's lovely because I just wear the fashions and they catch on. More than anything I enjoy getting ready for the show. I love it! I love going to the hairdresser on Friday morning; I love dressing up and putting make-up on and even dabbing on the perfume. It's just like going to a smashing party.'

Supermodel Twiggy regarded McGowan as her role model: 'I'd sit and drool over her clothes. She was a heroine to us because she was one of us,' she told Dominic Sandbrook in his book *White Heat*. And it was true; McGowan did look like the girl next-door or the sixth form school prefect you admired. Other fashion gurus such as Anna Wintour testified to her influence not only on them but on the British fashion scene. Inevitably, Cathy McGowan soon had her own boutique selling her own designs.

Ready, Steady, Go began in August 1963 and was soon attracting a big audience, being hugely popular with young people. It had all the energy, chaos, and enthusiasm of *Oh Boy* and is still remembered as one of the most popular and influential television pop shows of all time. The show gained its highest ratings on 20 March 1964 when it featured The Beatles being interviewed and performing *It Won't Be Long, You Can't Do That* and *Can't Buy Me Love* – the latter being a hit at the time.

At Granada Television, producer Johnnie Hamp also dipped a toe in the water in November 1963 with a studio-based, hour-long pop programme, *It's Little Richard*, which also featured The Shirelles and Sounds Incorporated. In many ways it was a forerunner to *Ready, Steady, Go*, being filmed in a large studio with a dancing audience surrounding the pop stars. Little Richard was a sensation and the programme had huge ratings. The following year, in June 1964, Hamp repeated the exercise, this time featuring American rockers Jerry Lee Lewis and Gene Vincent, with Lewis surrounded by half-crazy dancing teenagers. Hamp recalls that the audience came mainly from Manchester University and the Manchester clubs Oasis and the Twisted Wheel. There was a particular dress code. 'The ticket for the show,' says Hamp, 'demanded leathers, sweaters, shades and no ties.' Nobody wearing a tie was to be allowed in. Also featured on the show were The Animals. Hamp remembers that Jerry Lee Lewis began his session sitting at the piano, but by the end, as it got wilder and wilder, he had discarded his jacket and tie and was standing on the piano, waving his arms and shaking his hips. The show was a sensation. Rock 'n' roll had probably never been better than this. The two shows have long been regarded by some as possibly the best live television rock 'n' roll ever.

And what of The Beatles? Leslie Woodhead, then a young researcher working on the regional news programme at Granada Television in Manchester, recalls their first ever television appearance:

'The guy who was running us said, find the most traditional and untraditional music things that are happening in our region. So I lined up the The Brighouse and Rastrick Brass Band. We went and filmed them. Then I remember asking a fellow researcher on *People and Places*, "What's the thing that's most unlike The Brighouse and Rastrick Brass Band in our area?" And he said, "I've heard there are these kids in Liverpool who are making a bit of a noise. Why don't you ring up a man called Epstein and see what's possible?"

'So I called and talked to Brian, met him in the Adelphi Hotel in Liverpool, went down to the Cavern Club, was completely blown away on a winter evening in '62, we agreed that we would come and film with them and we did that in August '62 in the Cavern Club, a lunchtime session, which became the first film ever made with The Beatles.

'I was fascinated by The Beatles, and followed them around the northern clubs as long as they were still playing the northern clubs, but we couldn't transmit the film because the Brighouse Band would have broken the local programmes budget for a month if we'd paid them full MU [Musicians Union] rates, so we were stuck with this half a film of The Beatles, and finally Brian Epstein collared me when I went to a concert – they were playing with Little Richard at the Tower Ballroom in New Brighton – and said, "When are you going to put the boys on TV?" And he wasn't kidding. He had me pinned against a wall. So the only thing we could do, since we couldn't say, "Brian, we've only got half a film, we can't put the boys on television," was to get them into the studio, which we did – and they did their first TV on *People and Places*, and then several more visits to both *People and Places* and *Scene at 6.30*, so that established that relationship.'

They later made numerous appearances on British television, including the Royal Command Performance at the London Palladium in front of the Queen. In February 1964, on the *Ed Sullivan Show* on CBS in America, they drew a record television audience for the United States of 73 million viewers. Then in June 1967, in a mammoth satellite link-up of nineteen different nations, they sang *All You Need Is Love* before most of the European continent.

The Rolling Stones also made one of their first television appearances on *Scene at 6.30* at Granada. Presenter Brian Trueman remembered it well:

'They came in and they were late and they were scruffy. They were quite noisy. They came in and they smelt a bit as well! I think they'd been in the van driven back from Germany or something and they smelt a bit. They made a fuss and messed up the dressing room but we did a studio piece and after that David Plowright, head of programmes, said "Right! That's it. A disgusting bunch. They're not coming inside this building again!!" He just wrote them off! Of course they did come back!'

Chapter 17

'We played it because we loved it'

Britain in the 1950s was far from the multicultural society that it is today. The *Windrush* immigration into Britain, beginning in 1948, had gradually accelerated throughout the 1950s as the nation looked to its Commonwealth countries, or Empire as it then was. In particular, it focused on the West Indies, for skilled and unskilled workers. There were jobs advertised for nurses, bus drivers, production-line workers and doctors. The Asian influx into Britain never really began until the 1960s.

So even into the early 1960s, Britain was still a largely white population. Yet despite immigrants arriving and being employed in vital sectors of the economy, not everybody was welcoming. Both the West Indian and Asian immigrants faced a multitude of problems, including housing, employment and blatant racism. Even the trade unions were obstructive. There were anti-immigration demonstrations in many parts of the country, while the prominent Conservative MP and former Minister of Health, Enoch Powell, made a damning speech in April 1968. In what became known as the 'rivers of blood' speech, he predicted the most appalling consequences of Britain's immigration policy.

Liverpool, however, had a long-standing black community. The Chinese population in the city had also been there for generations, mainly seamen, who either jumped ship or simply decided to settle in the city. Similarly, West Indian and West African seafarers had settled, many of them Somalis. Some of these communities went back decades. Primarily, they settled in the Toxteth (Liverpool 8) area of the city, close to the docks, where they could find work. Over the years, they opened their own clubs and community centres, often featuring their own music and musicians. But although the black community existed in substantial numbers, it went almost unrecognized in the city centre and confined itself to its own area, largely explained by the racism which its members had to confront if they ventured outside of Liverpool 8. For many decades there had been trouble, which eventually exploded onto the streets of Liverpool in 1981. But that is another story.

Liverpool had, interestingly, boasted two black champion boxers in the 1950s. The Nigerian-born Hogan 'Kid' Bassey, who had lived in Liverpool for most of his life, became world featherweight champion in 1957 and was always roared on by a passionate Liverpudlian crowd at The Liverpool Stadium, home of boxing on Merseyside, while Jamaican Joe Bygraves fought with distinction in the heavyweight division. Despite having lived in Britain for over ten years, Bygraves was barred from fighting for the British title and instead had to be content with the Empire crown.

Prior to The Beatles, black American music was largely unknown in Britain. Almost the only recognized black music in the early 1950s was West Indian calypso, which had briefly been popular, making it to the charts with hits such as 'Cricket, Lovely Cricket', which celebrated the famous Lords Test Match victory of the 1950 West Indian cricket team over England. Other calypso hits appeared later in the 1950s, the most popular being Harry Belafonte's 'Banana Boat Song'. There was also a black American vocal singing group called The Platters who had hits with 'Smoke Gets in Your Eyes' and 'The Great Pretender', and more notably a black boy band called Frankie Lymon and the Teenagers, whose record 'Why Do Fools Fall in Love' was a massive hit in 1956.

Plenty of teenagers also knew of Little Richard, who had top ten hits with 'Lucille', 'Good Golly Miss Molly' and 'Tutti Frutti' in the mid-1950s, but few other black artistes were familiar to British youngsters. But it was thanks to merchant seamen from Liverpool, known as the 'Cunarders', returning home with armfuls of records that they had purchased in the deep south of America or New York that black music slowly began to filter through. Initially it was in Liverpool itself, where groups like The Beatles, The Searchers, The Undertakers, The Big Three and Howie Casey and the Seniors began to play their music in the city's various music venues.

Not only did they play Little Richard songs, but also Chuck Berry numbers, such as 'Sweet Little Sixteen', 'Johnny B Goode', 'Roll Over

Beethoven' and 'Maybellene'. Berry hailed from St Louis in Missouri and was less well known. At the time, he was serving a three-year sentence in an American prison for having abducted a 14-year-old girl across the border 'for the purpose of having sexual intercourse with her'. Berry had pleaded his innocence, claiming that it was a racist slur. His imprisonment meant that he was unable to either record or even promote his own music. As a result, Berry went almost unnoticed outside of Liverpool.

Another popular, though lesser-known American group was The Coasters, with favourites such as 'Searchin'', 'Yakety Yak' and 'Poison Ivy'. They also played Bo Diddley numbers like 'Pretty Thing' and 'You Can't Judge a Book by Its Cover'. The music was rock 'n' roll as well as rhythm and blues. Some groups also played American Blues music, again an import from the sailors. Howlin' Wolf, Muddy Waters and Memphis Slim all contributed compositions that would be heard regularly at venues like the Cavern. Some of them later came over to Liverpool and played at the Cavern itself. Almost all these artistes were black and had recorded on small-time independent record labels, rarely achieving any national, let alone international recognition. Indeed, it wasn't until The Beatles had brought them to the attention of a wider audience that American teenagers became aware of rhythm and blues music.

It was The Beatles who did more than any other group to promote this black American music, particularly that of Chuck Berry, to a wider audience. They recorded Arthur Alexander's 'Anna' on their first album, a particular favourite of John Lennon's. In 1987, Paul McCartney said that 'if The Beatles wanted a sound, it was R&B. That's what we used to listen to and what we wanted to be like. Black, that was basically it. Arthur Alexander.'

Some years ago, McCartney also spoke about how The Beatles' music was influenced by Liverpool's different ethnic sounds. In particular, he mentioned 'calypsos via the Liverpool Caribbean community', which, he added, 'was the oldest in England'. McCartney claimed that sailors and immigrants made Liverpool a 'melting pot' of different ethnic sounds, adding that 'we took what we liked from all that'.

One of the most important, but lesser known, influences on The Beatles at the time was a certain Lord Woodbine, who had been born Harold Phillips in 1928 in Trinidad. He served in the RAF, and then in 1948 arrived in England on the *Empire Windrush*. He settled in Liverpool, where he worked (amongst other things) as a lorry driver, barman, decorator and builder. Lord Woodbine was a gifted musician, and his influence on Britain's black musical culture has never been fully acknowledged. He started and led one of the very first steelpan bands in Britain, the All-Steel Caribbean Band. He was also one of the first calypso singers to perform in Britain, and later Hamburg. Calypso singers are often referred to as 'Lord', while the 'Woodbine' part of his name came from a calypso he wrote about characters named after cigarettes.

Lord Woodbine, who was also known as Woody, was the business partner of Allan Williams, who worked in the early years as The Beatles' agent. Woodbine ran two clubs in Toxteth: the Cabaret Artistes' Social Club and then the New Colony. The Beatles played at both these clubs, and for a week or so played live musical accompaniment to a stripper at the Cabaret Artistes' Social Club. The young Beatles often socialized and drank with Woodbine, occasionally spending the night on the floor at his New Colony Club on Berkeley Street. Woodbine also helped arrange their first Hamburg trip, and went there with them.

John Lennon and Paul McCartney were intrigued with Woody and his calypso music. In 2008, McCartney recalled those times in *Mojo* magazine: 'Liverpool being the first Caribbean settlement in the UK, we were very friendly with a lot of black guys – Lord Woodbine, Derry Wilkie – they were mates we hung out with.'

In 1998, *The Observer* newspaper ran an article by Tony Henry that emphasized Woodbine's role in the musical development of the group and criticized writers on The Beatles for overlooking or downplaying this. Henry interviewed Woodbine before he died, as well as several of his contemporaries in Liverpool 8. The article detailed Woodbine's close involvement with The Beatles, although it focused more on the professional side than the music.

In an interview with the BBC's *Upfront* programme, Beatles academic James McGrath argued that Liverpool's black culture most definitely 'played a role in the Beatles' history' and that 'the importance of black Liverpudlian musicians has not yet been recognized ... but there's too much oral evidence on all this for it to be ignored.'

The Somali-Irish guitarist Vinnie Tow has also been acknowledged as showing John and Paul the seventh chord in the Chuck Berry style. John was always asking Vinnie, 'Show me this, show me that'. The Guyanese guitarist Zancs Logie was another willing teacher. In 1995, Woodbine told the writer Derek Murray: 'Zancs was always showing Lennon something. Until he died he was proud of how he taught Lennon to play guitar.' He transformed The Beatles from the Buddy Holly style of three-chord music to more playing sophisticated fifteen-chord numbers.

Other Liverpool contemporaries of the period suggest that Woodbine's role has been exaggerated, though notably not by Woodbine himself. Nonetheless, there is no denying that the calypso music of Woodbine was an influence on John and Paul, and that this, coupled with the black music of America and being taught some of the more complicated chords of Chuck Berry and Bo Diddley, expanded their musical horizons.

Although Thelma McGough does not remember Lord Woodbine, she does recall that that the main black musician around John and Paul at the time was Derry Wilkie, who went to Hamburg even before they did. Thelma remembered: 'Before he went to Hamburg, Derry was a male model at the art college while John and I were there.' Wilkie certainly hung around with The Beatles. He had been born in Liverpool in 1941 and lived in Upper Parliament Street in the Toxteth area. As a teenager, he joined a local band called The Hy-Tones, but soon teamed up with another band who were without a singer and they became known as Derry Wilkie and the Seniors, with Wilkie singing Little Richard-style. They soon became one of the most popular Liverpool bands of the time, playing all the clubs and often on the same billing as the lesser-known Beatles. The band were soon signed up to go to Germany and became the first British band to go to go to Hamburg, where they played for much of the summer of 1960 and were later joined by The Beatles.

Anyone who went to the Cavern in the years before The Beatles became widely known will testify that there was a dichotomy. On the one hand, there would be nobody there from an ethnic background, while on the other, The Beatles would spend the night playing numbers made popular by black musicians. These were the songs that resonated most with their Liverpool fans – basic rock 'n' roll, twangy guitars and a solid beat, with their sessions always ending with *Twist and Shout*.

There is no doubt that The Beatles wanted to create a sound that had black roots. They clearly loved the black music of Chuck Berry and company. Some years later, an article in the *New York Times* accused them of 'ripping off' black music. John Lennon was outraged at the accusation. He said they played it because they loved it, not because they wanted to steal it.

Chapter 18

The Fifth Beatle

George Best was young, good-looking and wore his hair long, like The Beatles. He was also stylish, always sporting the latest fashion trends. But more importantly, he was a brilliant footballer, playing with a swagger and style that matched his appearance. At Manchester United he became a fan hero, while elsewhere others just watched in envy and at times in disbelief as he tore opposition defences to pieces. Best was a winger who could dazzle with his mazy runs. At times the ball seemed to be stuck to his bootlaces. He was soon wearing the colours of Northern Ireland, and within a couple of years Manchester United were First Division champions.

If Best was a hero on the football field, he was a newspaper's dream off it. He was constantly spotted with attractive young women on his arm, including at one time Miss Great Britain. Everywhere he went, the paparazzi followed. He frequented the discos, and was rarely photographed without a bottle of champagne at his table. He later owned a nightclub in Manchester, called Slack Alice, as well as a fashion boutique in the centre of the city. 'Is he a player or a playboy?' asked the *People* newspaper. Best relied with his trademark Irish charm: 'I spent a lot of money on booze, birds, and fast cars. The rest I just squandered.'

The truth was that every young teenage lad wanted to be George Best, whether it be as a footballer or a playboy. And every teenage girl just wanted George Best.

Youth had already been given its opportunity on the football field in the Fifties when Manchester United manager Matt Busby began to introduce a crop of young players at Old Trafford into the first team, many of them aged under 21. They became known as the Busby Babes and would go on to win the First Division championship as well as appearing in two FA Cup finals and a European Cup semi-final. It was the first time any manager had introduced so many youngsters into a side, and United had quickly gone on to become the finest team in English football. Indeed, they were set to not only dominate the Football League for the next decade, but looked likely to become a major force in European football as well. Then in February 1958 tragedy struck when their plane returning from a European Cup quarter-final fixture in Belgrade crashed on take-off at Munich airport, killing eight players, two of the club's training staff and the club secretary. Eight leading football journalists also died, along with two air crew members and two other passengers. Not only Manchester but the entire football world went into mourning for their lost youth.

The Busby Babes, however, left a legacy, with football clubs more inclined to give youth its chance. More and more teams discarded their older players and began to nurture their youngsters. It was a trend that would continue throughout the 1960s. What's more, it would continue happening at Manchester United.

George Best, who was born in Belfast in Northern Ireland just after the Second World War, began to show promise as a footballer from his early years. At the age of 15, a Manchester United scout, Bob Bishop, saw Best playing for a local team and immediately informed United that he had spotted 'a genius'. United promptly invited him over to Old Trafford for a trial, where he was duly signed up, initially as an amateur. Best quickly impressed, turned professional, and in September 1963, at the age of 17, made his first team debut in the 1–0 league win against West Bromwich Albion. A legend was thus born. Over the next decade, George Best would be considered the finest footballer to ever come out of Northern Ireland, and one of the finest to have played in the English Football League.

In March 1966, he had almost single-handedly destroyed Benfica in Lisbon, scoring twice as Manchester United won their European Cup quarter-final second leg 5–1. That performance thrust Best onto the world stage, with the Portuguese press dubbing him the 'Fifth Beatle'. No other footballer, indeed no other sportsman, in Britain had ever received such adulation and publicity.

But drink and fame would eventually prove his undoing. Sadly, Best had a destructive streak. He liked his drink, inevitably stayed out late and skipped training, frequently testing the patience of Manchester United manager Matt Busby. In the 1970s and 1980s, the demon drink would lead him into considerable trouble, with a prison sentence (for drink-driving and assaulting a police officer) and numerous stays at rehab centres.

Yet despite the excesses, most of the time he could still produce the goods on the football pitch. When he was at the top of his game in the Sixties, he was irresistible, helping United to league, FA Cup and European Cup glory. He was the most famous footballer of his era, not just in Britain but in Europe, with leading clubs including Real Madrid and Juventus coveting his signature. He was British football's first pop star, his mischievous smile regularly splashed across many a front page.

Best was the changing face of British football. There had been plenty of exceptional young footballers before him, but somehow they always looked and acted older. They had earned at most the maximum wage of £20 a week, and their lifestyles reflected that. Best, however, was highly paid, single and free to do whatever he wished. He also spoke his mind. He thus epitomized the changing face of British youth.

Best, however, was not the only young sportsman hitting the headlines. In 1964, a young black boxer from Loiusville, Kentucky, defeated reigning world heavyweight champion Sonny Liston to become the new world title holder. Liston has been the most feared heavyweight since Rocky Marciano, having already battered popular champion Floyd Patterson in a first-round knockout to take the title. Liston was reckoned to be invincible, a champion who would be around for years. But on a steamy night in Miami in 1964, 22-year-old Cassius Clay pulverized Liston into submission, with the former champion unable to come off his seat for the seventh round. In their return fight fifteen months later, Clay floored Liston in the first round and the fight was over after just two minutes and twelve seconds.

America adores its heavyweight champions, and over the years had a virtual monopoly on the heavyweight crown. Joe Louis, Rocky Marciano, Floyd Patterson, Jack Sharkey, Max Baer, Gene Tunney and Jack Dempsey had all been American heroes. But when it came to Clay, America found it difficult to salute him as a hero.

It is conveniently forgotten that early in his career, Clay was not a popular figure in America. He was the most controversial black sportsman since Jack Johnson, another heavyweight champion who had shown 'two fingers' to white America. Clay was labelled a loudmouth, arrogant, a man who paid no heed to authority and, unlike so many champion boxers, had no links with the mafia. He also made rash predictions about the outcome of his fights. And many of his predictions came true, annoying the American fight press even more.

Four things, however, really set Clay apart from all his predecessors. First, he was an outstanding boxer; fast, deadly, always dancing on his toes and with seemingly limitless energy. Second, he was not a black man who was going to sit back and assume his place as a second-class citizen in his country, as had so many other black sportsmen, Jack Johnson apart. Third, he refused to serve in Vietnam. Clay had been drafted into the US Army, with the expectation that he would do his duty in Vietnam. But Clay had other ideas and was prepared to go to prison in order to avoid fighting in Vietnam. 'I ain't got no quarrel with them Vietcong,' he famously said, also later pointing out that 'no Vietnamese ever called me nigger'. And finally, Clay changed his name to Muhammad Ali in respect of his religion.

In America, the anti-war movement saw him as a role model. Other famous Americans had been drafted into the army at the peak of their careers, such as Joe Louis and Elvis Presley, but they had all accepted their fate with dignity and pride. But the Vietnam War was more confusing and ambiguous. Ali was instantly denounced by the newspaper columnists and TV pundits. They wrote that he was not a patriot, he was aiding the enemy, he was too big for his boots, he was dangerous, he was a bad example to America's youth, and so forth. Even the FBI began to take an interest. He was placed under surveillance, his phone was tapped and he was followed, and a fat file was soon built up.

Clay, or Ali as he was known by then, was the most important draft resistor in the United States. His case made headlines across the world, polarizing opinion, but at the very least it did show that there were prominent people who were prepared to put their principles before their fame and fortune. None of this won him many friends in the United States, though it did attract admiration elsewhere, particularly in Britain, where there was a considerably stronger and more accepted anti-war movement.

In his biography of Ali, David Remnick recounts how many young Americans – particularly black Americans – were overjoyed that someone, at last, was standing up to the authorities and refusing to be drafted into a war they did not believe in. For many, it was a cathartic moment. 'Ali's refusal to go to Vietnam touched young people, especially African-Americans,' wrote Remnick in his book *King of the World*. Ali was young, black, intelligent and a famous sportsman. If *he* was prepared to go to prison for his beliefs, then others would follow suit. It was a theory that the American authorities were all too well aware of, and they needed to take evasive action.

The black American essayist Gerald Early wrote:

> 'When he refused, I felt something greater than pride. I felt as though my honour as a black boy had been defended, my honour as a human being ... and I felt myself, little inner-city boy that I was, his apprentice to the grand imagination. The day that Ali refused the draft I cried in my room. I cried for him and for myself, for my future and his, for all our black possibilities.'

In 1967, Ali was convicted by an all-white jury and sentenced to five years' imprisonment for his refusal to join the army, but his case went to appeal and he was allowed out on bond. Nonetheless, his boxing license was stripped from him, and between 1967 and October 1970, when arguably he should have been at the peak of his ability, he did not fight. In the event, he did not go to prison, and in 1971 the US Supreme Court overturned his conviction. Ali was finally on the way to becoming a hero in his own nation, particularly among young people. As the Vietnam War ground to a stalemate and eventual American withdrawal, Ali's convictions took on a new significance. It was not surprising that when the Beatles visited America, they met up with Ali and had their photograph taken with him.

In England, sport also had its awkward squad. Chief among these was Jimmy Hill, a young Fulham footballer who, as chairman of the Professional Footballers' Association (PFA), led the campaign against the maximum wage for footballers. Hill was intelligent, articulate and persuasive. He argued that the maximum wage policy, which stood at £20 a week and had been in force for over sixty years, was an anathema in the modern footballing world. British footballers were being lured abroad by the promise of astronomical salaries, and if the £20 maximum continued, many more would be tempted to go and play in the likes of Italy and Spain. In 1961, the Football League, after considerable haggling, accepted the players' argument and backed down. Players were now free to earn whatever they could negotiate with their club.

Nevertheless, there was still a further dispute to be settled. Up to this point, footballers had signed a binding contract with their club that the players called a 'slave contract' as it bound them to the club for life. They were especially not allowed to ask for a transfer, although if the club wished to sell them onto another club, they could do so without even asking the player's permission. Indeed, many players did not learn that they had been sold to another club until after the deal had been completed.

George Eastham, a young player with Newcastle United, had wanted to leave Tyneside and join Arsenal but had been refused a transfer by his club. Eastham then challenged the decision in the courts. In January 1961, the PFA, under Jimmy Hill, backed him and threatened strike action. It made headlines, with the *Daily Mirror* voicing full support for the PFA. The strike was set for 20 January, but after five hours of heated discussions between the parties that even involved the Minister of Labour, John Hare, the strike was eventually called off, the Football League having agreed to scrap the 'slave contract'. Players were now free to move as they wished. It was a massive victory that would have major repercussions for football in Britain. It had been largely brought about thanks to the young Jimmy Hill. Such was Hill's eloquence and persuasiveness that he was immediately offered a job on television, and went on to become the voice of TV football.

What was important was that this was another smack in the face for authoritarianism, and there were at the time few more authoritarian institutions than the Football League. It had taken a young man to overthrow sixty years of intransigence and conservatism. The Establishment had taken another blow.

During the 1960s, politics entered the sporting arena in a more prominent manner. Politics had always been there, particularly in the 1930s, but there had rarely, if ever, been any boycotts. The British Olympic team had entered the 1936 Berlin Olympics without any compunction, although they generally shied away from giving the Nazi salute. The same could be not said for the England football team who had faced Germany in a friendly game in Berlin in May 1938; on the orders of the British Foreign Office, they had all given the Nazi salute before the match kicked off, though clearly with some reluctance. One player could be seen looking down the line to check who was giving the salute before nervously raising his own arm. Their gesture caused an outrage in the British press, with a photograph splashed across the front pages which was said to have paved the way for Prime Minister Neville Chamberlain's later attempts at an appeasement policy with Nazi Germany.

Two political factors came into play in the world of sport in the Sixties, although both were intricately linked. The first was apartheid in South Africa and that nation's right to participate in world sport, and the second was the Black Power movement in the United States.

Apartheid in South Africa had become a major issue in the UK, reflecting the fact that South Africa had been a member of the British Commonwealth but had been expelled in 1961 due to its abhorrent racial system. As a Commonwealth country, South Africa inevitably played a number of typically British sports, particularly cricket, football, rugby union and athletics, and regularly participated at an international level in many of these sports. After South Africa's expulsion from the Commonwealth, a question mark was raised over its participation in international sport. A number of international sporting bodies, such as FIFA (representing football) and the International Olympic Committee, promptly expelled South Africa from participating at international level. In Britain, however, both the rugby union and cricketing authorities continued to invite South Africa to tour Britain. As a consequence, these tours became a controversial issue with many organizations, notably the Anti-Apartheid Movement, the Labour Party, trade unions and other left-wing bodies, as well as many students, and developed into a major focal point for demonstrations.

The most notable event was the D'Oliveira affair, when South African-born mixed-race cricketer Basil D'Oliveira was told that he would not be welcomed as a member of the England touring team in South Africa if selected. As a result, the England selectors at the MCC initially omitted D'Oliveira from the side, despite the fact that he had hit a dazzling 158 in the final Test against Australia. His omission from the forthcoming tour was consequently greeted with disbelief, especially as it was widely known that the South African government had warned about his inclusion. The MCC selectors, surely the most Establishment body in world sport, claimed that his omission was due solely to his poor form, but everyone else suspected otherwise. A few weeks later, England bowler Tom Cartwright pulled out of the tour with an injury, and with a media frenzy in full flow, D'Oliveira was chosen as his replacement. The England selectors were now making fools of themselves and were informed by the South Africans in no uncertain terms that D'Oliveira would not be welcome. South African Prime Minister John Vorster insisted that his country was not prepared to receive a team selected for political reasons. 'The MCC team is not the team of the MCC but of the anti-apartheid movement,' Vorster claimed. With the frenzy hitting the headlines every day, and with no guarantee that either the England team or D'Oliveira would be allowed into the country, the England selectors, after desperately trying to find a compromise, finally pulled out of the tour. Nevertheless, this was not before there had been further demonstrations and protests. By now, apartheid in South Africa and that country's role in international sport was under the spotlight.

In November 1969, the South African rugby union side began a tour of the UK which was to be one of the most bitter sporting tours in history. There had been repeated calls for the tour to be called off, but the rugby authorities had ignored all the pressure. The opening game against Oxford

University was originally scheduled to be played in Oxford itself, but with growing discontent and the threat of demonstrations, it was rearranged and instead played at Twickenham in London. The game was still greeted by a huge demonstration, mainly by Oxford University students who had journeyed down to London for the occasion. One student even hijacked the team coach and began to drive it away with a couple of startled Springbok players on it and wondering what on earth was going on. The coach didn't get far. Inside the ground, thousands of spectators turned their backs on the game, while a handful of students succeeded in invading the pitch, with one actually managing to shin his way briefly up a rugby post before crashing to the ground and into the arms of the police. Dozens of arrests were made, and from then on every game of the tour was greeted by huge demonstrations and disruption. The tour was successfully completed, but not without cost. Hundreds were arrested, the policing bill was enormous and Britain's reputation among the black Commonwealth countries was severely damaged.

The Springboks even faced demonstrations from the teams they played in the tour. Welsh flanker John Taylor opted out of playing in the match against South Africa, while coach Carwyn James refused, as a protest, to come out of the dressing room during his team's match. Students had played a major part in the protests, organizing marches and demonstrations in London, Leicester, Cardiff, Manchester, Bristol and elsewhere.

Both the D'Oliveira and Springboks conflicts were between the old order, who saw apartheid as acceptable and an issue that could only be changed through talking, and young people, who demanded direct action and were prepared to face arrest and the wrath of the older generation in support of their views.

The most prominent protester was a young Peter Hain. Nineteen-year-old Hain, whose family had been exiled from South Africa because of their opposition to apartheid, was the principal organizer behind the Stop the Seventy Tour (which successfully campaigned against the all-white South African cricket team's tour of Britain in 1970), thereby cutting his teeth in the world of politics. Hain was a Young Liberal, but would later become a prominent Cabinet Minister in the Labour government of Tony

Blair and Gordon Brown. Hain was vilified by much of the British press, who nicknamed him 'Hain the Pain', but as a young person he showed the energy and commitment to ensure that the rugby and cricket authorities would, in the future, think twice about ever inviting a white-only South African side to Britain.

The other Sixties political event surrounding racial matters that sent shockwaves around the world came in the 1968 Olympic Games in Mexico City, where the black American sprint medallists Tommie Smith and John Carlos gave the Black Power salute as they collected their medals. Smith had won the 200 metres sprint in a new world record time, with the Australian Peter Norman second and Carlos in third position. At the medal ceremony, as the American anthem was being played, the two Americans both raised a clenched black leather gloved fist to the sky. They were also shoeless as a mark of respect for black poverty, and both, as well as the Australian Norman, wore Olympic Project for Human Rights badges. You could almost hear white America shudder in anger as the duo raised their fists and bowed their heads. It was a symbol that was to reverberate around America and beyond, and even today is regarded as one of the most political gestures ever made at an Olympic Games. It came in a year when Black Power had asserted itself in the United States as a doctrine, and at a time of massive confrontation in many American cities. Detroit, Miami, Chicago and other cities all experienced demonstrations and violence that left large areas in flames. The American media was horrified; their gesture was regarded as an affront to the nation. When they should have stood proud, arm across chest, saluting the American flag, instead, as the star spangled banner was slowly raised, they were labelled as bringing shame on their nation and themselves. Their photos were splashed across the front pages of every American and European newspaper.

The Olympic Committee was also outraged at the gestures of Smith and Carlos, demanding that both men be suspended from the American team. When the American team refused, Olympic chairman Avery Bundage threatened to expel the entire USA track and field team from the games. As a result, the USA complied and Smith and Carlos were expelled. Once back in the United States, both men were ostracized by most American sports bodies and heavily criticized by the US press, although in later years there was more of an understanding of their gesture, particularly by the black community. Australian Peter Norman also found himself under heavy fire back home and was shunned by the athletics authorities, which even excluded him from their 1972 Olympics sprint team despite having easily qualified. All three were young men who had the strength to stand up for their beliefs, even though it brought an end to their sporting careers.

Chapter 19

The Beatles are Coming!

By 1964, The Beatles had taken Britain by storm. Beatlemania was everywhere. Nobody had seen anything like it before. Wherever they went, they were besieged. At concerts, thousands of hysterical girls out-screamed the onstage noise from the band's amplifiers. Barriers had to be erected outside theatres where they were appearing and police had to be brought in to control the crowds. And now The Beatles were about to invade the rest of the world.

During their formative years, The Beatles had played in Hamburg to small audiences in a dark cellar not unlike the Cavern, but apart from that had never ventured abroad. Then in October 1963 they played five concerts in Sweden. On the day they returned from the short Swedish tour, American TV host Ed Sullivan happened to be passing through Heathrow airport and was astonished to see thousands of screaming girls. 'What's going on?' he asked. 'It's The Beatles,' he was told, 'they're just coming back from Sweden.' The showman Sullivan, wise enough to realize that this was something big, promptly suggested booking them for his US show.

But before taking up their invitation to the USA, The Beatles had a three-week, eighteen-show residency at the Olympia in Paris in early 1964. Paris went wild for them. Their fame was suddenly spreading, not only beyond Liverpool and around Britain, but internationally.

Three weeks in Paris was immediately followed by their first visit to America. When The Beatles flew into New York, they were greeted by 4,000 screaming teenagers at JFK airport. The group had scored its first No. 1 US hit just six days before with 'I Want to Hold Your Hand', but still nobody expected a reception quite like this. And this was an America still shell-shocked and in mourning just a few months after the assassination of President John F. Kennedy.

First up was *The Ed Sullivan Show*. It might have been one of American TV's biggest shows, but even the producers were astonished at what happened. More than 50,000 people had applied to be part of the studio audience. Although it was difficult to hear the performance over the screams of teenage girls in the studio, an estimated 73 million US television viewers – or about 40 per cent of the nation's population – tuned in to watch. It was a record TV audience. Sullivan, who had made a sly dig at The Beatles and their style of dress when he introduced them, was almost speechless as the show ended. They were immediately booked for two more appearances that month.

In her book *Beatleness*, American sociologist Candy Leonard had no doubt that The Beatles had changed America: 'They were a non-stop influence in the USA for six years. When you think of the size of the baby boomer generation, they had this power on us for six years as consumers and protestors. The Beatles, they became very significant to the story of post-war American history.'

The group made their first public concert appearance on 11 February 1964 at the Coliseum in Washington, D.C., and 20,000 fans attended. The next day, they gave two back-to-back performances at New York's Carnegie Hall, and police were forced to cordon off the streets around the famous concert venue. America had seen nothing like it since the early days of Elvis. Most agreed that this was even bigger.

American journalist and Beatles fan James Rosen says: 'With their music, their very presence, their humour, their wit, their good looks, everything about them, helped the United States emerge out of that period of mourning [after the murder of President Kennedy] and really touched off the sixties as we think if it.'

History professor Melanie Tebbutt points out:

'Lennon, himself an early baby boomer, born in 1940, famously summed up the sense of a new global phenomenon most visible in Europe and the United States when he remarked of the Beatles in 1966 that they were "more popular than Jesus". Lennon was, in fact, commenting on a unique social phenomenon: Europe and North

America were the first societies to deal with a growing number of young people in their teens and early twenties who were demanding and creating lifestyles often opposed to those of their parents.'

Their singles and albums sold in their millions, and at one point in April 1964, all five best-selling US singles were Beatles songs. By the time The Beatles' first feature-film, *A Hard Day's Night*, was released in August that year, the Beatlemania epidemic had spread over almost all the world. Later that month, the four boys from Liverpool returned to the United States for their second tour and played to sold-out arenas across the country. By now, The Beatles were topping the hit parades in nearly every country in the world apart from those in the Soviet Bloc. But even there, it was impossible not to have heard of them. *A Hard Day's Night* played to packed cinemas, with queues stretching up and down streets around cinemas. The film would go on to gross £10 million, a huge amount for those times. Even Elvis was overshadowed. Some say he was even angry and jealous at their success.

After America, most of 1964 was spent touring abroad, with concerts in Denmark, the Netherlands, Australia, New Zealand, Sweden again and then back to America. Their second US tour in August 1964 took in twenty venues, beginning in San Francisco, and also included Las Vegas, Philadelphia, Boston, Los Angeles, New Orleans, Kansas City and Dallas before ending at the Paramount Theatre in New York. Many of those concerts were in stadiums playing to vast crowds. Within eight months of The Beatles' first appearance on *The Ed Sullivan Show*, the group had twenty-eight records in Billboard's Hot 100 Singles chart, eleven of those in the Top Twenty. They also had ten albums released worldwide, five of them on Capitol Records. The Beatles had really arrived, smashing box office, chart and audience attendance records everywhere, whilst creating mayhem and chaos wherever they went.

In his account of the second Beatles tour, *Ticket to Ride: Inside the Beatles' 1964 Tour That Changed the World*, broadcast journalist Larry Kane wrote of 'high drama, on the verge of violent and deadly chaos: Crowds awaiting the Beatles surge out of control, a fan gets shoved through plate-glass windows.' The Beatles were also beginning to get concerned, sometimes fearing for their own lives. They had worldwide fame, but were now wondering about its ramifications.

They were weary and needed a good rest after their travels, so spent the next six months in the UK; some of it on the road, some of it in the recording studio. Then in June 1964, they kicked off another international tour, beginning in France, followed by Italy and Spain before landing back in America. Their first gig there was at the Shea Stadium, home of the New York Mets baseball team. More than 56,000 people turned up, then a record crowd for a pop concert. It really was pandemonium.

The Beatles arrived by helicopter, looking on in disbelief at the vastness of the crowds both inside and outside the stadium as they approached. As the helicopter hovered tantalizingly overhead, the crowd went berserk. Dozens of security men had to guard the band as they pushed their way from their dressing room towards the dugout entrance. The Beatles were introduced to the crowd as they walked from the dugout area to the stage, with their fans going even wilder. Running towards the stage, they looked up in awe at the vast crowd. Girls were screaming, jumping up and down, climbing over barriers, rushing as far to the front as they could get, with the NYPD police battling to keep control. First aiders tended to those injured in the scramble or suffering from shock. Then, after a quick tune-up, the boys began. But in truth, they couldn't even hear themselves playing above the screams and shouts. It was to spell the beginning of the end of stadium tours for the Beatles.

Fox News Washington correspondent James Rosen said:

'It was like they sent a signal up to teenagers across the country, across the world, that it was okay to let it all hang out. The Beatles were a force for freedom, culturally, politically, in fashion sense, with their hair, the way they spoke their minds. That's why they were so revolutionary and they caught on so big.'

New Yorker editor David Remnick was also of the opinion that The Beatles had a major influence on American youth culture. Writing of Paul McCartney years later he said:

'[He] played a pivotal role in the rise of rock and roll, the invention of the teenager, youth culture, and the sixties. Not everyone took part in global Beatlemania – there were not many Black fans in the Shea Stadium news footage – but the band was at the center of the closest thing we'd ever had to a pop monoculture after the Second World War.'

The Beatles had certainly won the West, but they had yet to win in the East. The Beatles had conquered young people in Britain, the United States, France, Germany, Japan, Australia and most other countries, but had still to make their mark behind the 'Iron Curtain'. In 1961, a wall had been erected overnight in Berlin, after which freedom of movement between East and West descended into a new era of isolationism.

Throughout the Sixties, the Beatles were regarded as an anathema by the authorities in Eastern Bloc countries, who seemed to see all young people as vulnerable and easily corruptible, to the extent that they frowned upon and took action against any individuals attempting to break down cultural barriers. All Eastern Bloc countries needed to keep a tight rein on all possible influences that might emanate from the West, be it politics, culture or even sport. Soviet communism was best, they argued. Pop music was just one of the many forms of western culture that was prohibited. All western imports of culture – be it jazz, dance or pop music – were regarded as a seditious force and were made illegal. And that included The Beatles. Their music was forbidden, with a ruling that they were to never play in the Soviet Union. And nor did they.

But that didn't stop enterprising young people in the USSR from getting their fix of The Beatles. Radios were finely tuned, albeit illegally, to western music stations such as Radio Luxembourg, Voice of America and the BBC.

'The cold war was won by the West,' says Artemy Troitsky, 'not by nuclear weapons but by the Beatles.' Troitsky was one of numerous young Russians cited by Leslie Woodhead as loving The Beatles, tuning into their music on crackly radios.

One academic at the Institute of Russian History in Moscow told the documentary producer and writer Leslie Woodhead: 'Beatlemania washed away the foundations of Soviet Society. They helped a generation of free people to grow up in the Soviet Union.'

As a documentary filmmaker working for Granada Television, Woodhead had been the first person to film The Beatles in August 1962 when he made a black and white two-minute cameo film for Granada's evening magazine programme. Over the years, Woodhead visited the USSR on many occasions, often illegally, to make films about repression and samizdat dissidents in the country.

Years later, Woodhead's book *How The Beatles Rocked the Kremlin* told the story of the dissidents who spread the word about The Beatles. Woodhead himself smuggled the occasional Beatles tapes into the country, passing them on to the dissidents. Recordings also came from elsewhere, and each would be re-recorded, copied and smuggled out to a network of other Beatles fans around the country. Over time, thousands of copies would be made as each new album was released. The Beatles may have been illegal in the USSR, but if you knew the right people, you could get hold of their latest album almost as soon as it had appeared in the shops of London or Liverpool. Lyrics were also copied and passed on. Kids made scrapbooks of Beatles pictures, lyrics and drawings, and secretly hid them away. There were illegal gatherings of aficionados, and even a few 'copycat' bands which would play the occasional gig when the KGB wasn't looking or listening. It was a dangerous hobby, but if nothing else, young people have little fear. In the end, their movement grew, and when Mikhail Gorbachev succeeded Konstantin Chernenko as head of the USSR in March 1985, a new era of reforms was born. An official 'rock laboratory' was launched in Moscow, where young musicians could buy instruments and recording equipment. Then in March 1986, the state record label Melodiya released the first ever-complete Beatles recordings, though in limited numbers. Thousands of excited fans queued in disbelief.

In his book, Woodhead also quotes a leading dissident of the time, Boris Grebenshikov: 'The Beatles started to change the way people think, the way people feel.' The dissident Art Troitsky added: 'They alienated a whole generation from their communist motherland, and prepared Soviet kids for different human values. The message we took was we're free even though we live behind the Iron Curtain.'

Before long, the floodgates were opening. British and American bands even began to tour the USSR, although tours were generally limited to Moscow and Leningrad. Paul McCartney, at the request of some of the dissidents, recorded an album of classic R'n'B hits, specifically for release in the Soviet Union and as a gesture of thanks to his many fans there. 'The new spirit of friendship opening up in Russia,' McCartney said, 'had enabled me to make this gesture to my Russian friends and let them hear one of my records first for a change.'

Then in May 2003, 100,000 people gathered in Moscow's Red Square, not for some military parade or state funeral, but to hear McCartney, one of The Beatles, at last play live for them. A huge cheer went up as he hit the first chord: 'Back In The USSR'.

Elsewhere in Eastern Europe, there had been the same closed society. From Romania to Poland, East Germany to Czechoslovakia and from Hungary to Albania, The Beatles were *persona non grata*. There were no records in the shops, no tours, no mentions in the press, no songs played on the radio or television. Then in 1968, a series of events came from a totally unexpected and unpredictable source in communist Europe, with an upheaval in Czechoslovakia that threatened to shatter the Cold War politics of post-war Europe. Of course, somewhere in the mix of it all were young people and Beatlemania.

The seeds of the crisis were sown in January 1968 when reformist politician Alexander Dubcek was elected as First Secretary of the Communist Party of Czechoslovakia. Dubcek was a liberal and no fan of the authoritarian centrist system of the Soviet Union. Once in power, Dubcek began a series of reforms that would have devastating consequences. It became known as the Prague Spring, as a new nation seemed to be born. Many of the reforms were of a social nature, with a loosening of restrictions covering travel, the media and freedom of speech. Other changes brought about an easing of economic constraints and some political decentralization. Importantly, one of the reforms included loosening strict restrictions on the media – for the first time, young Czechs could listen to The Beatles on the radio.

For those in the West, these reforms were barely radical, but within the Soviet Bloc they constituted a serious threat to the system and to European communism. The Soviet Union was hardly delighted at the notion of such changes, fearing that if Czechoslovakia went ahead with them, then the rest of the communist block might follow suit; it was a serious challenge to Soviet power, and who knows where that could lead? Soviet leader Leonid Brezhnev quickly realized the danger of the situation and began discussions with Dubcek aimed at reining back any such reforms. But Dubcek was having none of it and remained intent on progressing his reforms.

The Beatles, of course, were never far away from the action. Their carefree, 'let's change the world' attitude had been exported around the world, and the Soviet Bloc was no exception. In May 1964, the British Ambassador in Prague had written a 'restricted' memo to the Foreign Office back in London pointing out the effects of Beatlemania in Czechoslovakia. He noted that 'its enthusiasts are apparently moved by it to spontaneous breaches of the peace in much the same way as British contemporaries.' There had, he said, been serious disturbances at a big beat band contest at the city's congress hall, which had to be broken up by the police and the hall cleared. This had in turn led to 'hoodlums roaming the streets', with fights and arrests made by the police. Meanwhile, guitars had become virtually unobtainable in the shops. The seeds for reform were being sown, and a few years later, Dubcek was responding to the drive for change and liberalism. But that was not what the Czech's Soviet masters had in mind.

As a result, on the night of 20 August 1968, 200,000 Warsaw Pact troops swept across the Czech border and pushed on into Prague. 'A day that will not be forgotten,' wrote Tony Benn in his diary. Such was the swiftness and force of the invasion that the Soviets met little opposition. A total of seventy-two Czechs were killed, but with large border areas still free and open there was a mass migration from the country, with over 70,000 people reported to have fled the Soviet tanks and made for freedom in Western Europe. That is not to suggest that there was no opposition.

Indeed, it was extensive, but it was generally non-violent. Most of the opposition came from the Beatle-loving young. Students stood on top of Soviet tanks waving the Czech flag, daring the Soviets to take action. Others gathered in the capital's main squares to voice their protests. There were sit-down demonstrations, while others defiantly bared their chests before the gun turrets of Soviet tanks. In one of the most remarkable and courageous incidents of the Prague Spring, Czech student Jan Palach publicly set himself on fire, later dying of the burns he suffered. Two other young people also set themselves on fire. 'It has had an explosive effect on an already explosive situation,' Violet Bonham Carter wrote in her diary. 'Crowds assembled in the Wenceslas Square and elsewhere in tears of grief and despair. Czechoslovakia is a nightmare – a Russian crime.'

Outside of Czechoslovakia, there were major demonstrations against the invasion, mostly co-ordinated by young people who saw the Soviet action as an authoritarian response to the Czechs' demands for greater freedoms. Even international communist parties were appalled, with many denouncing the invasion as anti-socialist. The reaction was much the same as it had been over the Hungarian invasion in 1956. Students marched in most capital cities across Western Europe to denounce the invasion. But it could only ever be a gesture. In truth, there was little the West could do. Nobody was suggesting a counter-invasion, and there were few effective measures that could be taken against the Soviets. The events only sought to emphasize the intolerable authoritarianism of the Soviet regime and the steps to which Moscow would go in order to maintain its control over the Eastern Bloc countries. It was a dire warning to every communist state in Eastern Europe that if they too dared to venture down the path of liberalism and reforms, then they would suffer the same consequences.

Once the Soviets had restored control, Alexander Dubcek was deposed, and in his place Gustav Husack was appointed First Secretary of the Czech Communist Party and also the country's president. Husack immediately began a process of 'normalization', which in effect meant reversing all the reforms of the Dubcek era. Additional powers were given to the police and army, while press censorship was reinstated. Young people were threatened and the Prague Spring was forced underground. The Beatles and western culture were sternly discouraged. As for Alexander Dubcek, he was promptly given a post as a forestry official somewhere out in the wilderness, far away from the reins of power and any ability to influence future events in Prague or elsewhere. Once the new regime had overturned all his reforms, Czechoslovakia – after its brief spring of reforms, optimism and rebirth – returned to its dull, authoritarian restrictions. But The Beatles and their music, as in other Eastern Bloc countries, had helped give birth to a counterculture that in 1989 would lead to the downfall of the Berlin Wall and all that it represented.

Chapter 20

Conclusion

If you were to ask any music lover where they would most liked to have spent their teenage years during the twentieth century, they would maybe answer New Orleans in the 1920s or Greenwich Village in the 1950s, perhaps even Manchester in the 1980s. But for many, the answer would be Liverpool in the 1960s. The combination of the Beatles, Merseybeat, the Cavern and two football clubs winning trophies galore was as good as it gets for any young person. This author can certainly testify that with disposable income in his pocket, weekly visits to the Cavern and other clubs, as well as to the football, was an experience that has never been bettered. Sadly, you often don't realize how good these things are until they are gone.

We can sometimes look back on our childhood or youth through rose-tinted glasses, imagining that everything was wonderful; forgetting the hardships and difficulties that most of us experience when growing up. But those memories of Liverpool in the Sixties not only continue to linger vividly in the mind for the fun they brought, but because they marked a major turning point in British social history, one that would have repercussions throughout most of the world.

Of course, not everyone was directly affected by The Beatles and their challenging counterculture. Those living in leafy rural areas did not enjoy the same kind of access to clubs and live music as those growing up in towns and cities. And those who didn't go to university didn't experience the student life of political debates, sit-ins and freedom from their parents. Not everyone imbibed in drug-taking; many were either totally opposed to the very notion of smoking dope or simply never came into contact with it. It might not have been too difficult to buy marijuana in London, but they were hardly selling it on street corners in most towns or villages, at least not during the 1960s. Furthermore, not everyone was indulging in the new sexual revolution. The pill wasn't readily available to many single women, while others feared pregnancy or were suffocated by too much Catholic guilt. Not everyone read Edna O'Brien or went to the theatre to see the latest kitchen-sink dramas, and of course not everyone liked The Beatles or even popular music.

There was also a discernible difference between the early and later Sixties. By 1968, cultural changes were easily identifiable, but it wasn't until the 1970s that many of the social changes came into practice. Legislation governing homosexuality, divorce and abortion had been passed, but took a few years before their effect was fully realized.

Nevertheless, most people did in many ways indirectly experience the new counterculture. It was difficult to escape what was happening on television, which was a shared universal culture. Nor could people entirely ignore the newspapers, with their daily reports of The Beatles or The Rolling Stones. And nor could people be unaware that abortion had been legalized, that divorce was easier and that homosexuality was no longer a criminal offence. Moreover, nobody could fail to notice that most young boys had suddenly grown their hair long or that young girls were sporting miniskirts and shopping at the likes of Biba.

The counterculture simply seeped into the nation's psyche.

The Beatles had begun as four working-class kids from Liverpool. Like so many Liverpool bands, they had bought their equipment on credit and set off on their dream to entertain local audiences. It seems inconceivable that they could ever have imagined the impact and influence they would have over the next few decades. Indeed, it's doubtful if that was what they would have wanted. They just wished to enjoy themselves, playing basic hard-core rock 'n' roll and the lesser-known rhythm and blues from America's south.

It's certainly true that their audiences, before the band became famous, were largely working class. They were boys and girls who, thanks to their jobs, had disposable income to spend on going to clubs in Liverpool, buying records and even guitars.

'A working class hero is something to be,' sang John Lennon, though ironically that was long after they had become famous and rich. They may have started out as a gang of working-class lads from the banks of the Mersey, embracing their backgrounds, but it wasn't long before they changed and more middle-class kids had taken them to their hearts.

In a *New Yorker* interview in December 1963, just as The Beatles were set to invade America, Brian Epstein was asked whether the band was a working-class phenomenon. 'I disagree with the sometimes expressed notion that their appeal is merely to the working classes,' he responded, adding interestingly that 'The Beatles are classless'.

By then it was true. In many ways, that had become the crux of their appeal. Their attraction went across class divides. Epstein might even have added that it also went across ages, and was even about to reach across national borders. It was Epstein himself who transformed them into a classless band. Instead of rock 'n' roll and rhythm and blues music, they began playing more melodic compositions of their own. And instead of the black leather gear, they were wearing suits. Epstein was an entrepreneur, an impresario who instinctively understood the music industry. He may have changed The Beatles from being what John Lennon reckoned was 'the best rock and roll band in the world' into something more gentrified, but without having done so The Beatles would probably never have experienced much success outside of Liverpool. Instead, they became the most famous band the world had ever known, probably the finest ever songwriters in the business.

In her book *Making Youth*, Melanie Tebbutt, Professor of Youth History writes:

> 'The sixties have been defined as a period of generational upheaval when the values of the older generation were contested culturally and politically ... This contempt for and rejection of established institutions encouraged political discord and stimulated interest in alternative beliefs and life-style: experimentation (with drugs, and sex); lack of inhibitions; personal freedom.'

There is no doubt that the 1960s was a unique decade. Even today, people talk of it as the decade of protest and hope; a decade inspired by young people. It was the coming together of so many ambitions and ideals; a decade of re-examination, when anything seemed possible. It's almost impossible for today's generation to realize the impact The Beatles had on the Sixties. Unless you experienced them, you can't begin to understand what was happening. It was an era when young people seized the initiative from an older generation, challenging authority and changing attitudes. They confronted the political ideologies of the past with their new radicalism, throwing out the social mores that had made life restricting for so many women, gay people and couples trapped in unloving relationships. They generated new ideas in art, music, drama, books and television, and even provoked the established religious orders in their search for new spiritual meanings.

Not only did all this bring about noticeable changes in Britain, but America too was caught up in the wave of upheaval. Vietnam, civil rights, drugs, universities; all became issues and challenges. After years of senseless warfare, America capitulated, finally withdrawing its troops from Vietnam, having achieved nothing but 58,000 dead GIs and hundreds of thousands more soldiers injured. It was America's youth who bore the brunt and led the rebellion against the war.

In Eastern Europe, authoritarian regimes, trying to stem the influence of The Beatles and their counterculture, sought to ban their records and any mention of them in newspapers and on the media. In Prague, it led to a new liberal government being overthrown by Soviet tanks. But it was always a battle against the tide of history. In the end, it would lead to their own undoing.

In her autobiography, American singer-songwriter Carole King summed up perfectly the impact of The Beatles on America and American youth:

> 'The world changed on my twenty-second birthday. It was February 9, 1964, when Gerry and I watched Ed Sullivan introduce the Beatles on his television show. I could barely hear the band over their screaming fans. By the time the Fab Four had finished their first number, teenage boys across America had resolved to let their hair grow and take up the guitar. The growing restlessness of young

Americans was fertile soil for the seeds of dramatic sociological transformation planted by the lads from Liverpool. Irreverent answers in interviews ... resulted in many young men realizing, Yeah! These guys look how I wanna look and they're sayin what I'm thinkin!'

In November 2023, the Beatles released a new single, 'Now and Then'. It was the last Beatles song, and the first Beatles record to be released since 1970. The song had been written by John Lennon in the late 1970s, recorded as a home demo and almost forgotten. But with the aid of new digital recording techniques, producers Paul McCartney and Giles Martin (the son of George Martin) were able to blend John's voice and George's guitar with new studio recordings from Paul and Ringo. It may not have been the Beatles' best number, but the single immediately shot into top ten charts around the world. In both Britain and America, it raced to number one within a week of release and clocked up more than 11 million streamings. It was as if the Beatles had never gone away.

When the city of Liverpool applied to host the 2023 Eurovision Song Contest, it was almost a foregone conclusion that it would be chosen. Apart from Manchester, what other city in Europe could possibly boast the same credentials when it comes to popular music? It was as if Europe was coming to pay homage to Liverpool. Every day, you can see in Mathew Street, where this book began, crowds still flocking to pay their respects to where the Sixties really started, where the sound of The Beatles music drifts eerily up from a cellar known as the Cavern.

Bibliography

Over the course of writing this book, I have consulted many books, websites and newspaper articles. There is such a plethora of books on The Beatles that it would take an entire book to just list them! However, I would like to draw attention to those books I have consulted in some detail or have referred to and even quoted from. They include the fiollowing:

Benn, Tony, *Diaries, Out of the Wilderness, 1963–7.*
Bonham Carter, Violet, *Daring To Hope, The Diaries of Violet Bonham Carter 1946–1969.*
Braine, John, *Room At The Top.*
Burns, Jimmy, *Papa Spy*
Castle, Barbara, *The Castle Diaries, 1964–70.*
Coleman, Ray, *Brian Epstein, The Man Who Made The Beatles.*
Coleman, Ray, *Lennon, The Definitive Biography.*
Connolly, Ray, *Being John Lennon.*
Crossman, Richard, *The Crossman Diaries.*
Crouch, Colin, *The Student Revolt.*
Debray, Regis, *Revolution in the Revolution.*
Dorril, Stephen, *Honey Trap.*
Dunn, Nell, *Poor Cow.*
Dunn, Nell, *Up The Junction.*
Dylan, Bob, *Chronicles.*
Hodgson, Godfrey, *America In Our Time.*
Kelly, Stephen F., *Red Voices.*
Kelly, Stephen F., *You've Never Had It So Good.*
Kelly, Stephen F. and Jones, Judith, *Forty Years of Coronation Street.*
Kidd, Harry, *The Trouble At LSE 1966–1967.*
King, Carole, *A Natural Woman.*
Kynaston, David, *On The Cusp, Days of 62.*
Lawrence, D.H., *Lady Chatterley's Lover.*
Leonard, Candy, *Beatleness.*
Lowe, D. and Whiteside, Thomas, in *New Yorker Book of the Sixties.*
Macmillan, Harold, *The Macmillan Diaries.*
Marr, Andrew, *A History of Modern Britain.*
Masters, Brian, *The Swinging Sixties.*

McGrath, James, unpublished PhD.
Mersey Beat newspaper.
Moran, Joe, *Armchair Nation: An intimate history of Britain in front of the TV*.
Morley, Paul, *The North*.
O'Brien, Edna, *August is a Wicked Month*.
O'Brien, Edna, *Country Girls*.
Pimlott, Ben, *Harold Wilson*.
Prior, Michael, *Dreams and Reality*.
Remnick, David, *King of the World: Muhammad Ali and the Rise of the American Hero*.
Richards, Keith, *Life*.
The Robbins Report
Robinson, John, *Honest To God*.
Sandbrook, Dominic, *White Heat*.
Tebbutt, Melanie, *Making Youth, A History of Youth in Modern Britain*.
Thompson, Phil, *The Best of Cellars*.
TUC Annual Reports, 1966, 1968, 1969.
Wilson, Colin, *The Outsider*.
Winstone, Ruth (ed.), *Events, Dear Boy, Events*.
Woodhead, Leslie, *How The Beatles Rocked The Kremlin*.
Worth, Jennifer, *Call The Midwife*.

Newspapers and periodicals
The Times, Daily Mirror, Sunday Mirror, Evening Standard, Guardian, Daily Mail, Daily Telegraph, Observer, Daily Herald, Financial Times, Police Review, Sheffield Star, Birkenhead News, Tribune, International Socialism, Black Dwarf, Spare Rib, New Statesman, Liverpool Echo, Mersey Beat, Jackie, Teen, The New Yorker.

Index

Aberson, Arielle, 167
Abortion, 44, 130, 132-33, 157
   Abortion Act (1967), 165-67
Alexander, Sally, 167
Argyll, Duke and Duchess, 151

Bacon, Francis, 47-8
Baez, Joan, 29
Beatles
   America, 31-2, 221-4
   BBC, 195, 198-200
   Beatlemania, 31, 220
   buying equipment from Hessy's, 174
   Cavern, 1-7, 22
   conscription fears, 89-90
   Coronation Street, 45-6
   counter-culture, 231-4
   Czechoslovakia, 226-9
   drugs, 108, 113-4
   Ed Sullivan show, 221-3, 233
   education, 85
   fashion, 170, 175-6, 185
   Granada Television, 188-9, 201-202
   Hamburg, 23
   Hard Day's Night (film), 222
   Harold Wilson, 56
   homes, 72-3
   homosexuality, 135, 138
   influence of R&B music and black culture, 205-8
   John Lennon and radicalism, 125-6
   John Lennon and Thelma Pickles, 11, 28
   Liverpool accents, 186
   Liverpool College of Art, 20
   Please, Please Me, 30
   politics, 27, 56-8, 102
   recording contract, 24-3
   religion, 128-30
   Soviet Union, 224-6
   The Quarrymen, 20
   The Silver Beetles, 10
   Yoko Ono, 144
Beatniks, 170
Beaulieu, Lord Montagu, 138
Beetles, Silver, 10

Benn, Tony, 98, 166, 227
Berry, Chuck, 17
Best, George, 185, 209-11
Beyond The Fringe, 190
Birkett, Jean, 70, 81-2, 84, 86-7, 155-6, 180
Black, Cilla, 2, 20, 178
Bogarde, Dirk, 138
Boothby, Robert, 8, 137
Bourne, Alex, 161
Boycott, Rosie, 167
Brown, Jane, 157
Busby Babes, 210
Butler, Cliff, 70

Campaign For Nuclear Disarmament, 103, 104-6
Capital punishment, 141-2
Carlos, John, 218
Carnaby Street, 184
Carter, Violet Bonham, 228
Cassius Clay (also Muhammad Ali), 211-3
Catholic Church, 130-3
Cathy Come Home, 76-7
Cathy McGowan, 199-200
Cavern club, 18-9, 22-3,
Church of England, 134
Civil Rights demonstrations, 118
Computerisation, 68
Conscription, 88-9
Contraception, 130-4
   contraceptive pill, 153
Cooley, Mike, 68
Coronation Street, 44-6, 187-8
Crossman, Richard, 140, 166
Cuba, 15

De Gaulle, General, 14
Devlin, Bernadette, 59
Driberg, Tom, 136
Drugs, 108, 172
   raid, 109-10
Dubcek, Alexander, 226-9
Dunn, Nell, 164
Dylan, Bob, 28-9, 113, 134
D'Oliveira, Basil, 216

Early, Gerald, 213
Eastham, George, 214
Eden, Anthony, 8
Education Act (1944), 79
Edwards, Tony, 26
Epstein, Brian, 2, 21, 24, 66, 72, 136, 201, 232
Eurovision Song Contest, 234
Everyman Theatre, Liverpool, 33-5

Finch, Janice, 189
Freeman, John, 189
Fury, Billy, 19
Fyfe, David Maxwell, 137

Gaitskell, Hugh, 55
Gaye, Marvin, 125
Germany, 14, 103
Gielgud, Sir John, 137
Gill, Freda, 68
Grade, Michael, 194
Graham, Billy, 127
Granada Television, 44, 98, 11, 186-8
Grebenshikov, Boris, 225
Greece, 13
Greer, Germaine, 167
Guevara, Che, 119-21

Hain, Peter, 217-8
Hair, 39-40
Haley, Bill, 3
Hamburg, 23
Hamp, Johnny, 200
Hard Day's Night, A (film), 43
Harry, Bill, 20, 45-6
Heffer, Eric, 57
Hill, Jimmy, 214
Hitchens, Christopher, 101
Hockney, David, 47-8
Hodge, Gavin, 159
Holly, Buddy, 17
Home ownership, 73-4
Home, Douglas Alec, 8
Homosexuality, 135-7
Honest To God, (book) 133
Humanae Vitae, 133, 157

Italy, 14

Jackie (magazine), 179-180
Jagger, Mick, 1-2, 27
Jazz, 18
Jenkins, Clare, 25, 27, 35, 42, 57, 94-5, 131, 145-6, 158, 160, 180-1

Jenkins, Roy, 140
John Moores Painting Prize, 46
Jones, Bob, 54, 65, 69-70, 86, 94, 109, 162, 183, 196
Jones, Judith, 64
Jung, Carl, 7

Kennedy, John, 14, 108
   assassination, 54
King, Carole, 233
Kirchherr, Astrid, 47

Labour Party, 57-8
Lady Chatterley's Lover trial, 11, 36-8
Larkin, Phillip, 38
Laski, Marghanita, 157
Lawrence, D.H., 11, 36
Leary, Timothy, 113
Leonard, Candy, 221
Little Richard, 19
Littlewood, Joan, 39
Liverpool College of Art, 46
Liverpool Institute, 20, 85
Liverpool poets
   Henri, Adrian, 33
   McGough, Roger, 33, 35
   Patten, Brian, 33
Liverpool music shops,
   Hessy's, 174
   NEMS, 21
London School of Economics, 98-9, 102, 141, 167

Macmillan, Harold 8, 11, 50, 62, 137
Maharishi Mahesh Yogi, 130
Marquee Club, 25-6
Marr, Andrew, 6, 161, 167
McFall, Ray, 19
McGough, Thelma (nee Pickles), 9, 11, 20, 23, 27-8, 72, 99, 147-8, 207
McGowan, Cathy, 177
McGrath, James, 207
McGuinness, Wilf, 88
Menand, Louis, 119
Mersey Beat newspaper, 20-1
Mini Minor, 65
Mods, 171
Montgomery, Viscount, 140
Motown, 118

New Yorker magazine, 119, 223, 232, 235
Nightclubs
   Birmingham, 25
   Liverpool,
      Cavern Club, 1, 9, 18, 20, 22-3
      Iron Door Club, 22

London, Marquee 25-6
Manchester, 24
Nixon, Richard, 14
Northern Ireland, 58-9, 140, 209

Oh Calcutta, 40
Ono, Yoko, 144
Orwell, George, 12
Osborne, John, 38
O'Brien, Edna, 42
O'Malley, Annie, 43, 62, 82-3, 111, 130-2, 152, 155, 160, 177-9, 181-3, 185
O'Rahilly, Ronan, 195

Palmer, Veronica, 146
Park Hill flats, Sheffield, 74-5
Parkinson, Christine, 24, 27, 30-1, 82-4, 94, 178
Platt, Stephen, 85
Pirate Radio, 195-7
Police Review, 173
Portugal, 13
Presley, Elvis, 5
Prior, Chris, 89
Prior, Mike, 92-3, 106-7
Private Eye magazine: 48-9
Profumo Affair, 50- 3
Proops, Marjorie, 149

Quant, Mary, 176-7
Quarry Bank School, Liverpool, 85
Quarrymen, 10, 20

Radio Luxembourg, 195
Ready, Steady, Go, 193
Religion, 127
Remnick, David, 213, 223, 236
Richard, Keith, 26, 85, 176, 195
Robbins Report, 91, 92
Rolling Stones,
  America, 176
  bad influence, 27
  Cavern, 1, 2, 23
  dress style, 176, 184-5,
  drugs and drugs charge, 108-110
  Granada Television, 176, 202
  Juke Box Jury, 198
  Marquee club and Middlesborough, 25
  Mick Jagger appearance on *World In Action*, 188
  politics, 102
Room At The Top, (book) 95
Rosen, James, 223
Ruskin College, Oxford, 99-101

Ruskin College, National Women's Liberation conference, 167

Sandbrook, Dominic, 199
Saturday Club, 195
Savage, Jon, 138
Scaffold, The, 34
Shankar, Ravi, 129
Shea Stadium, New York, 223
Sheffield Star, (newspaper), 154
Shrimpton, Jean, 178
Six Five Special, 198
Skiffle, 18
Smith, Tommie, 218
Soviet Union, 14
Spanish Civil War, 13
Steel, David, 165
Storm, Rory, 19
Student riots, Paris, 96-7
Sullivan, Ed, 220
Sutcliffe, Stuart, 10, 20, 46-8, 99, 170
Swinging Blue Jeans, 9

Tebbutt, Melanie, 221, 232
Teddy Boys, 169
Teen magazines, 179-180
That Was The Week That Was, 53, 190-1
Thomas, Andi, 149
Top of the Pops, 199
Trade Unions, 67-8
Troitsky, Artemy, 224-6
Trueman, Brian, 202
Turing, Alan, 136
Twiggy, 177-8

Ulysses, 40
Unemployment, 62-3

Vaughan, Frankie, 19
Vietnam War, 15, 115
  anti-war demonstrations, 97, 117

Weber Barbara, 7, 103
Weber, Manfred, 7
Whitehouse, Mary, 194
Wilkie, Derry, 206-207
Wilson, Harold, 27, 53-6
Wolfenden Report, 1954, 139
Women's Employment Survey, 1968, 147
Women's Rights, 60
Woodbine, Lord, 206
Woodhead, Leslie, 188, 201-2, 224-5
Wooler, Bob, 109
World In Action: 98, 102, 109, 117, 188
Worth, Jennifer, 163-4
Wyman, Bill, 2

Dear Reader,

We hope you have enjoyed this book, but why not share your views on social media? You can also follow our pages to see more about our other products: facebook.com/penandswordbooks or follow us on Twitter @penswordbooks

You can also view our products at www.pen-and-sword.co.uk (UK and ROW) or www.penandswordbooks.com (North America).

To keep up to date with our latest releases and online catalogues, please sign up to our newsletter at: www.pen-and-sword.co.uk/newsletter

If you would like a printed catalogue with our latest books, then please email: enquiries@pen-and-sword.co.uk or telephone: 01226 734555 (UK and ROW) or email: uspen-and-sword@casematepublishers.com or telephone: (610) 853-9131 (North America).

We respect your privacy and we will only use personal information to send you information about our products.

Thank you!